Ten Assessment Literacy Goals for School Leaders

Ten Assessment Literacy Goals for School Leaders

Steve Chappuis
Susan M. Brookhart
Jan Chappuis

FOR INFORMATION:

Corwin

A SAGE Company

2455 Teller Road

Thousand Oaks, California 91320

(800) 233-9936

www.corwin.com

SAGE Publications Ltd.

1 Oliver's Yard

55 City Road

London EC1Y 1SP

United Kingdom

SAGE Publications India Pvt. Ltd.

B 1/I 1 Mohan Cooperative Industrial Area

Mathura Road, New Delhi 110 044

India

SAGE Publications Asia-Pacific Pte. Ltd.

18 Cross Street #10-10/11/12

China Square Central

Singapore 048423

President: Mike Soules

Associate Vice President
  and Editorial Director: Monica Eckman

Publisher: Jessica Allan

Senior Content Development Editor: Lucas Schleicher

Associate Content Development Editor: Mia Rodriguez

Production Editor: Tori Mirsadjadi

Copy Editor: QuADS Prepress Pvt. Ltd

Typesetter: C&M Digitals (P) Ltd.

Proofreader: Barbara Coster

Indexer: Integra

Cover Designer: Candice Harman

Marketing Manager: Olivia Bartlett

Printed in the United States of America

Library of Congress Cataloging-in-Publication Data

Names: Chappuis, Stephen, author. | Brookhart, Susan M., author. | Chappuis, Jan, author.

Title: Ten assessment literacy goals for school leaders / Steve Chappuis, Susan M. Brookhart, Jan Chappuis.

Description: First edition. | Thousand Oaks, California : Corwin, [2021] | Includes bibliographical references and index.

Identifiers: LCCN 2021012522 | ISBN 9781071821947 (paperback) | ISBN 9781071821909 (epub) | ISBN 9781071821879 (epub) | ISBN 9781071821848 (pdf)

Subjects: LCSH: Educational leadership—United States. | Educational evaluation—United States. | Academic achievement—United States.

Classification: LCC LB2806 .C346 2021 | DDC 371.200973—dc23
LC record available at https://lccn.loc.gov/2021012522

This book is printed on acid-free paper.

SUSTAINABLE FORESTRY INITIATIVE

Certified Chain of Custody
At Least 10% Certified Forest Content
www.sfiprogram.org
SFI-01028

21 22 23 24 25 10 9 8 7 6 5 4 3 2 1

Contents

Web Contents   vii

Acknowledgments   xi

About the Authors   xiii

Overview   1

Chapter 1: Comprehensive and Balanced
Assessment Systems   9

Chapter 2: Clear Standards   29

Chapter 3: Standards of Assessment Quality   53

Chapter 4: Formative Assessment Practices   81

Chapter 5: Grading Practices   117

Chapter 6: Effective Communication   141

Chapter 7: Ethical and Appropriate Assessment Use   157

Chapter 8: Evaluation of Assessment Competencies and
Providing Appropriate Professional Development   179

Chapter 9: Analysis of Student Assessment Information   205

Chapter 10: School and District Assessment Policies   233

Appendix   245

References   257

Index   263

Visit the companion website at
resources.corwin.com/10GoalsLeaders
for downloadable resources.

Web Contents

Chapter 1: Comprehensive and Balanced Assessment Systems — 9

- Activity 1.1: An Abbreviated Assessment Audit Model — 21
- Chapter 1 Definitions — 27

Chapter 2: Clear Standards — 29

- Activity 2.1: Exploring the Relationship Between Learning Goals and Assessment — 41
- Activity 2.2: Learning Targets and Success Criteria — 45
- Activity 2.3: Recognizing the Formative Learning Cycle in Action — 47
- Chapter 2 Definitions — 50

Chapter 3: Standards of Assessment Quality — 53

- Activity 3.1: Connecting Your Own Experiences to the Keys to Quality — 67
- Activity 3.2: Auditing an Assessment for a Clear Purpose — 69
- Activity 3.3: Auditing an Assessment for Clear Learning Goals and Appropriate Sample Size — 70
- Activity 3.4: Practicing With Target-Method Match — 73
- Activity 3.5: Auditing an Assessment for Quality — 75
- Activity 3.6: Auditing an Assessment for Bias and Distortion — 77
- Chapter 3 Definitions — 78

Chapter 4: Formative Assessment Practices — 81

- Activity 4.1: Identifying Talking Points for Critical Components of Formative Assessment — 109

- Activity 4.2: Looking for Evidence of Effective Formative Assessment Practices in the Classroom   111
  - o Activity Chart 4.2A: Evidence of Formative Assessment Practices in the Classroom (online only)
  - o Activity Chart 4.2B: What to Ask Teachers (online only)
- Activity 4.3: Discussing Formative Assessment Practices With Students   113
  - o Activity Chart 4.3: What to Ask Students (online only)
- Activity 4.4: Establishing a School Baseline   114
- Chapter 4 Definition   116

Chapter 5: Grading Practices   117

- Activity 5.1: Grading Stories   134
- Activity 5.2: Grading Policies and Practices in My District   136
- Activity 5.3: Grading in Classrooms and Courses   137
- Chapter 5 Definitions   138

Chapter 6: Effective Communication   141

- Activity 6.1: Beyond the Report Card   154
- Chapter 6 Definitions   155

Chapter 7: Ethical and Appropriate Assessment Use   157

- Activity 7.1: Recognizing the Ethical and Appropriate Use of Student Assessment   167
- Activity 7.2: *The Classroom Assessment Standards*   172
- Activity 7.3: Assessment Accommodations   173
- Activity 7.4: Ethical and Unethical Test Preparation   175
- Chapter 7 Definitions   177

Chapter 8: Evaluation of Assessment Competencies and Providing Appropriate Professional Development   179

- Activity 8.1: Practicing With Teacher and Principal Evaluative Criteria in Assessment   196
- Activity 8.2: Personal Reflection on Classroom Assessment, Teacher Evaluation, and Professional Development   198
- Activity 8.3: Practicing Linking Evaluation Results to Professional Development Recommendations   200
- Activity 8.4: Verifying Teachers' Content Knowledge and Assessment Competence   201
- Chapter 8 Definitions   203

Chapter 9: Analysis of Student Assessment Information 205

- Activity 9.1: Internet Scavenger Hunt — 224
- Activity 9.2: Dipping Into Data — 226
- Activity 9.3: Scenario Discussions — 228
- Chapter 9 Definitions — 231

Chapter 10: School and District Assessment Policies 233

- Activity 10.1: Using School/District Policies to Support Quality Assessment — 241

Appendix: A Guide to Learning With the Book 245

Acknowledgments

The field of educational leadership is filled with talented individuals who often make a difficult job look easy. Somehow, things like paying attention to detail, having an educational vision or mind for the "big picture," working tirelessly, and drawing enjoyment and energy from students and adults alike all seem to combine into one caring and dedicated soul.

This book aims to help all school leaders, regardless of title or role, provide leadership though assessment literacy. In writing it we have been reminded of school leaders we have worked with in our careers who have made a difference in the lives of students and other educators, including ourselves. We could single out many others with equal respect and admiration; for the purposes of this book, we name just a few.

Dr. Beverly Long is in a league of her own when it comes to making a difference in assessment in her local district and in our own view of assessment, especially the assessment literacy needs of principals. On her watch, schools began building-wide work on learning targets and other formative assessment strategies, work that continued for over a decade and had a documented impact on student learning. She sees student well-being and student learning as the primary purpose of the work of all educators and championed the role of assessment in that work over the many years we had the privilege of working with her.

Over her long career with the Hawaii State Department of Education, friend and colleague Monica Mann was a constant and effective advocate for assessment practices that produce accurate and helpful information at all levels from the state department to the individual student. For over 30 years, she sought out, sponsored, and delivered transformational assessment literacy training for hundreds of educators throughout the islands—DOE staff, Complex Area superintendents, professional developers, instructional coaches, and teachers. Monica's leadership style embodied reflective practice: she listened carefully, responded thoughtfully, identified needs, and engineered action that resulted in productive change. Although she passed away in November 2020, Monica's work and passion live on in those who had the honor to learn with and from her.

Jim Whitford, as a building principal and a supervisor of principal interns, continues to be a role model in school leadership for many who work with him. His balance of good humor and serious dedication to the job, his uncanny and consistent behaviors of putting students first, and his approach to schooling and schools as places that both educate and nurture all set him apart as someone special. A building with Jim as a principal is a safe, loving, and rewarding teaching environment.

Our thanks to these leaders and the many others who have helped us along the way to this book.

About the Authors

Steve Chappuis has served as a school teacher and principal, and in district administrator positions responsible for curriculum, instruction, assessment, and principal supervision and evaluation. In the private sector he has helped small and large education service companies establish strategic plans for publishing and professional development in the area of student assessment. He has delivered presentations around the country to school leaders on the benefits of quality classroom assessment and how to implement local balanced assessment systems, and has authored and coauthored books and articles on these topics.

Susan M. Brookhart, PhD, is Professor Emerita in the School of Education at Duquesne University. She is also an independent educational consultant, professional developer, and author. Dr. Brookhart's interests include the role of both formative and summative classroom assessment in student motivation and achievement, the connection between classroom assessment and large-scale assessment, and grading. She was the editor in 2007–2009 of *Educational Measurement: Issues and Practice*, a journal of the National Council on Measurement in Education. She is the author or coauthor of 20 books and numerous articles and book chapters on classroom assessment, teacher professional development, and evaluation. She serves on several editorial boards and research advisory panels. She has received the 2014 Jason Millman Award from the Consortium for Research on Educational Assessment and Teaching Effectiveness and the 2015 Samuel J. Messick Memorial Lecture Award from Educational Testing Service.

Educator and author **Jan Chappuis** began her career as an elementary and secondary teacher, after which she became a curriculum developer in English/language arts, mathematics, social studies, and world languages. She joined Assessment Training Institute in 2001, working with Rick Stiggins and Steve Chappuis to write books and develop workshops focused on classroom assessment practices that support learning. Currently an independent consultant, she presents both nationally and internationally and is best known for her work in translating assessment research into practical classroom applications.

Jan is the author of *Seven Strategies of Assessment for Learning* (2nd ed., 2015) and coauthor of *Classroom Assessment for Student Learning: Doing It Right, Using It Well* (3rd ed., 2020), *An Introduction to Student-Involved Assessment for Learning* (7th ed., 2017), *Creating and Recognizing Quality Rubrics* (2006), and *Understanding School Assessment: A Parent and Community Guide to Helping Students Learn* (2002).

Overview

In 2016 Congress passed the Every Student Succeeds Act to replace the 2001 No Child Left Behind (NCLB) Act, perhaps best known for placing high-stakes importance for both schools and students on the results of a single test. Even though it is now five years removed, NCLB and the requirement for schools to make adequate yearly progress influenced assessment in American schools in ways that have not been fully realized or successfully managed yet today.

NCLB triggered the adoption of new levels of testing in schools and districts, most of them voluntary. Test publishers and software companies saw the movement and pursued the profit, trying to capitalize on anything remotely "formative." The K–12 market filled with options for benchmark, interim, short-cycle, and common assessments. But whatever the test was called, whether purchased off the shelf or developed in-house, a standardized test or a home-grown common assessment, built from an item bank, taken online or with paper and pencil, schools and districts raced to generate the data they believed they needed to help them get to adequate yearly progress. Given the stakes, it's little surprise that schools did what was thought necessary to discover if they were or were not on the road to the levels of achievement required.

Along the way, many schools discovered gaps in what was taught and what was tested, and had to grapple with why and what to do about it. Others discovered that the results of any assessment are only as good as the quality of the assessment itself. And they found that multiple measures don't help without first attending to the conditions that need to be in place for all assessments to produce accurate results. The move to new levels of interim assessment happened so quickly that many schools had difficulty laying the foundation of assessment literacy required to make it all work. For some it was trial and error: some testing issues were unforeseen and managed, while others went either unnoticed or unaddressed. Teachers and schools became overloaded with data and were mostly unprepared to use the results in ways that help students learn. And in the classroom, two competing forces became more apparent than ever: the use of instructional time spent preparing students for tests external to the classroom that largely measured what was practical to test in a large-scale format seemed in conflict with the commitment to teach a well-rounded, rich curriculum (Au, 2007). Across all levels of education (states, districts, schools, and classrooms), assessment balance became difficult to achieve.

The Assessment Literacy and School Leadership Connection

As authors, our primary interest in writing this book comes from the ongoing need we see to promote and strengthen assessment literacy in educators at all levels. NCLB's side effects may have helped put a spotlight on the need for assessment literacy, but that need was always there, and it persists today.

We see fundamental assessment literacy as part of the complex equation of what makes an effective teacher. The role of the principal is largely in providing direction and exercising influence (Leithwood & Louis, 2012). Some scholars believe that the concept of "instructional leadership" has remained vague and undefined. However, we assume that it entails the principal taking responsibility for the programs of curriculum, instruction, and assessment in the school. It follows then that, in respect to establishing assessment literacy, responsibility rests with school leaders to provide opportunities for teachers to learn to become assessment literate, and to support them in the classroom as they transfer what they have learned into everyday instruction. For that to happen, school and district leaders must also be assessment literate. For many, that means continuing to learn while on the job, an activity that most principals are happy to engage in and model for others.

Assessment Literacy

What does it mean to be assessment literate? In the box below is the definition (Chappuis & Stiggins, 2020) we promote when discussing assessment literacy.

> *Assessment literacy is having the knowledge and skills needed to gather accurate information about student achievement and use the assessment process and its results to effectively improve achievement.*

The shortcut we've used as a reminder of the definition's two big ideas is "doing it right and using it well," and it can be applied to assessments of all types and for all purposes, formative and summative, criterion and norm referenced, and in all grade levels and subject areas.

Because students experience the vast majority of assessments as part of daily classroom instruction, our emphasis in this book tilts in the direction of classroom assessment literacy. In large part our reasoning is that improved learning through the use of assessment has been shown at the classroom level, where the rewards of formative assessment are greatest. Ideally, all preservice preparation for teachers would include coursework in assessment literacy, and in-service professional development would build on that. But that is not yet the case, and the longer it is not the case, the more problematic some of the omissions in teacher preparation become. Those omissions end up becoming issues that can often confront and confound building administrators. For principals who are not assessment literate, the resolution to such issues is harder to find, as exemplified below.

Poorly constructed assessments mismeasure student learning and exacerbate inequity. The link between instruction and assessment is as strong, or should be, as the link between the written curriculum and instruction. Like curriculum and instruction, assessment can be done either well or poorly. Done well, it measures student learning accurately and results can be used to promote further learning. Done poorly, students are indeed harmed. For example, a faulty test score from a poorly constructed summative test leads to a faulty final grade. Similarly, a faulty formative assessment can lead to inappropriate feedback to students and errors in what comes next in instruction. For some students the desire to learn is linked to learning success; if success is undermined by poor assessment, we put at risk the entire notion of "incentive to learn." Imagine students saying, "There were too many trick questions on the test" or "That test had nothing to do with what was in the book and homework," or the most common catch-all, "That test was grossly unfair!" If such familiar complaints are too often blown off as "kids being kids," it is a sign of assessment literacy work yet to be done.

Assessment practices in general do not yet meet student information needs. An assessment-literate educator knows how to involve students in the process of gathering and using assessment information so they develop the habit of self-assessing and learn to adjust their strategies and efforts as needed to gain success. For some teachers and principals the concept of students being at the front of the line of all of the many users of assessment information is novel and even hard to grasp. But the notion of student engagement in the lesson is an instructional strategy with research to back it up, and principals are often on the lookout for it as they observe them in classrooms. Involving students in the assessment process is a logical extension of a strategy that many teachers already employ. Research suggests that students who understand the characteristics of good work and learn how to use those characteristics for their own self-assessment experience learning gains. But it also suggests that continuing, on-the-job professional development is needed for teachers to establish their formative classroom practices (Educational Testing Service, 2018).

Unsound grading practices harm both learners and learning. Grading is both an information delivery tool and a process. But as with other functions in schooling we've previously noted, grading can be done well or done poorly. Even though sometimes difficult to distill, if assigned properly, test and report card grades can relay the status of student learning in relation to the goals of instruction, in real time or aggregated over time. If grading is done poorly, the quality of the information is at best uneven, and students can't get out of the way of what essentially becomes inaccurate information about their learning. When variables that have nothing to do with how well students have learned, such as attendance, effort, and attitude, are allowed to enter the grading process, the need for assessment literacy becomes clear.

Assessments in many schools and districts are disjointed, occurring in isolation instead of as a part of a comprehensive and balanced assessment system. We will explore balanced assessment systems more in Chapter 1, but it is important to note at the outset that assessment literacy for all staff is more likely to take hold and thrive when all assessments are viewed as a part of a larger system of assessments, each with a clearly defined purpose and role. And each assessment in such a system is based on what has been or will be taught vis-à-vis the established learning goals, meaning that the space between curriculum, instruction, and assessment is undetectable. More than ever, we need to be prepared to answer the question "Why does my child have to take this test?" or "What exactly does this test measure?" In a balanced system the answers to these questions are readily available and are communicated to all, with the principal playing the point guard in the distribution of information.

School Leadership, Instruction, and Assessment

Evidence continues to show the connection between student learning and effective leadership from the building principal, and leadership is second only to classroom instruction as an influence on student learning (Leithwood & Louis, 2012). This body of research helps explain why leadership knowledge and skills specific to the area of classroom assessment are beneficial. The principal can ensure that assessments in the building and from outside the building are of high quality and, in the same vein, can call into question long-standing assessment practices that can adversely affect learning and learners. Assessment-literate principals can advocate for student involvement in the assessment process, provide high-quality feedback to teachers on their assessment practices, and encourage teachers to see the use of data as an opportunity to investigate causes and generate solutions rather than just calling out another problem.

Ten Assessment Literacy Goals for School Leaders

The vehicle we use in this book to link assessment literacy with school leadership is a set of 10 goals (see Table 1), all of which when acted on can contribute to individual and/or systemic assessment literacy. Each assessment literacy goal is focused on a main concept, bolded in the list in Table 1. We found it useful to pull these concepts out into their own list, where they can act as reminders of the big picture of each goal and the work ahead. Each of the next 10 chapter titles are drawn from this list.

1. Comprehensive and balanced assessment systems

2. Clear academic achievement targets

3. Standards of assessment quality

4. Formative assessment practices

5. Sound grading practices

6. Effective communication

7. Ethical and appropriate assessment use

8. Teacher evaluation and professional development

9. Analysis of student assessment information

10. Sound assessment-related policies

TABLE 1   Ten assessment literacy goals for school leaders

1. The leader understands the attributes of a **comprehensive and balanced assessment system** that includes large-scale assessment, school- or district-level assessment, and classroom-level summative and formative assessment, ensuring multiple measures of all valued learning goals.

2. The leader understands the necessity of **clear academic achievement goals**, aligned classroom-level learning targets, and success criteria used by students and teachers, and their relationship to the development of sound assessments.

3. The leader understands the **standards of quality** for student assessment and ensures that these standards are met in all school/district assessments.

4. The leader understands **formative assessment practices** and works with staff to integrate student-centered assessment for learning into classroom instruction.

5. The leader understands **sound grading practices** and works with staff to ensure that all students receive meaningful, accurate grades.

6. The leader **communicates effectively** with all members of the school community about student assessment.

7. The leader understands the conditions required for the **ethical and appropriate use of student assessment** and protects students and staff from potential misuse.

8. The leader **evaluates** teachers' classroom assessment competencies and uses that information to present and/or secure **appropriate professional development**.

9. The leader **analyzes student assessment information** accurately, uses that information to improve curriculum and instruction, and assists teachers in doing the same.

10. The leader develops and implements **sound assessment and assessment-related policies**.

The 10 assessment literacy goals serve as a guide for school leaders who wish to improve their own assessment literacy. In doing so, leaders will see how assessment can be used to improve student learning, and the steps they can take in their own system to help bring that about. The goals are intended for individual, group, or organizational use. Working with one or all of the goals at any level will help educators gain assessment literacy and, by doing so, influence the assessment literacy in the system where they work. The 10 assessment literacy goals can also be used for work at the systems level in the following ways:

- As a resource in planning and implementing a comprehensive and balanced system of assessments

- To inform assessment criteria for principal evaluation frameworks

- To clarify personal goal setting for formative principal evaluation systems

- To inform teacher evaluation criteria, observation, and feedback

- To inform school improvement planning and organizational goal setting

- As a resource for professional development: individual, small/large group, face-to-face presentation, online course, and so on

Looking Ahead

Each of the 10 chapters that follow will explore one of the assessment literacy goals in some depth. For each goal you'll find the following:

- Chapter learning goals

- Text that explains the goal: its relevance, applicable research, and leadership responsibilities

- Success indicators for the goal, describing what knowledge and actions look like when the goal is attained

- Personal portfolio entry suggestions

- Study guide questions

- Definitions of key terms, with each term appearing in bold the first time it occurs in the chapter

- Activities and resources to assist with understanding, implementation, and self-analysis of goal attainment.

The appendix provides ideas on how to use the book content and features in a professional development setting, as well as in a learning team model of study. It also connects each learning goal with features of the text. The appendix also includes a table that matches chapter learning goals to success indicators, activities, and study guide questions.

School and/or District Administrator Focus

As noted earlier, because of research focused on the effects of formative assessment in the classroom, and because of the positive impact school principals can have on school effectiveness and student learning, this book is focused primarily on the role of building administrators. The 10 goals, however, easily cross over from building to district administrators, and what the district administrator can do to operationalize a goal is often similar to what a school leader must do.

Resources Consulted

While our collective experience in teaching educators the principles of sound assessment aided as a resource for this book, we also reviewed some of the most recent instructional frameworks for teachers as well as professional standards for school administrators, with an eye toward what each contained regarding assessment knowledge and skills. Some were practically void on the topic. Listed below are those that we found most useful to help frame the 10 assessment literacy goals and also inform the indicators of success for each:

- *Assessment Literacy Standards*, Michigan Assessment Consortium

- *Professional Standards for Educational Leaders*, National Policy Board for Educational Administration

- *Evaluating School Principals: A Legislative Approach*, National Conference of State Legislatures

- *5D+ Rubric for Instructional Growth and Teacher Evaluation*, Center for Educational Renewal, University of Washington

- *Comprehensive and Balanced Assessment Systems*, National Panel on the Future of Assessment Practices, Learning Sciences Institute

- *Teacher/Principal Evaluation Program*, Office of the Superintendent of Public Instruction, Washington

Comprehensive and Balanced Assessment Systems

1

Assessment Literacy Goal #1: *The leader understands the attributes of a comprehensive and balanced assessment system that includes large-scale assessment, school- or district-level assessment, and classroom-level summative and formative assessment, ensuring multiple measures of all valued learning goals.*

A *system* is a set of parts working together—an interconnecting network. Our schools and districts function as systems, with multiple subsystems at work: if your school is wired for email communication and internet access, you access a system every day, in this case an actual network. An elementary textbook adoption acts as a system, linking one chapter to the next, one year to the next, building on what came before and preparing for what is yet to be taught. A well-written curriculum functions in the same way, omitting from instruction what is not essential and emphasizing what is most important for future learning success. In that way it is *comprehensive*—complete, containing all of the elements necessary for student growth in any given subject area over time.

Chapter Learning Goals

1. Understand the five levels of a comprehensive and balanced assessment system and what each level contributes to the system.

2. Recognize that learning goals form the backbone of a comprehensive and balanced assessment system.

3. Understand the function of assessment audits and how they are necessary to a comprehensive and balanced assessment system.

4. Recognize how classroom formative assessment acts as the foundation for a comprehensive and balanced assessment system.

A System of Assessments

This first assessment literacy goal for school leaders, building a **comprehensive and balanced assessment system**, serves as an umbrella for the other nine goals. If a school or district commits to all that it takes to develop such a system, many of the other goals begin to be concurrently acted on because they are necessary components of the system and a part of what it means to be assessment literate. Each of the other nine goals can be undertaken individually, but all of them fit into the larger context of a comprehensive and balanced assessment system.

We advocate for a systems approach to student assessment because it is in the best interest of the students we serve. It also is the best solution to the following questions often posed by school leaders:

- How can I ensure that assessments at all levels are used to improve teaching and learning?

- How do I determine if all assessments in place are necessary, are of high quality, and are linked to the same **learning goals**?

- How do I know that teachers are using assessment results to modify and improve instruction? How can I help them?

The answers lie in a planned, organized system of student assessment. Along with a foundation of assessment literacy and the tools needed to manage the system, the five levels of the system that we will describe, when working together, can help school leaders

- determine *the level of **alignment*** between all assessments in the system and the learning goals as defined by the written curriculum;

- ensure that *all valued targets* are assessed, not just those that are easy and quick to measure;

- *quantify and control* the number of assessments students experience;

- identify and *manage assessment redundancies*, finding gaps and overlaps, and eliminating assessments that do not contribute useful, relevant information;

- encourage the use of *multiple measures* of student learning to inform decisions; and

- emphasize the importance of using ***formative assessment*** *processes and results* in the classroom, regularly and purposefully, to cause learning, not just to report it.

Prerequisites

The effectiveness of any assessment system depends on the assessment literacy of those in the system. Having a wide range of assessments alone does not ensure accuracy of results or effective and appropriate use of information. For a balanced assessment system to work effectively, each assessment must meet standards of quality for accuracy and effective use. In Chapter 3 we'll discuss in more detail the following standards, which are the core of assessment-literate practice:

First, the purpose of the assessment must be established; the intended use of the information and the intended users are clearly defined.

Second, each assessment directly aligns to clearly defined goals of instruction. Without a foundation of clear learning goals, the system can't provide accurate information to any users of assessment results. It is this fidelity to established learning goals in every assessment that knits them into a system.

Third, each assessment in the system relies on an appropriate assessment method, and each method used adheres to criteria for sound assessment design.

Fourth, assessment results are communicated in timely, understandable, and actionable ways. The methods to communicate progress and results within and outside the classroom meet the information needs of all users, including students. Grading practices result in fair and defensible summaries of student achievement at a point in time.

Levels of Assessment in a Comprehensive and Balanced System

We have developed an organizing framework of five levels of assessment to make clear the different intended uses, or *purposes*, for each assessment in a balanced system (Figure 1.1). Both "big-picture" academic standards and a daily instructional program of aligned unit- and lesson-level learning targets are important in a balanced system. In this model the annual state test is positioned as one assessment inside a larger, comprehensive plan of assessments, while classroom assessment assumes a role that no other level of assessment can fulfill.

Although each level of assessment has a different purpose, they are not independent of one another. Each level collects information about student learning in differing degrees of detail, measuring the same set of learning goals at different levels of complexity. The assessment balance in the system is not achieved by having equal numbers of assessments at each of the five levels, or of summative and formative assessment events, or of multiple-choice items and performance assessment tasks, or of large-scale and classroom assessments. Rather, the concept of balance here refers to having the necessary information at the appropriate level of detail available to all users when they need it. A balanced system when in place is comprehensive and therefore can decrease the tendency to use any one assessment or assessment level to deliver results for multiple purposes.

Figure 1.1 shows the system we describe in the form of a hierarchical pyramid, with classroom formative assessment serving as the foundation of success for the four levels above it. Your school or district may already have an assessment system in place, or parts of one, or similar levels, perhaps with different labels. Whatever your present situation is, a thorough review of the current system and development of a plan for next steps are a large part of assessment literacy goal #1.

FIGURE 1.1   Five levels of assessment in a comprehensive and balanced system

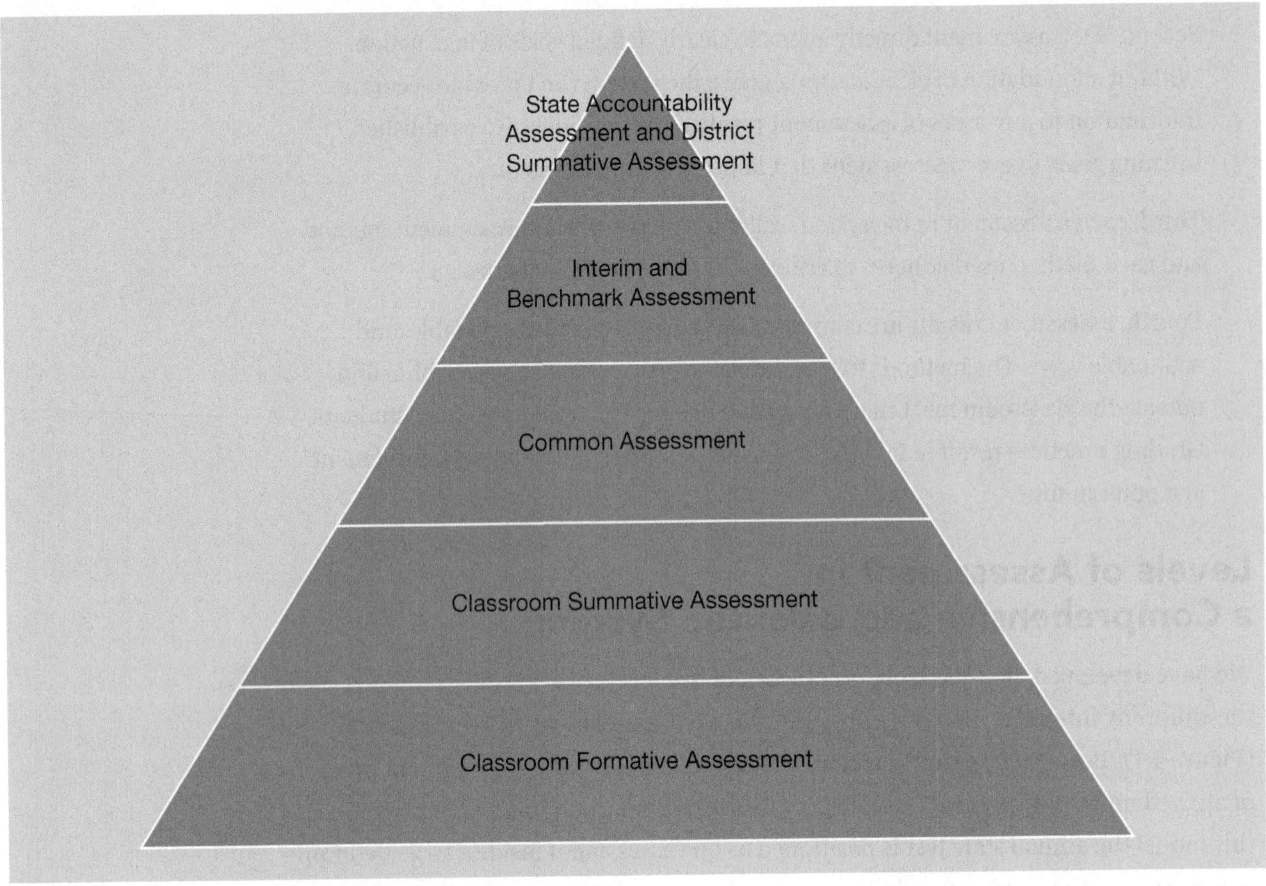

State Accountability
Assessment and District
Summative Assessment

Interim and
Benchmark Assessment

Common Assessment

Classroom Summative Assessment

Classroom Formative Assessment

State Accountability Assessment
and District Summative Assessment

This level of **summative assessment** is the least frequent in administration, furthest from the classroom, and the only level that the local district does not entirely control. The annual state accountability assessment is more about measuring system performance than individual student performance. Typically, state assessment results provide the broadest level of information about student learning: districts can be compared with one another, schools can be compared with one other, and groups of students can be compared. Assessments at this large-scale level typically group academic standards for reporting purposes rather than report student status on each and every standard. Given that limitation, it's not hard to see that the use of the information would also be limited, particularly as it relates to individual students. Even so, the list of users at this level is deep, with the possible exception of students: from policymakers to community members, to every level of state, district, and school leaders and teachers, accountability scores are an important contributor to assessing how the education system (in a state, district, or school) is performing.

Other large-scale standardized assessments that many districts give, usually on an annual or semi-annual basis, don't have the same high stakes attached to them and are often a vendor-published test of "basic skills." Although intended to mirror the learning goals of most states, they can really only do so to a certain extent given their reliance on selected response items, meaning that some valued learning goals go unassessed. Still, this type of norm-referenced assessment (see Chapter 9 for a full explanation) can play a role in providing a different kind of measure in that it reports whether students performed better or worse than a hypothetical student with an average score.

Interim and Benchmark Assessment

The users of information for this level of assessment are fewer in number, consisting mainly of school leaders and classroom teachers. That is largely because one of the primary purposes of interim/benchmark assessments is to monitor and improve student performance, typically two to four times a year, leading up to the state accountability test. Some districts refer to them as their "dip-stick tests," providing common data points on student learning and hopefully predicting state assessment performance results at the end of the year. This is best achieved when a district maps out its learning goals for the year by calendar and the interim assessments are matched to what has been taught during the period just prior to the assessment (Herman et al., 2010). When interim assessments are parallel in form to the state assessment and measure the same learning goals, their results of can be connected to progress toward the learning requirements of a state assessment (Brookhart et al., 2019; Educational Testing Service, 2018). This predictive purpose is one of four main purposes for which states and districts use interim assessments. They are as follows:

1. *Communicate expectations for learning:* Interim assessments help inform students, parents, and teachers what knowledge and skills are important. This is especially true if the assessments are not limited to traditional selected response formats.

2. *Plan curriculum and instruction:* If interim assessments are truly aligned with learning goals, if they are verified by a process and statement other than a vendor's claim, and if what is assessed is what has just been taught in the classroom, their results can be used to adjust curriculum and instruction to better meet student needs. Teachers and school leaders can identify content to reteach, differentiate instruction, and identify students who need additional support.

3. *Monitor and evaluate instructional and/or program effectiveness:* Just as individual students and student groups can be affected by the changes brought about in instruction due to an interim assessment, so too can programs (reading curriculum, math text adoption, instructional framework for teaching students writing, etc.) be evaluated using data from appropriately constructed interim assessments, and course corrections can be made as a result.

4. *Predict future performance:* Interim assessment results can assist teachers and school leaders in knowing how well students or groups of students are doing and how likely they are to be rated proficient on the state accountability test at the end of the year (Dadey & Diggs, 2019; Herman et al., 2010).

An interim assessment can serve more than one of these four purposes (Herman et al., 2010; Perie et al., 2007). But doing so requires careful consideration in assessment development or selection. As in other assessments, purpose plays an important role not only in successful and appropriate use of results but also in assessment design and development. An assessment designed to predict state accountability test performance is going to be different from an assessment that monitors the curriculum as taught. Whatever the purpose, when the data are reliable and reported in a timely way, the chances increase that results are likely to be actionable. For example, aggregating and reporting information differently for users in the system at various levels (student, classroom, grade, school, district) with item analysis should be a feature of all systems. Among other things, teachers can be provided data for individual students by content strand, by subgroups that perform similarly, either above or below expectations, and by individual classrooms, facilitating as many options as possible for intervention and assistance (Herman et al., 2010).

Given the four purposes listed above, with appropriate reporting formats, interim assessment results can have formative value if the right conditions are in place. This can be problematic, especially if an item bank is being used to construct the assessment and if that same item bank is "open" for items constructed locally. In such cases assessment literacy for item bank users becomes a must. If it is a quality assessment that yields accurate results, information can be gathered that can answer questions such as the following:

- Which students or groups of students need help, and with what standard or set of standards?

- Where should we focus instruction for the next interim? What needs reteaching?

- Do we need any regrouping of students? What other interventions are called for?

- Did items assess what hasn't been taught? Which ones?

Finally, in the process of designing a balanced assessment system, it is important to note at the outset that the research at this time does not provide much evidence showing significant increases in student achievement as a result of assessment at this level (Carlson et al., 2011; Dadey & Diggs, 2019; Jones, 2013; Konstantopoulos et al., 2013; Konstantopoulos, Li, et al., 2016; Konstantopoulos, Miller, et al., 2016; Leithwood & Louis, 2012). Of the four main purposes of interim assessments described above, the most common use found in research is for instructional purposes, even though few studies address the efficacy of the assessments themselves. Still, we agree that there are intuitive arguments for including this level of assessment in a local system. Properly constructed or selected interim assessments can play an important role by helping track and predict student performance and improve curriculum and instruction. This level of assessment may lead to a desired change in student learning, but it is not the change agent in and by itself (Dadey & Diggs, 2019; Perie et al., 2007).

Common Assessment

This level of assessment is flexible in purpose (summative or formative) and in the student population to be assessed. Common assessments are administered at regular time intervals, usually by subject-area or grade-level teams of teachers, with the results being applied to instructional improvement.

With regard to purpose, whether formative or summative, care must be taken on the front end prior to assessment design and administration and on the back end when it comes to using results. As with item bank use, which could also be an issue at this level, assessment literacy is another must-have for common assessment development. This is the first level we've looked at so far where students can be actively involved in using the assessment results. This is in part because the detail provided at this level is usually smaller-grained than that derived from an interim/benchmark assessment, although less granular than the daily-lesson detail that can be obtained through classroom assessment. And often, results can be returned more quickly than interim assessment results. Some of the questions that can be answered by the results of common assessments are similar to those that can be answered with interim/benchmark assessments. And if properly planned, common assessments also provide an opportunity to examine how students are thinking, as well as their understanding or misunderstanding of what has been taught at a chapter or unit level. They also provide opportunities for teachers to share best practices, track patterns in student responses, modify daily instructional planning as needed, and gauge where students are at a given time relative to the intended learning (Erkens, 2016).

The grouping of students participating in the assessment can be any of the following:

- Subject area by whole school

- Subject area by grade-level teams

- Subject area vertical teams

- Other identified student subgroups

This is also a level of assessment that the school leader can directly and positively influence. Most often, instead of buying an assessment product off the shelf, common assessments are developed and scored in-house by collaborative teams of teachers. This presents the principal with both an opportunity and a responsibility for assessment leadership, which may include actions such as the following:

- Maintaining the school's focus on established learning goals, using assessment and instruction terms and practices commonly understood by all staff members

- Providing the professional development support needed for item construction and task development (scoring procedures and analysis of results are a leadership responsibility at this level of assessment; some teachers report hesitation in developing common assessments, acknowledging their own need for assessment literacy [Erkens, 2016])

- Fostering collaborative teamwork at all stages of the assessment process, from development to action on results, decreasing teacher and assessment isolation

- Helping teachers respond to results with specific instructional plans of action

- Helping determine what instructional changes should be made for the next time the same content is taught versus what can be applied for immediate use in the classroom

Classroom Summative Assessment

A weekly spelling quiz, a chapter test in history, a unit project in science, or a term-long research paper—just about everything that goes into the gradebook is considered summative and is part of this level of assessment. This means that it is in some way evaluated and scored, and is what most people, and certainly students, think of first when they hear the term *classroom assessment*.

This assessment level has a very clear purpose: it verifies that students have met certain learning requirements, derived from the same learning goals assessed at the other four levels. It comes after the learning and assigns scores to the assessment results, which then feed into grades on report cards, which in turn feed into a host of other decisions made about students.

Although all the five levels we describe require care in the development and scoring processes, classroom summative assessment is the level where students can easily get caught crosswise, simply because a lot of things can go wrong. Consider the following:

- The grade on a test is only as reliable as the test itself. If test items are poorly constructed, student confusion results and student scores may not accurately reflect student learning.

- The directions on how to complete a problem or task could be vague and hard to follow, or a writing prompt may use wording beyond the grade-level vocabulary of the student. Either situation could contribute to a faulty score.

- On a collaborative project, students all receive the same grade, which is then factored into the final grade.

- Multiple-choice items on a test have more than one correct answer to choose from.

The good news is that assessment-literate teachers know how to avoid these pitfalls and others like them. They can match the learning targets that have been taught with quality assessment items and the proper assessment method. They can create tasks and scoring guides that meet standards of quality. And summative classroom assessment is another level in the system where principal leadership can play an important role. In Chapters 2–4 we'll provide more detail on what classroom teachers need to know and do for students to have sufficient opportunity to demonstrate what they know and can do, which is important for school leaders to know. This is an area of assessment where professional development can make a positive difference, school and district policies can make a difference, and both can make a contribution to student learning (see Chapter 10).

Classroom Formative Assessment

This level is the heart of the comprehensive and balanced system we describe because it is the level where the research showing the link between formative assessment and student learning is based. It is the only level of student assessment that is meant to be continuously ongoing, integrated into everyday instruction, serving mainly to improve and support learning (Brookhart et al., 2019; Chappuis & Stiggins, 2020). Like every other assessment level, it requires skill and knowledge for the assessment to be accurate and results useful. But it is frequently less formal than the other four levels, allowing teachers and students to work together during instruction to generate information about student learning that can be acted on immediately. It is not an off-the-shelf product or a different kind of "test." Instead, it is a set of teacher and student practices: teachers can diagnose learning needs, provide descriptive feedback, and plan next steps in instruction. Students can use formative assessment information to self-assess and set goals for their next learning, as well as track and reflect on their own progress. If this process is missing from the classroom or ineffectively implemented, all of the formative uses of assessment at the other levels will not combine to provide the learning gains that can be achieved with an assessment-literate classroom teacher. Chapter 4 provides more detail about this level of assessment and how school leaders can support teachers in their use of formative assessment.

A System of Assessments Is Dependent on a System of Learning Goals

You've no doubt noticed the common, connecting thread that runs through the five levels of assessment. It is the learning goals, their different expressions at each level, and their relationships among the five levels that make it a true system, instead of a collection of unrelated assessments. For example, if the state accountability test shows our district as weak in mathematics, we raise the question "Why don't our kids do as well in math as we want?" To answer that question, we need to look at smaller-grain-size information that will tell us what specifically they did or did not learn, at what level of depth, with what degree of success, and so on. Since state standards are assessed in smaller grain size (see Chapter 2) as the assessment levels get closer to the classroom, it is the alignment among the five levels that makes the coordinated assessments a coherent system: the five levels form a united whole.

Designing the System: Getting Started

One of the first steps in creating a balanced system is to conduct an *assessment audit* at both the school and the district level. An assessment audit maps the big picture of what assessments are currently in use that originate outside the classroom. Activity 1.1, at the end of this chapter, provides an abridged example of the tools and processes that go into an assessment audit. The audit produces an assessment inventory that provides information on what assessments are being given, what standards the assessments measure and at what grade level(s), their frequency or when they are given, how much time each one takes, what assessments are in place for special populations, and the assessment accommodations provided. An audit can also collect information on and catalog each assessment's purpose, the developer(s) of the assessment, the assessment format or methods used, the users of results, the type of data/report furnished, and the cost. If your district has a **comprehensive assessment plan**, there is already assessment guidance in the system, and some of the information needed for the audit can be accessed in the plan.

The condensed model for an assessment audit we provide can be adapted to fit local needs and interests. Other, more complete audit models can be found online at achieve.org, and an online search of states and districts that have completed assessment audits yields not just models but also auditing tools, a variety of process options and display options, and different points of data collection. Most models advise an inclusive approach with as many stakeholder groups as possible represented in the process, and also allow for some flexibility in what information is collected.

After the Audit

Once the audit is conducted, the management of a system of assessments can be more methodical. School leaders, district personnel, and other stakeholders involved in the process begin to analyze the information collected via the inventories. The analysis may reveal gaps and redundancies relative to assessing established learning goals or, worse, a total misalignment. There may be a mismatch between the uses of results and the purpose of the assessment. There may be an absence of test and item specifications, which will likely raise questions about any assessment offered in that condition. Or gaps might be found in an assessment imbalance by grade level or by subject area. The redundancies may lead to some assessments being eliminated, or assessments that are not of high quality might be identified. The audit results can be compiled into a report and then developed into an action plan for next steps and considerations. Individual school inventories can also be merged with district audit information for a comprehensive picture, school by school, giving building administrators similar options for action and improvement. In summary, a comprehensive assessment plan based on high-quality assessments, assessment balance, users and uses, and multiple measures becomes a stronger management tool when it is informed by the results of assessment audits.

Extending the Use of Audit Results

The information collected through the audit process is also useful when aligning a local system with a state assessment system and ensuring that they work together, keeping the mutually shared learning goals front and center. Assessment audit results also are valuable when communicating with parents about standardized test administration and results. Once each assessment's audit data (time, purpose, use of results, standards assessed, methods used, scoring procedures, etc.) are cataloged, districts and schools can use the information to create communications to parents to help them understand what is assessed, when, and for which purposes.

Beyond conducting an assessment audit as described above, and modeled in Activity 1.1, audits for other purposes can yield additional, detailed information that can contribute to improving various components of the system—as indicated by the following examples:

- Any assessment can be audited for standards of quality (detailed in Chapter 3). In some audit models and processes, but not in all, this is called for by default.

- Any curriculum or set of standards can be audited for a balance of the four types of learning goals (see Chapter 2).

- A classroom instructional curriculum can be audited against state/district standards and local learning goals to help ensure alignment of what is taught and what is assessed.

- A text series and supplemental materials can be audited for alignment with and support of the learning goals.

- Classroom assessment practices and instruments can be analyzed for a balance of formative and summative assessment, in the types of learning goals assessed, and in the appropriate assessment methods used.

- Methods for communicating results to assessment users can be evaluated for clarity and effectiveness.

Finally, an evaluation protocol for assessments is available for schools or districts from SCILLSS (Strengthening Claims-Based Interpretations and Uses of Local and Large-Scale Science Assessment Scores). Titled *Ensuring Rigor in Local Assessment Systems: A Self-Evaluation Protocol*, it is designed for interim assessments developed by test vendors and is available at www.scillsspartners.org.

Closing

Whether it is system performance or student performance, whether it is a large-scale assessment or a formative assessment embedded in classroom instruction, it is not possible to know how well the system or the students in it are doing unless all assessments are of high quality. We can avoid the "garbage in, garbage out" syndrome produced by unsound assessments by ensuring assessment-literate staff and a coherent system of assessments founded on a commitment to the learning goals of the district. Clear instructional targets for students and assessment literacy for staff are the cornerstones of a balanced system. When the classroom is brought into balance with formative strategies that help students learn, partnered with high-quality summative assessments to measure learning, it mirrors what we hope to achieve in the larger organization. In this way, students can become the primary users of assessment information. Without their direct involvement in the formative assessment process, the gains in student learning shown by research are less likely to materialize.

 ## Success Indicators for Assessment Literacy Goal #1

The school leader

- can describe a model for a comprehensive local assessment system and can speak to components of the system such as assessment balance, coherence of learning goals, accurate assessment, and student involvement;

- can explain why classroom formative assessment acts as the foundation of the system; and

- can explain the differences and similarities among the five levels of assessment.

 ## Study Guide Questions

1. Why does a solid foundation of assessment literacy weave through the components and functions of a comprehensive and balanced assessment system?

2. What are some strategies a school leader could use to ensure that assessment results are used for instructional improvement?

3. As a result of reading this chapter, has your conception of *summative assessment* and *formative assessment* changed or remained the same? If changed, how so?

4. In your own words, how would you define the term *balanced assessment*?

5. Of the five assessment levels described, what levels are currently in use and working as defined in the text?

6. After reading this chapter, what comes to mind as the first thing you would need to either know or do?

Personal Portfolio Entry Suggestions

- Assessment audit inventories, reports, and/or action plans

- Annual assessment calendar by school/district

- Instructional materials' alignment to learning goals analysis/report

- Professional development initiatives or calendar related to assessment literacy

- Staff memos regarding school or district assessment plan implementation

- Site council minutes related to assessment matters

- Schoolwide action plan or district strategic plan

- Personal/professional goal-setting examples regarding assessment

- Faculty meeting agendas dealing with assessment issues

- Minutes of leadership team meetings

- Department/grade-level reports regarding common assessment results, and so on

Activity 1.1
An Abbreviated Assessment Audit Model

Learning Targets for the Activity

- Understand the process used and information required to complete a formal assessment audit.

- Understand the type of information yielded by an audit and how it can be used to further quality assessment practice.

Purpose

The purpose of this activity is for participants to experience a simplified version of an assessment audit. Doing this activity will help demonstrate how some components of an assessment audit function, and can help you tailor the experience (create different grids, adjust column categories, etc.) to your local program for future audits.

The activity has three parts. Each part contains a blank table grid to fill out with your relevant information. Please note that this may not be a group activity in the traditional sense. Different participants may take responsibility for different sections, some of which require analysis and more time than a group activity allows. Once all the information is gathered and the forms are completed, groups can then process the information with the prompts provided.

(Continued)

(Continued)

Time

Variable: multiple sessions over the course of a day or longer, plus prep time to gather the necessary materials.

Materials Needed

- School calendars or other documents that detail or list the assessments being administered to students, and the district Comprehensive Assessment Plan, if one exists. You'll also need a copy of state standards and district learning goals by subject and grade level. Note that this activity may involve gathering information from a variety of sources.

Suggested Room Setup

Tables and chairs for groups of up to eight members.

Part 1: A Model for Identifying Gaps in Your Assessment Plan

Please note that this exercise relates *only to the top three levels* of the five shown in Figure 1.1. It does not pertain to classroom assessment, either summative or formative. The column headings are flexible, and as many as desired can be added.

Directions

1. Once you have gathered your assessment documentation, begin to enter the details according to the column headings. Start with only district-level assessments for a district perspective or school-level assessments for a building-level perspective.

2. Examine the chart once completed; what stands out in each column? Make notes of what the participants conclude from their observations.

3. Next, identify which columns seem to generate the most discussion. For example, in looking at the two columns for standards and district curriculum, do there seem to be redundancies in the measurement of certain content standards?

4. What do you notice about the amount of testing time, the comparison of time across the different subject areas, or the testing schedule in relation to the calendar or school year? Does a picture form of who are the predominant users of the results? How much information might make its way to the classroom for instructional use or improvement?

5. Do the results say anything about the comprehensiveness of the assessment system currently in place? That is, is there evidence that all valued learning outcomes are being assessed, or does it appear to be only those that are easily measured? How can you tell?

Part 2: Record of Required State, District, and School Assessments

The previous organizer was meant to focus on the overall picture of assessment within your system external to the classroom. This organizer assists in narrowing the focus to the use of assessments across grade levels and content areas. This organizer can be used separately for the district, for a set of schools, or for just a single school. This activity is a precursor to part 3, which will select only one subject area for further examination.

You can adapt this grid just as you could the one from part 1. You might want to know more about the mix of summative and formative assessment, the mix of assessment methods, or the similarities and differences between locally developed assessments and assessments purchased off the shelf from a test publisher. You can also start to get more specific about the learning goals being assessed and those omitted.

Directions

1. Using the same assessment documents as needed for part 1, and completed in Figure 1.2, list the assessments by the grade level administered and the content area being measured, using Figure 1.3 to record the results.

2. Next, examine the results first for anything that stands out regarding what is being measured across grade levels and content areas. Do some grade levels or content areas appear more heavily affected than others? Is that important or not, planned or happenstance? Is there balance in meeting informational needs—who is requiring the information and when?

Note: Developed with Dr. Linda Elman.

Part 3: Assessments in a Content Area

This organizer is another way to look at some of the information displayed in Figure 1.3, and it allows you to narrow your analysis from part 2 and determine the assessment picture across any single given content area. For example, if you choose to look at only the math assessments administered during the year, by grade level, for the top three levels of the pyramid in Figure 1.1, this would be one way to display that information. Remember that this model is focused on assessments that do not originate in the classroom.

Directions

1. Using the completed Figures 1.2 and 1.3 and any other necessary information, begin to fill in the cells of Figure 1.4 according to the column headings.

2. Analyze the table for balance in purpose, users, and grade levels tested.

3. Do the assessments inform all the various users of the assessment information, or are they more focused on a few users?

4. Does the assessment information meet all users' needs?

5. Do you have any observations about the grade-level spread of the assessments?

(Continued)

(Continued)

FIGURE 1.2 Identifying gaps

NAME/FORM OF EACH ASSESSMENT ADMINISTERED	GRADE LEVEL(S) TESTED	TIME OF YEAR GIVEN	TOTAL TESTING TIME	SPECIFIC STATE STANDARDS ASSESSED BY THIS INSTRUMENT[a]	CONNECTION TO THE DISTRICT LEARNING GOALS[b]	ASSESSMENT METHOD(S) USED	INTENDED USES AND USERS OF TEST RESULTS	COMMUNICATION OF RESULTS

[a]This column can contain more information than the cell can hold, and a separate attachment is needed. Beyond the identification of the standard by number or strand, it is important to have the full written standard.

[b]This cell asks for a rating (1-2-3 or Strong-Medium-Low, etc.) for representation of each of the state standards identified in the previous cell in the district learning goals for that subject and grade level. Depending on the assessment, this can be a lengthy task and is best completed separately by users familiar with both the standards and the learning goals.

FIGURE 1.3 Assessment balance across grade levels and content areas

GRADE	MATH	LANGUAGE	READING	SCIENCE	SOCIAL STUDIES	OTHER	TOTAL STATE REQUIREMENT	TOTAL SCHOOL REQUIREMENT	TOTAL
Grade 2									
Grade 3									
Grade 4									
Grade 5									

(Continued)

(Continued)

FIGURE 1.4 Assessment in a subject area across grade levels

NAME OF ASSESSMENT	PURPOSE	USERS OF RESULTS	DISTRICT LEVEL	SCHOOL LEVEL	COMMON ASSESSMENTS	TIME NEEDED	TIME OF YEAR GIVEN	K	1	2	3	4	5	6	7	8	9	10	11	12

Definitions

Alignment: Refers to the extent to which what is assessed is a match with what is taught in the classroom.

Comprehensive and balanced assessment system: A program of assessments, practices, and guidelines, all founded on the learning goals of the system and designed to meet the information needs of all users of assessment results in order to both document and improve student learning.

Comprehensive assessment plan: A written description of the philosophy of and approach to student assessment in the organization, including purposes, stakeholders, and uses of results. It also describes the types of assessments used, provides information on scoring and educator training, and includes a list of assessments used.

Formative assessment: A collection of formal and informal processes that teachers and students use to gather and share evidence for the purpose of guiding next steps toward learning and for helping students become self-directed learners.

Learning goal: A statement of what students should know and/or be able to do after instruction. This book will use the term *learning goal* as a general term for intended learning outcomes at any level of specificity, from large- to small-grained, and of any temporal duration, from short-term to long-term.

Summative assessment: The use of assessment information to certify that students have met certain learning requirements, usually at the end of an instructional unit, a lesson, or some other fixed period of time, such as a course, semester, or year.

 This chapter's online resources are available for download from **resources.corwin.com/10GoalsLeaders**

Clear Standards

2

Assessment Literacy Goal #2: *The leader understands the necessity of clear academic learning goals, aligned classroom-level learning targets, and success criteria used by students and teachers, and their relationship to the development of sound assessments.*

Any consideration of assessment begs the question "assess what?" A classic theory of curriculum, instruction, and assessment sees them as the three vertices of a triangle, where the curriculum says what will be taught and what will be assessed. The triangle is typically depicted as an equilateral triangle, showing that all three are equal in importance and that they must match: what is planned should be taught, and what is taught should be assessed. Of course, today local curricula do not stand alone but represent state standards. And we know that instruction does not simply deliver curriculum but also interprets it as learning goals are transformed into classroom lessons. We also know that assessment that occurs during instruction can be used to alter that instruction. While these complexities render our simple triangle somewhat of an oversimplification, it is not a bad image to keep in mind as you think about assessment. Student learning goals, in all their forms, must be clear to both teachers and students so that they can provide a meaningful basis for both instruction and assessment.

Chapter Learning Goals

1. Understand how state standards are deconstructed into smaller-grain-size learning goals in the curriculum in use in your building/district.

2. Describe how state standards and the learning goals in your district's curriculum are assessed in your building/district.

3. Understand the role of student-friendly learning targets and success criteria in connecting classroom-level instruction and learning with broader learning goals.

4. Understand how clear academic learning goals form the basis for developing sound assessments.

A leader who understands the importance of clear academic learning goals, aligned classroom-level **learning targets** and **success criteria** used by students and teachers, and their relationship to the development of sound assessments has command of two basic concepts. One is that learning goals express intentions about what students should learn, at various levels from general to specific. The second is that a learning goal constitutes the **domain of learning** from which assessments can be designed and to which assessment results are generalized.

Think of it this way. A clear learning goal expresses what students should know and be able to do after instruction. You can't ask students to show they know and can do every possible task the learning goal implies, so you select a sample of tasks from that universe and ask students to do those things; this sample of all possible things you could ask students to do makes up your assessment. If your sample was a representative one, you can reason that student achievement on the whole learning goal is well represented by their performance on your assessment.

For the sake of illustration, let's use a very concrete example, where the domain is limited and the possibilities are not infinite. Suppose a third-grade teacher wants to assess whether their students have memorized the multiplication facts from 0 to 9. It would be possible to give the students a test with all 100 facts on it and find out for each student what percentage of them the student can recall. It would also be possible to select a smaller number of those multiplication facts, say 30 of them, and make a shorter test. If the sample is representative—not all easy facts or hard facts, and not all facts from one number family, but a nice balance—then you could conclude that the students' performance on your 30-fact test would be a reasonable indicator of how they would do if they were given all 100 facts. In other words, you could generalize from how students do on 30 facts to how you would expect them to do on all 100 facts.

Most learning goals are more abstract than memorizing math facts, and often the possibilities for test items or performance tasks that match a given learning goal are infinite. Still, the principle is the same: assessment questions and tasks are always a sample from all possible items or tasks that match the goal. You generalize from students' performance on that sample to arrive at an estimate of their achievement for the whole learning goal. In other words, learning goals control both assessment design and interpretation. The clearer the learning goals are, the more straightforward it is to write or select assessment items or tasks that match the goal (assessment design) and to generalize from students' performance on your assessment to some statement about their level of achievement (assessment interpretation).

Where Do Learning Goals Come From?

It is only within the past 100 years that educators began to realize that articulating learning goals was important. Before that, educators mostly saw learning in terms of topics of study and student compliance with the assigned exercises. In the 1940s, Ralph Tyler and his colleagues revolutionized both curriculum theory and educational evaluation by insisting that education be based on defining appropriate objectives, establishing and delivering learning experiences, and then evaluating whether the objectives had been achieved. As common as this goal-driven approach to educational assessment sounds today, it was revolutionary at the time.

From the 1950s to the 1970s, educators took the use of curriculum-based assessment of learning objectives further. A widely used **taxonomy** of educational objectives (Bloom et al., 1956), behavioral objectives, mastery learning, and measurement-driven instruction (Bloom et al., 1971) all pushed Tyler's principle of evaluating curriculum and programs by how well learning goals were achieved down to the level of small-grained, classroom-level lesson objectives. This moved the principle into the classroom, where teachers, and not administrators, had control over their lessons' learning targets and assessments.

In the 1970s the minimum competency testing movement began as a reaction to a pervasive dissatisfaction with public education. The "competencies" tested were learning goals of a sort, but they were mostly basic-skills minimums. The educational reform movement of the 1980s, partly inspired by the publication of *A Nation at Risk* by the U.S. National Commission on Excellence in Education in 1983, advocated rigorous and measurable standards and high expectations for all students. In the 1990s this reform movement morphed into what has come to be called the "standards movement" (Porter, 1993). States developed standards for achievement and outcomes-based accountability policies. The NCLB era centralized this thinking. The Common Core State Standards in English Language Arts and Literacy in History/Social Studies, Science, and Technical Subjects and Common Core State Standards for Mathematics (Common Core State Standards [CCSS] Initiative, 2020) were an attempt to regularize standards somewhat. Spearheaded in 2010 by the National Governors' Association and the Council of Chief State School Officers, this movement garnered more state support in 2010 than it has as of this writing, but the general principle that states should have standards in content areas seems firmly established for the foreseeable future. More recently, the Next Generation Science Standards (https://www.nextgenscience.org/) and the College, Career, and Civic Life (C3) Framework for Social Studies State Standards (https://www.socialstudies.org/c3) have provided guidance for state standards in their respective content areas.

What Are Learning Goals, and Where Can I Find Them?

The goal is the place where you aim the football or the hockey puck. It's "something to shoot for." A goal is something one strives for. In education, learning goals describe what students will know and be able to do after instruction and learning take place. They describe outcomes (e.g., "I can explain why objects float or sink"), not inputs (e.g., "I will watch a video on floating and sinking"). There are many reasons for this, but probably the easiest to remember is that there is no guarantee than any particular input (e.g., watching a video, reading a textbook, doing an experiment) will lead to the desired learning.

Learning goals are the basis for both instructional decisions about what methods to use to help students achieve the goals and assessment decisions about what methods to use to check on student progress toward or arrival at the goals. As described above, learning goals (often organized in curriculum documents), instruction, and assessment should work together and should align with one another. When these three elements do not match, students may be intended to learn one thing, taught another, and assessed on something else. This renders assessment information useless and ultimately harms students and their learning. The key to all this starts with learning goals.

Terminology

State standards are learning goals, but they are broad in scope. They define general intended learning outcomes (e.g., "CCSS RI [Reading Informational Text] 2.8: Describe how reasons support specific points the author makes in a text"). The outcomes described are at a large grain size. Because of state accountability policies, state standards become the basis for local curriculum, again at a broad level. Standards are deconstructed into learning goals of smaller grain sizes until they reach levels suitable for teaching and learning. Figure 2.1 shows how learning goals differ in grain size, using general terms for the learning goals. Different states and districts use different terms for the levels of learning goals under state standards.

FIGURE 2.1	Learning goals come in different grain sizes	
State standard	Describe how reasons support specific points the author makes in a text.	
Unit learning goal	Students will understand that reasons can be based on facts, research, logic, and sometimes appeals to authority or emotion, depending on the text.	
Teacher instructional objective	The student will be able to identify facts in informational text and describe how the author relates them to the main idea.	
Learning target	I can find the facts in an article and explain how they support the author's main point.	

Source: Images from Pixabay.com.

Typically, some sort of curriculum document relates the smaller-in-scope learning goals to the state standards. These subsumed learning goals may have several levels themselves. **Unit learning goals**, which may be known by different terms in different districts, may be more focused goals that feed into the broader goals (e.g., "Students will understand that reasons can be based on facts, research, logic, and sometimes appeals to authority or emotion, depending on the text"). **Teacher instructional objectives** within a unit, which again may be known by different terms in different districts, may be more focused still (e.g., "The student will be able to identify facts in informational text and describe how the author relates them to the main idea"). The instructional objectives from a series of lessons should form a learning trajectory that leads to broader unit goals and state standards. The important principle to understand is that broader standards are deconstructed into goals of smaller grain sizes, until they arrive at descriptions of what students should know and be able to do that are of an appropriate size for instruction. In a comprehensive assessment system (see Chapter 1), assessment happens at all levels.

Another example may be helpful to illustrate the variation in learning goal grain size and terminology. Some districts unpack curriculum directly from standards to what they call learning targets, which may be of a grain size that requires one lesson or a sequence of lessons, omitting the intermediate level labeled "unit goals" above. Figure 2.2 presents an example from a district workshop in North Carolina.

FIGURE 2.2   Example of two levels of learning goals.

NC STANDARD COURSE OF STUDY
GRADE 7 ELA
READING FOR INFORMATION

Standard: *RI 7.8: Trace and evaluate the argument and specific claims in a text, assessing whether the reasoning is sound and the evidence is relevant and sufficient to support the claims.*

Student learning targets:

I can identify an author's argument in an informational text.

I can identify the author's specific claim(s) in an informational text.

I can identify evidence that supports the author's argument(s) and specific claim(s) in an informational text.

I can assess whether the author's evidence is relevant and sufficient to support the claim(s).

I can trace the author's argument(s) and claim(s) in an informational text to determine their overall effectiveness.

I can evaluate the author's argument(s) and claim(s) in an informational text, determining whether the reasoning is sound and logical.

Standard: I can trace and evaluate the argument and specific claims in a text, assessing whether the reasoning is sound and the evidence is relevant and sufficient to support the claims.

Source: Allison H. Ormond, PhD, National Board Certified Teacher, North Carolina.

Note: NC, North Carolina; ELA, English language arts; RI, Reading Instruction.

Despite variations in terminology and number of levels, the principle remains the same. Curriculum documents in most districts use the term *standard* for broad learning goals and describe smaller-grain-size learning goals under them. These may be presented differently in different content areas, but the purpose of stating these learning goals is the same. They all describe what students should know and be able to do after instruction and therefore inform both instructional planning and assessment design and interpretation.

Grain Sizes and Classroom Instruction

The smaller the grain size of the learning goal, the closer it gets to classroom learning. Assessments can be based on learning goals at any level of the hierarchy (see Chapter 1). For example, a state accountability assessment may sample lightly from a broad domain (e.g., "Reading"), with the goal of reporting achievement over all the reading standards. A unit test or **performance assessment** may set questions and tasks for students that tap their understanding of just the instructional objectives related to that unit.

A learning target is a student-friendly version of an instructional objective. It is sometimes more focused, depending on the complexity of the instructional objective. Let's use this social studies standard as an example: "Compare and contrast democracies with different forms of governments." This standard is composed of several instructional objectives—defining the characteristics of several forms of government, determining the salient features on which to base comparisons, describing similarities and differences between any two forms of government, and supporting claims of similarities and differences with examples. Let's say a teacher's instructional objective is "Define the characteristics of a monarchy and an oligarchy." The student-friendly learning target will be "I can define the characteristics of a monarchy and an oligarchy." However, if the instructional objective is "Determine the salient features on which to base comparisons of different forms of governments," the student-friendly learning target might be "I can determine important features common to monarchies and oligarchies on which to base comparisons." In the first case the learning target is a straightforward restatement of the instructional objective from the student's point of view. In the second case the learning target has been focused on a specific case from the more general instructional objective. A learning target describes the learning that students and teachers will aim for—hence the "target" metaphor—in a lesson (Moss & Brookhart, 2012).

Learning Targets With Success Criteria

Learning targets help students participate in a formative learning cycle ("Where am I going? Where am I now? Where to next?")—that is, to be proactive and self-regulated instead of passive recipients of, and compliers with, teacher directions. Learning targets are most effective when they are stated in language that a student who has not hit the target would understand, mapped clearly to a task that gives evidence of student learning (the assessment), and coupled with student-friendly success criteria that students and teachers can both use during learning (for formative assessment) as well as afterward (for summative assessment).

Success criteria are the most powerful aspect of **lesson learning targets**. They help students form a clear concept of what the target means and give them a way to monitor their progress toward the target. In the words of the *target* metaphor, they show students how to aim the bow. Using more clinical language, success criteria operationalize the way to get to the target. They provide both students and teachers language with which to talk about the learning—which is a more important point than one might think—and qualities to look for in the work. Success criteria are not scores or grades (e.g., 80%, B) but rather characteristics of the work (e.g., "includes descriptive adjectives"). These characteristics can form the basis for student self-assessment and teacher feedback during learning (i.e., for formative assessment). They can become the basis for scores or grades after instruction (i.e., for summative assessment). For example, in the lesson about analyzing an article from Figure 2.1, success criteria might include the following: "I state the author's main point clearly. I find facts in the article that support that point. I tell why the facts are convincing to me." Or the success criteria might be in the form of a more general rubric about reading expository text that would transfer to other tasks assessing the same learning goal: using text-based evidence, using relevant details, clear reasoning, logical organization, and so on. The point is that success criteria flesh out the learning target for students and at the same time facilitate both self-assessment and teacher feedback.

What Are Some Different Kinds of Learning Goals?

Learning goals can be classified according to what kind of learning they describe. The kind of learning you want to assess helps you identify the assessment methods you need to use, because different methods are more or less appropriate for different kinds of learning goals, as we will see later in this chapter.

There are several different ways of classifying learning goals. In your university courses you may have studied the new Bloom's taxonomy (Anderson & Krathwohl, 2001). The new Bloom's taxonomy describes different kinds of learning goals using two dimensions, according to what kind of knowledge is invoked (called the Knowledge dimension, with four categories) and what kind of thinking is invoked (called the Cognitive Process dimension, with six categories). Learning goals, and the assessments that tap them, can then be classified into a four-by-six table defined by the categories of these dimensions. This is one way of looking at what kind of learning goal you want to teach and assess and what kind of assessment will match those intentions.

Here, we will use a four-category taxonomy for learning goals (Chappuis & Stiggins, 2020). This way of sorting learning goals more easily supports selecting an assessment method that matches the learning goal. The four categories are as follows:

- **Knowledge learning goals** specify the facts, concepts, and procedures students will learn and understand. These facts, concepts, and procedures are usually discipline specific.

- **Reasoning learning goals** specify the thought processes students will learn to apply. They may be cross-disciplinary.

- **Performance skill learning goals** specify the physical performances or demonstrations in which students will develop proficiency.

- **Product learning goals** specify the artifacts students will be able to produce.

These goals are related hierarchically. When a student reasons, for example, they use facts (knowledge) to support their arguments. When a student executes a performance skill, for example, making a wet mount slide of cheek cells for a microscope, they use knowledge about the parts of the microscope and needed supplies and reasoning about how best to assemble the supplies and collect and mount their specimen. When a student produces a product like a term paper, they may analyze, compare, classify, or evaluate (i.e., they use reasoning) facts and concepts (knowledge) to arrive at that product.

How Are Learning Goals Deconstructed for Curriculum, Instruction, and Assessment?

If learning goals are the aim or outcome of instruction, teaching and learning are how students get there. To use a metaphor, learning goals are the destination, instruction is the GPS navigation directions, and learning is what students do as they walk or drive on the path. Like GPS directions, instruction doesn't usually go directly to a destination "as the crow flies." There are turns and landmarks along the way. The journey can be deconstructed into smaller journeys, and drivers can check their progress along the way. Simpler journeys have fewer stops along the way. More complex journeys have more stops.

In a similar sort of way, as we said in the previous section, broad state standards are usually deconstructed into learning goals that are simple enough to support a unit-sized journey, and unit goals are deconstructed into teacher instructional objectives that form the basis for instruction and into student-friendly learning targets that define the learning for students. But something else happens as well when state standards are deconstructed into smaller goals for instruction and assessment, which turns out to be important for instruction and assessment.

When broad state standards are deconstructed, they can—and often do—end up subsuming learning goals of two or more types: knowledge, reasoning, performance skill, and product. In fact, this is true most of the time, and the exceptions would be very unusual standards; for example, some state history standards simply specify the facts students are expected to know because they live in the state. It is best to expect that, in general, broad standards include more than one type of learning goal.

This, of course, has implications for instruction, because how you teach knowledge of facts differs from how you teach reasoning and performance skills. And it has implications for assessment, which we take up in the next section. The purpose of this section is to make the case that many kinds of learning goals are woven into state standards, so to plan curriculum, deliver instruction, and—most germane to our assessment literacy goal—assess learning, you have to know what these are. Perhaps the best way to show this is to give an example.

A third-grade writing standard in the category Text Types and Purposes (CCSS, 2020) reads as follows:

1. Write opinion pieces on topics or texts, supporting a point of view with reasons.

    a. Introduce the topic or text they are writing about, state an opinion, and create an organizational structure that lists reasons.

    b. Provide reasons that support the opinion.

    c. Use linking words and phrases (e.g., *because, therefore, since, for example*) to connect opinion and reasons.

    d. Provide a concluding statement or section.

Writing an opinion piece is a product goal. To deconstruct the standard in order to teach and assess it, students would need to be able to

- understand specific vocabulary and concepts (*opinion, reason, organize, linking word, conclusion*)—knowledge;

- distinguish between opinions and reasons—reasoning;

- formulate an opinion about a topic or text—reasoning;

- formulate reasons that support an opinion—reasoning; and

- organize the opinion and reasons into a written product that includes stating an opinion, using linking words to connect the opinion and reasons, and writing a conclusion—product.

Goals from other writing standards—for example, goals about doing research to present knowledge or goals about using standard language conventions—may also be invoked. But we think it is enough for you to see that the teacher would not just ask students to begin by writing an opinion piece. They would teach other goals along the way. Similarly, there would likely be performance assessments: students might be asked to produce several different opinion pieces in the unit. But there might also be other assessments along the way—for example, an exercise in distinguishing opinions and reasons, or a discussion about what constitutes strong and weak support for an idea.

How Are Learning Goals Assessed?

Two ideas are important for understanding how learning goals drive assessment. The first is that the type of learning goal helps suggest which assessment method is the most appropriate—that is, which assessment method will likely yield information that is the most meaningful and accurate for decisions to be made about that learning goal. The second is that the learning goal defines the content domain from which assessment questions and tasks are sampled. We focus on the former here. The next chapter (assessment literacy goal #3) will take up how to ensure that an appropriate sample of questions and tasks is drawn from a learning domain.

Assessments have two parts: tools (sometimes called assessment instruments) and processes. We are used to thinking of the tool as the assessment itself (e.g., someone may refer to a unit test as an "assessment"), but the process is also important. For example, a well-constructed unit test administered at the end of a unit after giving students enough notice for them to have time to study and where students have enough time to take the test in a quiet classroom would likely be an effective assessment because both the tool and the process were of high quality. The same unit test if given without notice or after the wrong unit of instruction would likely be ineffective; a high-quality tool cannot rescue a flawed process, and vice versa. For this discussion we are going to focus on the tools or assessment instruments, but before we do that, we just wanted to confirm that you realize there is more to assessment than a set of questions.

Many different varieties of questions and tasks exist, but for our purposes we can think of four general categories: (1) **selected-response items**, (2) **constructed-response exercises**, (3) performance assessment, and (4) **personal communication**. We will define each one first and then show how some assessment varieties are more suited to some types of learning goals than to others.

1. *Selected-response items* include multiple-choice, true/false, matching, and fill-in items. These formats require that students recognize and choose a correct answer.

2. *Constructed-response exercises* include short-answer and extended-response exercises and show-the-work math or science problems. These formats require that students generate their own answer to a question or prompt.

3. *Performance assessment* is assessment of a student process or product, or both, using observation and judgment based on criteria. Performance assessments have two parts: a task or tasks and rubrics or some other scoring scheme.

4. *Personal communication* involves gathering information about what students know through oral interaction. Personal communication includes asking questions during instruction, listening during student discussion, giving oral exams, and interviewing.

You can probably see how understanding the nature of the learning goal will help you select an appropriate assessment method—one that is capable of yielding meaningful and accurate information—just from reading the descriptions of the different assessment methods. To assess whether students know the year in which the Battle of Hastings was fought (1066), a knowledge learning outcome, you could simply ask them, using a selected-response or fill-in format. To assess whether students can explain the consequences of the Norman conquest of England, you could pose a constructed-response exercise. To assess student understanding in more detail, you could assign a product like a term paper or written report. This kind of thinking has been called "target-method match" (Chappuis & Stiggins, 2020, p. 106). Figure 2.3 evaluates the target-method match for four types of learning goals and four assessment methods.

FIGURE 2.3   Target-method match

TYPE OF LEARNING GOAL	SELECTED RESPONSE	CONSTRUCTED RESPONSE	PERFORMANCE ASSESSMENT	PERSONAL COMMUNICATION
Knowledge	*Good* Can assess isolated elements of knowledge and some relationships among them	*Strong* Can assess elements of knowledge and the relationships among them	*Partial* Can assess elements of knowledge and relationships among them in certain contexts	*Strong* Can assess elements of knowledge and the relationships among them
Reasoning	*Good* Can assess many but not all reasoning targets	*Strong* Can assess all reasoning targets	*Good* Can assess reasoning targets in the context of certain tasks in certain contexts	*Strong* Can assess all reasoning targets
Performance skill	*Partial* Good match for some measurement skill targets; not a good match otherwise	*Poor* Cannot assess skill level; can only assess prerequisite knowledge and reasoning	*Strong* Can observe and assess skills as they are being performed	*Partial* Strong match for some oral communication proficiencies; not a good match otherwise
Product	*Poor* Cannot assess the quality of a product; can only assess prerequisite knowledge and reasoning	*Poor* Cannot assess the quality of a product; can only assess prerequisite knowledge and reasoning	*Strong* Can directly assess the attributes or quality of products	*Poor* Cannot assess the quality of a product; can only assess prerequisite knowledge and reasoning

Source: Chappuis, Jan; Stiggins, Rick J., *Classroom Assessment For Student Learning: Doing It Right - Using It Well, 3rd Edition* (Figure 4.3, p. 106) © 2020. Reprinted by permission of Pearson Education, Inc.

Note: Strong—the method works for all learning goals of this type; *Good*—the method works for many learning goals of this type; *Partial*—the method works for some learning goals of this type; *Poor*—the method does not work for any learning goals of this type.

In summary, learning goals express intentions about what students should learn, at various levels from general to specific. In other words, they are intended learning outcomes or statements of what students should know and be able to do after instruction. Learning goals therefore should influence both instruction and assessment. A learning goal influences assessment design and interpretation in two ways. First, you choose the assessment you are going to use based on its ability to yield meaningful and accurate results for the type of learning outcome you have. Second, the learning goal defines the domain from which assessment questions and tasks are sampled and to which assessment results are generalized.

 ## Success Indicators for Assessment Literacy Goal #2

The school leader

- ensures that school curriculum documents are aligned with state standards;

- ensures that school curriculum documents are easily accessible to staff;

- secures staff training in the use of classroom materials relative to state standards;

- differentiates for staff teaching the written curriculum from teaching a textbook;

- monitors lesson plans and classroom instruction for clear communication of learning targets;

- publishes learning goals/targets for parents in student-friendly language; and

- provides staff training in selecting or creating assessments that are matched to the learning goals.

 ## Study Guide Questions

1. Think back over the study of academic learning goals that you did for this assessment literacy goal. What did you find most interesting about the examples you reviewed and discussed? Did anything surprise you?

2. After reading this chapter and doing the activities, you may be more familiar with the learning goals in your building and district. Can you identify any that do not rise to the level of "clear standards"? That is, are any of the learning goals unclear, or are any of the learning goals likely to be interpreted in different ways by different administrators and teachers? What might your next step be to address this issue?

3. Are the assessments in use in your building/district well matched to the learning goals they were intended to assess? Did you notice any assessments that were not good matches to their goals? What might your next step be to address this issue?

4. What are some ways you could engage teachers in your building/district to build their lessons on student-centered learning targets and success criteria? Or if this is already in progress in your building/district, what are some ways you could support and enhance this work?

Personal Portfolio Entry Suggestions

- Examples of learning goals in your building or district, annotated according to grain size, cognitive level, and other characteristics described in this chapter

- Samples of lesson plans that show a clear connection between learning goals, instruction, and assessment

- Statements of learning goals prepared for parents

- Test blueprint from a common assessment

- Collaborative Inquiry Guide for Learning Targets and Success Criteria from Activity 2.3, filled in, accompanied by your notes from the collegial feedback session and a written statement of the professional learning goal you set for yourself, the success criteria you identified, and what you have done to pursue the goal

- Further work by subject-area or grade-level teams on unpacking standards, developing units, or mapping curriculum

- Agendas or memos where learning goals are the focus

- Any personal/professional goal related to learning goals and clear targets

 ## Activity 2.1
Exploring the Relationship Between Learning Goals and Assessment

Learning Target for the Activity

- Explain how clear academic achievement standards are the basis for developing sound assessments.

Purpose

In this activity school leaders analyze the relationship of one assessment to the learning goals it is intended to assess. The purpose of doing this analysis is to prepare school leaders to think in this way about the other assessments in use in the building/district as well and to demonstrate the importance of understanding the link between learning goals and assessment.

Time

Approximately one hour

(Continued)

(Continued)

Materials Needed

- Choose an assessment in use in your building/district. For this exercise use a formal assessment: a test or performance assessment. Include the scoring directions (e.g., a test scoring key, rubrics). Select an assessment with enough substance that it can be used with the protocol below. The assessment can be projected electronically or provided as a print copy to each participant.

- A copy (electronic or printed) of the state standard(s), teacher instructional objectives, and any other learning goals for which the chosen assessment is intended.

- A copy (electronic or printed) of the protocol "What's in an Assessment?"

- Chart paper and markers

What's in an Assessment?

This protocol can be used to analyze assessment exercises or instructional tasks for what they require students to know and be able to do, and for their match with intended learning goals.

Step 1. Selecting a Facilitator

Select a participant to serve as the facilitator. The facilitator will ensure that the steps are followed in order and that all participants have an opportunity to speak. If the group wishes, they can designate a scribe to take notes.

Step 2. Presenting the Assessment

The group describes the assessment. What are its features and formats?

- What assessment method is used (selected response, constructed response, performance assessment, or personal communication)? Does the assessment use more than one method?

- What type of items, exercises, tasks, or prompts does it present to students?

- Are there directions, and what do they say?

- What scoring methods and directions are provided with the assessment?

- Does the assessment explicitly reference a learning goal? If so, what is it? If not, is one implied in the title of the assessment?

- What other descriptive information about the surface features of the assessment seem salient? For example, is there anything about the length or look of the assessment that would strike students?

- How are students intended to respond to the assessment (e.g., by writing answers on the page, doing a class presentation, writing an essay on a word processor)?

Step 3. Trying the Assessment

- Participants should attempt to do the assessment themselves if it is possible within the time and space available. If not, they should "do" the assignment as a thought experiment: what steps would students take as they work their way through the assessment?

Step 4. Analyzing the Assessment Content

- What content knowledge (facts, concepts, and/or procedures) would students need to have for this assessment? Make sure you have teased out all the content knowledge that seems to be required, whether or not it is relevant to the assessment topic. Record your results on chart paper.

- What cognitive levels would students activate for this assessment? Participants can use Bloom's taxonomy, Webb's depth of knowledge, or a simple dichotomy (recall or basic comprehension vs. higher-order thinking), depending on how student thinking is usually discussed in your building/ district. Record your results on chart paper.

- For any descriptive scoring key (e.g., rubrics or point schemes), note the content knowledge and cognitive level as well. Record your results on chart paper.

Step 5. Analyzing the Intended Learning Goals

- In this step you will analyze the content knowledge and cognitive levels stated or implied in the learning goal(s) the assessment is intended to assess. Please remember that since the assessment is a sample of everything that could be asked, the results from step 5 may not match those of step 4 exactly. Please bracket and save any observations about the relationship between the assessment content and the learning goals for step 6; for now, just analyze the intended learning goals.

- What type of learning goals are involved (knowledge, reasoning, skill, and/or product)?

- What content knowledge (facts, concepts, and/or procedures) do these learning goals say students need to know? Record your results on chart paper.

- What cognitive levels do these learning goals say students need to activate? Record your results on chart paper.

Step 6. Comparing Intended Learning Goals and Assessment

- Using the results you have recorded on chart paper, identify areas where the assessment exercises students are asked to do, and the credit they will get from the scoring scheme for doing them, match the intended learning goals. Compare the content and cognitive-level descriptions for the assessment with those for the learning goals. Use green markers to identify exact (or very close) matches and yellow markers for inexact matches, highlighting the parallel and nonparallel language on the assessment and learning goal charts.

- Using the same chart paper results, identify areas where the assessment exercises students are asked to do, and the credit they will get from the scoring scheme for doing them, require something from students that is not in the intended learning goals. Use red markers for this.

(Continued)

(Continued)

- Finally, using the same process, identify areas where the intended learning goals require something from students that is not in the assessment. Use purple markers for this.

Step 7. Interpreting the Relationship Between the Learning Goal(s) and the Assessment

- Evaluate the "target-method match" (see Figure 2.3). Is the assessment method a match to the learning goal?

- Evaluate the representativeness of the assessment exercises or tasks as a sample from the domain described by the learning goal(s). Are the content and cognitive levels in the assessment a reasonable representation of the domain? Remember that the assessment does not have to ask students everything possible, just be a representative sample of the intended learning.

- Evaluate whether the assessment requires irrelevant knowledge and skills that could cause the assessment to misrepresent students' status on the learning goals.

Step 8. Debriefing

Participants, led by the facilitator, discuss how well the protocol process worked and what they have learned by following it.

Suggested Room Setup

Arrange tables and chairs to accommodate a small group.

Directions

Complete each step in the order below:

1. Participants receive their materials: the assessment and its scoring guide, the learning goal(s) the assessment is intended to measure, and the protocol handout "What's in an Assessment?"

2. The group designate a facilitator. The facilitator and participants follow the protocol.

Closure

Closure is built into step 8 of the protocol.

Activity 2.2
Learning Targets and Success Criteria

Learning Target for the Activity

- Explain the role of learning targets and success criteria in connecting classroom-level instruction and learning with broader learning goals.

Purpose

This activity provides some additional information about learning targets and success criteria and a description of how they are used in one district.

Time

One hour

Materials Needed

- *Reading:* Moss et al. (2011).

- Survey, on a slide with prepared questions or a printed version, or entered into a questioning app (e.g., Socrative). If printed, make two copies for each group member.

- Flip chart and markers or interactive whiteboard

	STRONGLY DISAGREE	DISAGREE	AGREE	STRONGLY AGREE
1. Students who do not know the intention of a lesson expend precious time and energy trying to figure out what their teachers expect them to learn.				
2. Learning targets get their power from sharing them with students.				
3. What you ask students to do in a lesson helps communicate to them what you intend them to learn.				
4. Success criteria describe for students what good work looks like.				
5. Learning targets and success criteria affect student motivation as well as achievement.				

(Continued)

(Continued)

Suggested Room Setup

This is a small-group activity. Sit around a table where everyone can comfortably see and hear one another.

Directions

Working in small groups, complete each step in the order below:

1. Give everyone two copies of the survey (if printed) and a copy of the article or electronic access to it. If the survey is on a slide, project it.

2. Before reading the article, each group member individually completes the five-question survey. Summarize the group results on a flip chart or whiteboard, or project the summary from the questioning app. For each question note how many people selected each option (strongly disagree . . . strongly agree).

3. Individually, read the article "Knowing Your Learning Target." Using a highlighter, highlight the *one sentence* in each section that you think most clearly conveys the main idea of the section. If you are reading the article electronically, write the sentence down. If two or more sentences seem to be relevant, force yourself to select the one of them that, in your estimation, conveys the main idea most clearly. You should end up with eight highlighted sentences, one for each of these sections: (1) What Is a Shared Learning Target? (2) The Dangers of Flying Blind (3) Constructing a Learning Target (4) Beginning to Share (5) The Power of Meaningful Sharing (6) Designing a Strong Performance of Understanding (7) Explaining the Criteria for Success and (8) Empowering Every Student.

4. One of the group should volunteer to be the facilitator in a discussion of each section in turn. First, the facilitator should have each group member share the sentence they selected as the main idea and explain why. Follow-up questions should probe areas of agreement and disagreement. A scribe should make notes on a flip chart or whiteboard.

5. The facilitator then asks a final question: "How do learning targets and success criteria contribute to clear standards, the theme of this assessment literacy goal?" Participants should reference the information on the flip chart or whiteboard to support their answers.

6. After the discussion has ended, the participants individually fill in the survey again. Again, summarize the group results on a flip chart or whiteboard, or project the summary from the questioning app. For each question note how many people selected each option (strongly disagree . . . strongly agree). Compare these results with the results obtained before the reading and discussion. Notice any patterns and try to explain them.

Closure

The group reaches closure by facilitating a discussion based on this question: What did I learn from this activity that is important for me to know in my role as a school leader?

Activity 2.3
Recognizing the Formative Learning Cycle in Action

Learning Target for the Activity

- Be able to tell whether the learning target and success criteria are functioning within a lesson to support student learning.

Purpose

This activity gives school leaders practice with the concept of a learning target and success criteria and thus with the idea that learning goals are not just for teachers but for students as well. The observational aspect of this activity helps school leaders "know it when they see it." The aspects of this activity related to collegial conversations and professional learning goals help school leaders practice what it means to be a leading learner, which is the kind of leadership that has been shown to support classroom formative assessment practices.

Time

Variable (takes more or less time as needed), in three segments: (1) pre-observation conversation with the teacher, 10 minutes; (2) observation of a lesson, 20 minutes; and (3) collegial feedback session, 15–20 minutes.

Materials Needed

Collaborative Inquiry Guide for a Learning Target and Effective Success Criteria

Suggested Room Setup

For this activity the school leader will work with one teacher. The purpose is formative, and the aim is that both will learn something about learning targets and success criteria. Ideally, the school leader identifies a teacher who is already using a learning target theory of action in their lessons and who wishes to go deeper. The observation portion of this activity (part II) occurs in their classroom, and the consultation portions (parts I and III) occur in a mutually convenient and comfortable location. It would be possible to do this activity with a teacher who is just trying out learning targets, with longer preparation time in part I.

Directions

Part I: Pre-Observation Conversation

Identify a teacher, in your building or elsewhere, who is working on using learning targets with their students. The purpose of the pre-observation conversation is for you and the teacher to explore your current understandings of learning targets and success criteria, to get some background on the lesson you will be observing, and to identify what you will be looking for when you observe. Think of yourself and the teacher as each participating in a formative learning cycle where the goal is to understand learning targets and success criteria more deeply. This pre-observation conversation allows you to define your current understandings and be more precise about exactly what each of you wants to learn next. The observation will identify aspects of the lesson that are observable and serve as information for the collegial feedback conversation, which should help both you and the teacher answer the questions "Where am I now?" and "Where to next?"

(Continued)

(Continued)

Collaborative Inquiry Guide for a Learning Target and Success Criteria

LEARNING TARGET

Unless students are using a learning target to aim for and assess their understanding, the teacher may have a learning intention for the lesson, but the classroom learning team (students and teacher) does not have a learning target for today's lesson. Use this inquiry guide to look for the characteristics of a learning target and evaluate if the classroom learning team is guided by one throughout today's lesson.

	YES	SOMEWHAT	NO
Is there a description for students—via words, pictures, actions, or some combination of the three—of exactly what they are going to learn by the end of today's lesson? *Explain your choice:*			
Is the description of learning shared in developmentally appropriate language that all students can understand? *Explain your choice:*			
Is the description of learning stated from the point of view of a student who has yet to master the content, skill, or reasoning process that makes up the learning target for today's lesson? *Explain your choice:*			
Does today's lesson have a specific performance of understanding—what the students do, make, say, or write—that translates the description into action for the students to deepen their understanding, help them aim for mastery, allow them to self-assess the quality of their learning, and provide both the teacher and the students with evidence of the students' level of understanding? *Explain your choice:*			

SUCCESS CRITERIA

Success criteria, or "student look-fors," describe learning quality in such a way that students can recognize and use them to plan, produce, and improve the quality of their work as they are learning and working during today's lesson.

	YES	SOMEWHAT	NO
Do the criteria connect to the learning target for today's lesson? *Explain your choice:*			
Are the criteria about learning rather than assignment completion? *Explain your choice:*			
Could the criteria apply to more than one assignment—if the criteria describe learning, the quality should generalize to other similar work (e.g., "My sentences all end with periods," *not* "I put a period after 'boy'"; "I labeled my answers," *not* "I wrote 'square inches' after all the area problems"). *Or* if the criteria are specific to the performance of understanding, is it because the learning is specific too (e.g., "I can describe the construction of the Transcontinental Railroad")? *Explain your choice:*			
Are the criteria appropriate for the level of student understanding, observable to both you and your students (publicly stated), and definable in terms students can understand and use to judge the quality of their performance? *Explain your choice:*			

SUCCESS CRITERIA (CONTINUED)			
Are the criteria distinct from one another—that is, are they separate qualities that can be regulated and assessed for quality? *Explain your choice:*			
Do the criteria form a complete set—that is, when taken together (if there is more than one) do they describe the whole of the learning goal the performance is intended to develop and assess? *Explain your choice:*			
Do the criteria exist along a continuum of quality—that is, do they describe work on developmental continua so that students can self-assess and set next-step goals to improve their work? *Explain your choice:*			

Source: Adapted by permission from Figure 5.4 (p. 83) and Figure 7.1 (p. 121) of *Formative Classroom Walkthroughs: How Principals and Teachers Collaborate to Raise Student Achievement,* by Connie M. Moss & Susan M. Brookhart. Copyright © 2015 ASCD.

Use the Collaborative Inquiry Guide for Learning Targets and Success Criteria as the basis for your discussion. The teacher may be able to foreshadow some of the things you could be looking for when you observe. Be very clear with the teacher that the end result of this activity is that you should both understand learning targets and success criteria more deeply and have a sense of what work you should both do next to increase your knowledge and skill even more. You may need to make this point very emphatically because some teachers may be used to seeing "observation" as a summative, evaluative tool. No matter what you observe, you are the *learner* in this activity, not an evaluator. Of course the teacher will learn too, which is why the activity has value for them as well.

After you and the teacher have discussed your understandings of learning targets and success criteria and have reviewed the Collaborative Inquiry Guide, ask the teacher to select a lesson or portion of a lesson that will last at least 20 minutes that would be a good candidate for this kind of formative walk-through. Make an appointment to visit their classroom at that time.

Part II: Formative Walk-Through

Arrive at the appointed time to observe the classroom lesson. Take a copy of the Collaborative Inquiry Guide with you, and fill it in as you notice things. Do more than just check the boxes (Yes/Somewhat/No); make sure to explain your choice using evidence you observed during the walk-through.

This evidence should be based in what the *students* are doing. This may feel counterintuitive if you are used to classroom walk-throughs that focus on what the teacher is doing. The key to finding out whether a learning target is living in a lesson is to look at what the students are doing. Are they trying to learn something, or is compliance with teacher directions their main focus?

Observe for about 20 minutes. If for some reason your visit must be cut short, do another visit later when you can spend the full 20 minutes.

Part III: Collegial Feedback Session

After your observation, set up a time to talk briefly with the teacher. To prepare for this conversation, review the Collaborative Inquiry Guide.

(Continued)

(Continued)

To start the conversation, ask the teacher what they noticed about the learning target and success criteria in the lesson you observed. Ask them what they were trying to accomplish with the lesson and what they thought happened. Join in the conversation by sharing what you observed, which should be recorded in the "Explain your choice" sections of the Collaborative Inquiry Guide. Finally, each of you should set a next professional learning goal based on what you have observed and discussed together. The teacher's next professional learning goal should be something *they* identify as their likely next step (e.g., "I'd like to work on identifying ways in which my students could use success criteria more easily"), not something you tell the teacher they ought to do next.

Your next professional learning goal should be something related to the learning target for this activity: "I understand the role of learning targets and success criteria in connecting classroom-level instruction and learning with broader learning goals." For example, you might decide, "I want to understand how students experience learning goals and success criteria in my building." Identify an action plan—what are you going to do to pursue your goal? Identify success criteria—how will you know you are moving toward your professional learning goal?

Closure

Follow up with the professional learning goal and action plan you set for yourself in part III. Reflect on what you are learning.

Definitions

Constructed-response exercises: Item formats that require that students generate their own answer to a question—for example, short-answer and extended-response exercises and show-the-work math or science problems.

Domain of learning: A description of all possible questions and tasks implicated by a standard or other learning goal.

Knowledge learning goals: Facts, concepts, and procedures, usually discipline specific, that students will learn and understand.

Lesson learning target: A description in student-friendly language of what students will be trying to learn in a lesson.

Performance assessment: Assessment of a student process or product, or both, using observation and judgment based on criteria. Performance assessments have two parts: a task or tasks and rubrics or some other scoring scheme.

Performance skill learning goals: Real-time demonstrations, presentations, or physical performances that students will learn to carry out.

Personal communication: Gathering information about what students know through oral interaction—for example, asking questions during instruction, listening during student discussion, giving oral exams, and interviewing.

Product learning goals: Artifacts students will be able to produce.

Reasoning learning goals: Thought processes students will learn to apply.

Selected-response items: Item formats that require that students recognize and choose a correct answer—for example, multiple-choice, true/false, matching, and fill-in items.

State standards: Descriptions or statements about expectations for student learning, usually organized by content area and grade level, that have been officially adopted by state departments of education to apply to all public education in the state.

Success criteria: Qualities that students and their teachers will look for in students' work as evidence of the level of student learning.

Taxonomy: An organizational scheme in education applied to classifying learning goals by levels of complexity.

Teacher instructional objective: Descriptions or statements about what students will know and be able to do after one lesson or a series of lessons within a unit of instruction.

Unit learning goal: Descriptions or statements about expectations for student learning for a portion of the curriculum, typically for a unit of instruction.

 This chapter's online resources are available for download from **resources.corwin.com/10GoalsLeaders**

Standards of Assessment Quality

3

Assessment Literacy Goal #3: *The leader understands the standards of quality for student assessment and ensures that these standards are met in all school/district assessments.*

Being able to assess student learning for both summative and formative purposes is an essential aspect of teaching well. Yet assessment is often still seen as separate from teaching, used only to evaluate achievement at the end of instruction. We see this when every piece of work a student does "counts" toward the final grade. Historically, assessment has been deemed the province of "experts" rather than classroom teachers. We can be certain that teachers need to understand the standards of assessment quality if they are creating their own assessments and assignments. It might seem plausible to believe that we could leave this knowledge in the hands of commercial developers and simply buy already prepared assessments, such as tests and quizzes that come with textbook materials or items from an item bank, thereby ensuring quality. However, this is not the case. Results from both teacher-made and commercially prepared assessments and assignments can mismeasure achievement for a whole host of reasons. Teachers and school leaders must have a working knowledge of the standards of quality for each type of assessment used to ensure both accuracy and effective use of the information, whether assessments are locally created or not.

Chapter Learning Goals

1. Describe the five keys to quality assessment, understand how they relate to one another, and know why they should underpin assessments at all levels.

2. Conduct an audit with teachers to identify the strengths and weaknesses of an assessment according to quality indicators.

When we use the word *assessment*, we are not just referring to tests, quizzes, and projects that contribute to the summative grade. Everything teachers ask students to do—every assignment, every task, every activity—is or can be an assessment; that is, students' responses provide information about their level of understanding, competence, or mastery of the learning at the heart of the assignment, task, or activity. That information can and should be used formatively to guide next instructional steps. Therefore, when we talk about classroom assessment quality, we are concerned with *all* work students are given to do, as well as all tests, quizzes, tasks, and **scoring guides**.

Standards for Classroom Assessment Quality

The model we recommend using for determining assessment quality is the five keys to classroom assessment quality (Chappuis & Stiggins, 2020; Stiggins et al., 2004). The model was developed over many years, with content drawn from the measurement field that has been adapted to fit the classroom context. The first three keys lay out the conditions necessary for accuracy, and the last two explain the conditions needed for effective use (Figure 3.1). The model can be used both to guide assessment development and to audit an assessment for quality.

In the explanations that follow, we will identify typical problems that you as a school leader might have noticed within each key. The solution to each problem lies in developing teachers' assessment expertise. Chapter activities are designed to help do that.

Key 1: Clear Purpose

Creating a quality assessment begins with a clear answer to the question "Why are we conducting this assessment/giving this assignment?" Stated a different way, how do we intend to use the results? Who else will use the results? What will they do with them? For example, the results of a practice assignment may be used by both the teacher and students to determine what further instruction or practice is needed. The results of a quiz may be used by the teacher to target further instruction to individuals or groups. The same results may be used by students to self-assess: "What am I good at? What do I need to work on?" These are formative uses of assessment results. Teachers may also give assignments with the intent of using the results summatively—to contribute to the final grade.

Problems immediately crop up when the purpose of an assessment is not established and communicated. An interim assessment intended to inform instruction may be given without planning sufficient time to offer additional instruction, so the results are sometimes recorded as a summative score and included in the final grade. An opportunity for further learning, needed by perhaps many students, is thus lost.

Another typical problem arises with assignments. Teachers sometimes give practice work as homework without checking whether students know enough to practice independently. Then, when students turn their work in, it is evaluated and figured into the end-of-term grade. This illustrates a confusion of purposes. If the work is truly intended as practice (a formative purpose), students should have experienced at least a bit of guided practice prior to being sent off to do it without help. When they turn the work in, they should receive feedback about strengths and next steps, rather than a grade.

FIGURE 3.1   Five keys to classroom assessment quality

Key 1: Clear Purpose (Accuracy)

Who will use the information?

How will they use it?

Therefore, what type of information will be required?

Key 2: Clear Learning Goals (Accuracy)

Are learning goals clear to teachers?

Are learning targets clear to students?

Do learning goals form the basis of instruction?

Key 3: Sound Design (Accuracy)

Do the assessment methods used suit the learning goals?

Are items, exercises, tasks, and scoring guides of high quality?

Does the sample represent learning appropriately?

Does the assessment control for bias?

Do teachers know how to create assessments for formative use?

Key 4: Formative Usefulness (Effective Use)

Do formative assessment results guide next instructional steps?

Do students receive and act on feedback?

Do students offer accurate feedback to peers?

Are students engaged in accurate self-assessment and productive goal setting?

Key 5: Effective Communication (Effective Use)

Is formative assessment information tracked as needed?

Are students engaged in tracking, reflecting on, and sharing learning progress?

Is summative assessment information recorded according to the learning represented?

Is summative assessment information combined and summarized appropriately to reflect current level of achievement?

Source: Adapted from Chappuis, Jan; Stiggins, Rick J., *Classroom Assessment For Student Learning: Doing It Right - Using It Well, 3rd Edition* (Figure 2.1, p. 23) © 2020. Reprinted by permission of Pearson Education, Inc.

Differentiating between formative and summative use at the outset contributes to design decisions made later in the assessment development or selection process. You can't build or select an assessment that will provide accurate, useful information without knowing first how the information will be used. The design adage "Form follows function" applies here: the structure of the assessment (the "form") is driven by the intended use of its results (the "function").

Activity 3.2 helps teachers think through the conditions needed for effective formative use when planning an assessment.

Key 2: Clear Learning Goals

The second question to be addressed in the assessment design or selection process is "What learning goals are to be assessed?" Without clear learning goals—an established set of achievement expectations to be taught and learned—teachers cannot write or select appropriate test items, exercises, tasks, or scoring procedures. And assignments become busy work—activities that when completed do not yield evidence of learning anything of substance. Additionally, as we have seen in Chapter 2, clear learning goals are the foundation of assessment method selection—not all methods will yield accurate information about all types of learning goals.

Assessment problems arise in the absence of clear learning goals. In fact, the majority of problems we have encountered with accuracy of classroom assessments can be traced back to a lack of clarity of the intended learning. For example, students may see some items on a test as unfair in that they were not part of what the teacher taught or communicated as learning expectations. This is a common occurrence when teachers are using tests they did not prepare and have not checked to be sure the tests assess what they taught. This is an equity issue: students with more "educational capital"—those who are more widely read, who have a richer array of educational experiences, who have confidence in their ability to suss out the type of answer that might be called for—are much more likely to get such items right. Both struggling and strong students who get these items wrong receive misinformation about their success at learning, which can harm subsequent motivation. "This test isn't fair" can easily turn into "This teacher isn't fair" and then "I won't do well in this class."

Activity 3.3 is designed to help teachers audit their assessments for the match to what was taught.

Key 3: Sound Assessment Design

The previous two keys, Clear Purpose and Clear Learning Goals, have outlined decisions at the assessment planning stage. Key 3 concerns the development stage. Do our items, tasks, and scoring guides adhere to standards of quality? Have we sampled learning appropriately? Have we controlled for factors that can introduce **bias and distortion**? Knowing how to answer each of these questions is at the heart of key 3.

Adhering to Standards of Quality

Each of the four principal assessment methods—selected response, constructed response, performance assessment, and personal communication—has its own set of guidelines to ensure accuracy.

Selected-response assessment. Selected-response assessment formats include multiple-choice, true/false, matching, and fill-in items. Each has its own strengths and weaknesses. For example, multiple-choice items with carefully crafted distractors can provide diagnostic information identifying misconceptions or flaws in reasoning. Yet lack of understanding of how to write such distractors can lead to students getting the right answer for the wrong reason, a source of mismeasurement. It is easier to write multiple-choice items to assess recall than conceptual understanding or reasoning, so without assessment literacy the cognitive challenge of the item may not match that of the learning goal. Matching items that assess recall are easy to construct and score, but they can yield inaccurate information about achievement if they allow for correct responses through the process of elimination. And true/false questions are easy to score but can be difficult to write clearly so students know what they are judging to be true or false.

3 crazy answers to 1 understandable answer means they'll pick the right one but won't know why its correct.

Each item type has its own guidelines for development. The quality checklist for selected-response items shown in Figure 3.2 begins with general guidelines for all formats, offers guidelines for each item type, and concludes with guidelines for formatting test items, writing directions, and planning testing time.

FIGURE 3.2   Selected-response test quality checklist

1. *General guidelines for all formats*
   _____ Keep wording simple and focused. Aim for the lowest possible reading level.
   _____ Ask a question.
   _____ Avoid providing clues within and between items.
   _____ Correct answers should not be obvious without mastering the material tested.
   _____ Highlight critical words (e.g., MOST, LEAST, EXCEPT, NOT).

2. *Guidelines for multiple-choice items*
   _____ State the whole question in item stem.
   _____ Eliminate repetition of material in response options.
   _____ Be sure there is only one correct or best answer.
   _____ Keep response options brief and parallel.
   _____ Make all response options the same length.
   _____ Do not use "all" or "none of the above."
   _____ Use "always" and "never" with caution.

3. *Guidelines for true/false items*
   _____ Make them entirely true or entirely false as stated.
   _____ Write a simple declarative sentence.

(Continued)

FIGURE 3.2   (Continued)

4. *Guidelines for matching items*

_____ Provide clear directions for the match to be made.

_____ Keep the list of trigger items brief (maximum length is 10).

_____ Include only homogeneous items.

_____ Keep the wording of response options brief and parallel.

_____ Provide more responses than trigger items.

5. *Guidelines for fill-in items*

_____ Ask a question.

_____ Provide one blank per item.

_____ Do not make the length of the blank a clue. *(giving the answer w/o them knowing why its right)*

_____ Put the blank toward the end.

6. *Formatting test items*

_____ Be consistent in the presentation of an item type.

_____ Keep all parts of a test question on one page.

_____ Avoid crowding too many questions on one page.

_____ Order items from easy to hard.

_____ Arrange items by learning goal, or group similar formats together.

_____ Avoid misleading layout.

7. *Writing directions*

_____ Write clear, explicit directions for each item type.

_____ State the point value of each item type.

_____ Indicate how the answer should be expressed (e.g., whether the word *true* or *false* should be written or *T* or *F*; whether numbers should be rounded to the nearest 10th).

8. *Time*

_____ Make sure the test is not too long for the time allowed.

Source: Adapted from Chappuis, J., & Stiggins, R. J., *An Introduction to Student-Involved Assessment for Learning, 7th Edition* (Figure 5.10, p. 131) © 2017. Reprinted by permission of Pearson Education, Inc.

Constructed-response assessment. Constructed response exercises can take one of three forms: short-answer exercises, extended-response exercises, or interpretive exercises (Chappuis & Stiggins, 2020). Short-answer items call for a brief response and have one or a few possible right answers. Extended-response items call for a response at least several sentences in length or in the case of mathematics a multistep solution to a problem along with an explanation. They have a greater number of acceptable answers or paths to attain a correct answer than short-answer items. Interpretive exercises assess mastery of targeted patterns of reasoning with the content knowledge provided in the task itself. They can have a short-answer or extended-response format. Constructed-response exercises can be scored with a scoring list assigning points to each desired response or feature or with a **rubric**, depending on the learning goal they address.

Problems with this method arise first in writing the exercise, which should be brief and clearly worded, while giving students enough information to frame a desired response.

"Discuss photosynthesis," while brief, does not frame the task in a way that all students who understand photosynthesis will be able to answer successfully. "Explain the causes of the French Revolution" would be difficult to accomplish in an extended-response format without at least a few parameters, including clarifying what is expected by "explain." Teachers must know how to devise constructed-response exercises such that students who have learned the material are able to write a satisfactory response and students who haven't won't be able to bluff their way through it.

Second, the type of scoring guide for constructed-response assessments must be chosen carefully. Should the exercise be scored with a list of all possible correct answers or desired features, along with instructions on how points will be awarded? A *task-specific* rubric describing features of quality vis-à-vis the learning goal as they appear in a single exercise? A *general rubric* describing features of quality as they apply across all exercises focused on the learning goal? Unclear scoring **criteria** and criteria that don't directly address the learning goal both lead to an inaccurate appraisal of student learning.

The characteristics of a high-quality constructed-response assessment are summarized in Figure 3.3.

FIGURE 3.3   Quality guidelines for constructed-response assessments

Quality of the Exercises

- Is constructed response the best assessment method for this learning goal?
- Do the exercises call for focused responses?
- Is the knowledge to be used clearly indicated?
- Is the reasoning to be demonstrated (if any) clearly indicated?
- Is the exercise itself written at the lowest possible reading level: will all students understand what they are to do?
- Will students' level of writing proficiency in English be adequate enough to show you what they know and can do?
- Is there anything in the exercise that might put a group of students at a disadvantage regardless of their knowledge or reasoning level?
- Are there enough exercises to provide a defensible estimate of student learning on intended learning goals?

Quality of the Scoring Guide(s)

- For the knowledge aspect of the response, is it clear how points will be awarded? If a task-specific rubric is used, does the exercise clearly call for the features described in the highest level of the rubric?
- For the reasoning portion of the response (if any), does the rubric capture the essence of high-quality thinking at the highest level? Does it identify flaws in reasoning at the lower levels?
- Does the rubric sufficiently represent the intent of the learning goal(s)?

Scoring Considerations

- Is the total number of exercises to be scored (number of exercises on the assessment times number of students responding) limited to how many the rater(s) can accurately assess within a reasonable time span?
- If the scoring guide is to be used by more than one rater, have the raters worked together to ensure consistent scoring?

Source: Adapted from Chappuis, Jan; Stiggins, Rick J., *Classroom Assessment For Student Learning: Doing It Right - Using It Well, 3rd Edition* (Figure 5.7, p. 161) © 2020. Reprinted by permission of Pearson Education, Inc.

Performance assessment tasks and rubrics. The first requirement of a high-quality task is that it aligns directly with the intended learning goal and is written so that it elicits the intended performance or product. A second requirement is that it provides enough, and the right kind of, information to guide students' actions. A third is that it adheres to guidelines for feasibility and fairness. A fourth is that it samples the learning goal appropriately for the intended use.

Many problems arise with performance assessment because of an unclear or inappropriate task. It can be tempting to make one grand task intended to cover a host of learning goals, rendering it extremely difficult for students to complete and perhaps difficult to score for all of the intended learning goals. Or, without attention to the learning goal(s) to be assessed, efforts to make a task engaging for students can lead to the inclusion of extraneous requirements that may cause many to stumble. In an effort to maximize success, the task can include so much guidance that completing it has devolved into direction following, with the more complex components of the learning goal having been thought through for the student. Or the context of the task may be accessible to some students (e.g., baseball statistics) and foreign to others. Good tasks are not easy to write; they require adherence to a specific set of guidelines, such as those shown in Figure 3.4.

FIGURE 3.4   Characteristics of a high-quality performance task

Criterion 1: Content of the Task

- *Alignment to the learning goal:* Aligns to the intended learning goal and elicits the right performance or product
- *Information provided*
  - Learning to be demonstrated
  - Form the performance or product is to take
  - Materials to be used
  - Timeline for completion
  - Reminder of the criteria used for evaluation
- *Context:* Provides as realistic a context as possible

Criterion 2: Feasibility and Fairness

- *Time allowed:* How much time will students have?
- *Resources required:* Necessary resources and materials are available to all.
- *Instructions:* Directions are clear and unambiguous.
- *Level of scaffolding:* Information points the way to success without "overhelping."
- *Help allowed:* Directions specify what assistance will be permitted and from whom.
- *Choice:* If choice is offered, all options are equivalent.

Criterion 3: Sample Size

- *Use of information:* How many tasks will be assigned? Does this task sample adequately for the intended use?
- *Coverage of the learning goal:* Does the breadth of the task or the number of tasks adequately cover the breadth of the learning goal?

Source: Adapted from Chappuis, Jan; Stiggins, Rick J., *Classroom Assessment For Student Learning: Doing It Right - Using It Well,* *3rd Edition* (Figure 7.3, p. 225) © 2020. Reprinted by permission of Pearson Education, Inc.

There is no shortage of rubrics to be found on the internet, but relatively few meet standards of quality to ensure an accurate appraisal of student achievement. For example, a rubric may be labeled as an oral presentation rubric, but the content may include factors that aren't important to success at giving an oral presentation. Or it may not include everything of importance. Does the rubric structure match the intended use (formative or summative)? Is the number of criteria sufficient to make the judgments needed? Does the number of levels fit the learning goal's complexity and its intended use? What kind of detail is included? Do the descriptors provide an accurate picture of quality? Are they sufficiently robust to serve the intended use of the information?

One problem with the rubrics we frequently encounter is the mismatch between their content and the intended learning goal. If students are to be writing a book review to express an opinion and support it with examples, whether they use 12-point font should not figure in the rubric. Surface-level features of a performance or product that do not pertain directly to the learning goal should not be scored. A second, seemingly ubiquitous problem is when the language of the rubric uses "counts" as a measure of quality when the number of instances is not germane to successful demonstration of the learning goal. There is no rule that governs how many sentences a paragraph must have to be considered a good one, so a writing rubric should not count sentences as an indicator of quality. As another example, consider a rubric for display of information from a scientific inquiry. It describes level 4 as having four pieces of information, level 3 as having three pieces of information, and so on. It does make scoring simple, but using such a rubric would result in no picture of students' ability to communicate results effectively—the information shared could be inaccurate, poorly organized so it is difficult to interpret, or incomplete. On the other hand, sometimes "counts" do count. In an oral presentation, the number of disfluencies ("like," "you know," "um") does affect the quality of delivery, so "few disfluencies" would be an indicator of quality. A third issue is with clarity of the descriptors: the language in a rubric's performance-level descriptions should be clear enough to support consistent scoring from one teacher to another and, within one teacher's class, from one student to another.

To be a good consumer of rubrics as well as a good rubric developer, teachers need to be familiar with the characteristics of a high-quality rubric, as shown in Figure 3.5.

FIGURE 3.5 Characteristics of a high-quality rubric

Criterion 1: Content of the Rubric

- *Alignment to learning goal:* Criteria and descriptors focus only on key factors of quality.

- *Match to essential elements:* Everything of importance is included; unimportant factors are omitted.

(Continued)

FIGURE 3.5   (Continued)

Criterion 2: Structure of the Rubric

- *Number of criteria:* Number matches the complexity of the learning goal and intended use of information.

- *Independence of criteria:* Content in the criteria does not overlap.

- *Grouping of descriptors:* Descriptors are assigned to the appropriate criterion.

- *Number of levels:* Number fits the learning goal complexity and intended use.

Criterion 3: Descriptors in the Rubric

- *Kind of detail:* Descriptors provide an accurate explanation of the characteristics of quality.

- *Content of levels:* Content is parallel across levels.

- *Formative usefulness:* Descriptors identify strengths and areas needing work in sufficient detail to guide further action.

Source: Adapted from Chappuis, Jan; Stiggins, Rick J., *Classroom Assessment For Student Learning: Doing It Right - Using It Well, 3rd Edition* (Figure 7.7, p. 246) © 2020. Reprinted by permission of Pearson Education, Inc.

Personal communication as an assessment method. This method can be conducted in a variety of formats—instructional questions and answers, class discussions, conferences, interviews, and oral examinations—for both summative and formative purposes. Each format has its own set of quality standards. For example, teachers ask instructional questions to probe understanding or to encourage thinking and deepen learning. For this format to be successful, teachers need to know how to frame questions, pose them so that students have opportunity to think before answering, use strategies for calling on students that maximize engagement, and listen and respond effectively.

Engaging students in class discussions as a way of assessing learning has its own set of challenges, which can be met when teachers understand what they are and how to deal with them. It is especially important to clarify the learning goal to be assessed within the context of the discussion, to prepare discussion questions carefully to elicit evidence of the intended learning, to ensure that all students have opportunities to participate, and to have a high-quality rubric on hand to guide the assessment. Without thoughtful planning, the question-and-answer portion of a lesson may consist solely of "on-the-fly" correct-answer recall questions. Without protocols to ensure that all students are thinking about the question and all have opportunities to respond, too often only a few students actively participate, and the rest hope they won't be called on, thus limiting the value of this form of instruction.

Sampling Learning Appropriately

Every assessment is only a subset of all the questions we could have asked or tasks we could have assigned to get a good measure of level of achievement on any given learning goal. The **sampling** task is to gather as little information as is needed to lead to a confident conclusion about the aspect of learning being evaluated. As explained in Chapter 2, we gather information from the **sample** and then generalize to the level of mastery of the domain it represents.

Problems with accuracy attributable to inattention to sampling arise all too frequently. For instance, a teacher may assign the odd-numbered problems without checking to see which instructional objectives are left out. This may result in students completing one item for one learning goal and four for another. Whether the information is to be used formatively or summatively, chances are we do not have a broad enough sample with the one item to accurately judge the level of achievement. Or a teacher may use a test that comes with the textbook without checking to see if it is a representative sample of what they taught and what they expected students to learn. Some learning goals may be overrepresented, others may be underrepresented, and some may be missing altogether. Additionally, the number of points for each learning goal may not represent its relative importance within the whole. (Activity 3.3 explains a protocol you can use with teachers to help them learn to attend to sampling issues.)

So how much is enough? We would love to be able to say that four is the magic number or that if you triangulate, you have will have a sufficient sample size, but that would not be true. The answer to "How much is enough?" requires consideration of four factors (Chappuis & Stiggins, 2020):

1. *The assessment purpose:* Higher-stakes decisions require a more robust sample size. A quick check for understanding relies on a relatively small sample of questions, whereas a unit test requires a larger number of items per learning goal.

2. *The nature of the learning goal:* More complex goals require a larger sample size than simple goals. For example, you would not need as much evidence to assess proficiency with the use of periods at the end of sentences as you would to assess mastery of the use of subject and object pronouns. To determine proficiency in writing, the sample would need to include several examples each of different kinds of writing.

3. *The assessment method:* Each assessment method carries its own sampling challenges and recommendations. The more information provided by each assessment event, the fewer instances will generally be required to represent the domain in question. One multiple-choice question does not provide the same coverage as one constructed-response exercise. We may need fewer constructed-response items because they provide greater coverage of the learning goal.

4. *The students themselves:* Let's say students answer a series of questions addressing the same learning goal. Some get them all right, some get them all wrong, and some get half of them right and half of them wrong. For which group would you need to provide a greater sample to get a stable estimate of level of achievement? It would be the half-right, half-wrong group. You know you have gathered enough information if you can confidently predict how the student would do on the next question without giving it.

Avoiding Bias and Distortion

Even after adhering to standards of quality in developing or selecting an assessment, problems that interfere with accuracy of results can still crop up. These are known as sources of bias and distortion. Figure 3.6 shows a list of barriers to accuracy that can occur within the student, within the assessment context, and within the assessment itself. The best way to avoid them is to eliminate them before giving the assessment. If we believe that an assessment's results have been distorted by a source of bias, we should not use them, for they will be an inaccurate measure of the student's learning. There is no defensible reason ever to misrepresent achievement.

FIGURE 3.6   Potential sources of bias and distortion common to all assessment methods

Barriers That Can Occur Within the Student

- Language barriers
- Emotional upset
- Poor health
- Physical handicap
- Peer pressure to mislead assessor
- Lack of motivation at the time of assessment
- Lack of "test-wiseness" (i.e., understanding how to take tests)
- Lack of personal confidence leading to evaluation anxiety

Barriers That Can Occur Within the Assessment Context

- Insufficient time allotted
- Noise distractions
- Poor lighting
- Discomfort
- Lack of rapport with assessor
- Cultural insensitivity in assessor or assessment
- Lack of proper equipment

Barriers That Arise From the Assessment Itself

- Directions lacking or vague
- Poorly worded questions
- Misleading layout
- Poor reproduction of test questions
- Missing information

Source: Chappuis, J., & Stiggins, R. J., An *Introduction to Student-Involved Assessment for Learning, 7th Edition* (Figure 4.16, p. 104) © 2017. Reprinted by permission of Pearson Education, Inc.

Key 4: Formative Usefulness

We use the assessment process and assessment results formatively when our purpose is to guide next steps in teaching and learning, as we have seen in Chapter 1. High-impact formative assessment practices, as identified by researchers such as Heidi Andrade, Paul Black, Susan Brookhart, Dylan Wiliam, John Hattie, Gary Latham, Edwin Locke, D. Royce Sadler, and Lorrie Shepard, include the following:

- Diagnosing student learning needs and planning instruction to meet the needs

- Offering feedback effectively and giving students opportunities to act on it

- Teaching students to self-assess and set goals designed to lead to further learning

→ instructional goals

Once teachers have a firm grasp of these practices, they need to understand how to design an assessment event or instrument to carry them out. An assessment can adhere to the standards of quality described in key 3 and still not be suited to formative use. A common misconception is that a large-scale assessment, because it is developed by assessment experts, is a good model for classroom assessments. That may not be the case, especially if the intended use in the classroom is formative. Rubrics used for large-scale summative purposes often do not provide the detail necessary to pinpoint specific strengths and problems. So teachers need to know how to modify them or supplement them with different rubrics addressing the same learning goals if the intent is to use the results diagnostically. The 6+1 Trait Writing Rubric is a good example of a rubric structured for formative use, and one that can be used summatively as well. We will address formative assessment more fully in Chapter 4.

Key 5: Effective Communication

Assessments provide information, which is then communicated to the intended users of that information. Students, parents, the community, and other schools, in the case of transferring and graduating students, all need results communicated using language and concepts they understand. Assessment-literate educators know how to keep track of formative assessment information and what information to record. They know how to explain what "formative" means to parents, why some information won't be figured into the final grade, and how that benefits student learning. They help parents understand formative results and use them to guide parent actions to be taken in support of their child's learning. On the summative side, assessment-literate educators know how to derive fair and defensible grades—which information to use and how to combine and summarize it to accurately reflect the current level of a student's achievement. We will address grading practices more fully in Chapter 5.

Activity 3.4 offers practice in determining the appropriate assessment method for the type of learning goals taught. Activity 3.5 takes participants in depth into guidelines for quality for each assessment method, applying them to evaluate an assessment of their own. Activity 3.6 raises awareness of sources of bias and distortion that may reside undetected in teachers' assessment instruments and practices.

Summary

When an assessment is of high quality, it produces accurate information and the results are communicated effectively both to support and to report student learning. Accuracy of information relies on three keys to quality:

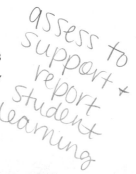

assess to support & report student learning

1. *Clear purpose:* Intentionally identifying the purpose of the assessment—what decisions the results will inform and who will be making them

2. *Clear learning goals:* Clearly defining learning goals, aligning instruction to those goals, and selecting the appropriate method by which to assess them

3. *Sound assessment design:* Knowing how to design or select items, exercises, tasks, and scoring guides that adhere to quality guidelines; how to determine an appropriate sample size; and how to avoid potential sources of bias and distortion that will render results inaccurate

Effective use of information encompasses the last two keys to quality:

1. *Formative usefulness:* Being able to carry out high-impact formative assessment practices regularly during instruction to guide teaching and learning for the teacher and the student, respectively

2. *Effective communication:* Communicating formative and summative assessment results accurately in terms that ensure all recipients understand them

Only when the five keys to assessment quality are part of the working knowledge of teachers and leaders will we have a sound assessment system in place, one that promotes students' academic well-being and raises achievement for all.

⭐⭐ Success Indicators for Assessment Literacy Goal #3

The school leader

1. purpose
2 learning goals
3 assessment design
4 form. usefulness
5 effect. comm

- can describe the five keys to classroom assessment quality;

- can explain how each of the keys contributes to assessment accuracy and effective use;

- can offer a compelling rationale for the importance of following the guidelines within each key;

- understands the conditions necessary for effective formative use of the assessment process and its results;

- knows how to audit an assessment for the match to what was taught;

- can determine the appropriate assessment method(s) to use based on the types of learning goals taught;

- knows how to audit an assessment for standards of quality; and

- identifies sources of bias that can distort assessment results.

Study Guide Questions

1. Think back over your study of the five keys to classroom assessment quality. What did you find most interesting? What was new information to you? Did anything surprise you? If so, why? *digging deeper into the creation of assessment questions*

2. The concluding sentence in this chapter reads, "Only when the five keys to assessment quality are part of the working knowledge of teachers and leaders will we have a sound assessment system in place, one that promotes students' academic well-being and raises achievement for all." Select one key, and think of a problem you have seen or experienced due to incomplete understanding of the requirements of the key. Then compose a compelling reason to attend to the requirements of that key.

3. After reading the chapter and doing the activities, you will likely be more familiar with sources of mismeasurement in the assessments used in your building and perhaps in your district. Which ones strike you as the most important to address first? How might you do that?

 Personal Portfolio Entry Suggestions

- Written responses to any of the study guide questions

- Artifacts from any of the chapter activities

- Planned or past professional development offerings addressing assessment quality

- School protocols in place for assessment design

 ## Activity 3.1
Connecting Your Own Experiences to the Keys to Quality

Learning Target for the Activity

- Know why the five keys to quality assessment should underpin assessments at all levels.

Purpose

By discussing the impact on students of sound and unsound assessment practices through the filter of the five keys to classroom assessment quality, participants come to understand the necessity of each key for student academic well-being.

(Continued)

(Continued)

Time

45–60 minutes

Materials Needed

- The description of the five keys to classroom assessment quality found in this chapter

Suggested Room Setup

Tables and chairs for small groups (content or grade-level teachers may prefer to work together)

Directions

Participants can do the reading in advance of the activity or during it. At the outset of the activity, ask participants to form discussion groups of three, and appoint a note taker. Then ask them to do the following:

1. Think of a time when you yourself were assessed and it was a positive experience. What made it positive? What impact did that have on you? Share your experience and answers to the questions. Note taker: Keep track of the answers to the two questions (10–15 minutes).

2. Now think of a time when you were assessed and it was a negative experience. What made it negative? What impact did that have on you? Share your experience and answers to the questions. Note taker: Keep track of the answers to the two questions (10–15 minutes).

3. Read the descriptions of the five keys to classroom assessment quality, noting connections to the positive and negative experiences shared in your small group (15–20 minutes). Or if participants have previously read the section, ask them to review it, looking for connections to the positive and negative experiences shared in their groups (10 minutes).

4. In your small group compare your positive experiences with the descriptions of each of the five keys to assessment quality. Which of the keys contributed to your positive experience? (You can also do this as a large-group discussion.)

5. Now compare your negative experiences with the descriptions of each of the five keys to assessment quality. What problems with one or more of the keys contributed to your negative experience? (You can also do this as a large-group discussion.)

Closure

Small-group/team discussion: which of the keys to quality are the most in need of attention in your own assessments? Why?

Activity 3.2
Auditing an Assessment for a Clear Purpose

Learning Target for the Activity

- Know how to help teachers plan intentionally for formative use when planning an assessment event or instrument.

Purpose

Educators sometimes confuse formative and summative uses of assessment information. This activity helps participants think through the conditions needed for effective formative use when planning an assessment.

Time

45–60 minutes

Materials Needed

- An assessment instrument or a description of an assessment protocol intended for formative use brought by each participant

- Electronic or paper copies of the form shown in Figure 3.7

FIGURE 3.7 Auditing an assessment intended for formative use

Name of Assessment

1. Who will use the information?
   ___ Teacher
   ___ Student
   ___ Other

2. How will the information be used?
   ___ To plan instruction
   ___ To differentiate instruction
   ___ To offer descriptive feedback to students
   ___ As the basis for student self-assessment and goal setting
   ___ Other

3. Does the instrument or event meet the following conditions for effective formative use?

   ___ The instrument or event provides information of sufficient detail to pinpoint specific problems, such as misunderstandings, so that the teacher, and students if appropriate, can make good decisions about what next steps to take.

   ___ The results are available in time to take action with the students who generated them.

(Continued)

(Continued)

Suggested Room Setup

Tables and chairs for small groups (content or grade-level teachers may prefer to work together)

Directions

Have participants use the form in Figure 3.7 to answer the following questions about their assessment:

- Who will use the information?

- How will they use it?

- Does the instrument or event meet the necessary conditions for effective formative use?

Closure

Ask participants to discuss the following questions:

- What new ideas came to you while you were doing this activity?

- What changes to current practice might you make?

Activity 3.3
Auditing an Assessment for Clear Learning Goals and Appropriate Sample Size

Learning Target for the Activity

- Know how to help teachers determine whether an assessment accurately represents the learning goals taught.

Purpose

One of the first places a classroom assessment's accuracy goes astray is in the match to the intended learning. Creating or selecting a test without having a plan, known as an **assessment blueprint**, can result in mismatches between instruction and assessment. The assessment will not likely measure what you intended it to measure, which is known as a **validity** problem. If you have ever faced an exam yourself that did not match what you thought were the most important aspects of the course you were taking, you know what that feels like from the student's point of view. When we make a plan for an assessment, whether we intend to create the assessment ourselves or use one developed by someone else, we are making the advance decisions about validity—what the test will cover and how much weight each learning goal will have. In the following activity the leader works with teachers to analyze a test they have given in order to determine its match to the intended learning goals and examine the sampling choices made.

Time

45–60 minutes

Materials Needed

- A copy of one of each participant's assessments, as described in the following directions

- Copies of the blank assessment blueprint shown in Figure 3.8

Suggested Room Setup

Tables and chairs for small groups (content or grade-level teachers may prefer to work together)

Directions

Ask participants to bring a selected-response or constructed-response assessment they have given to students in the past or one they plan to give in the near future. Then have them follow these steps to audit it for clear learning goals and appropriate sample size.

1. *Analyze your test item by item.*

   Using the form in Figure 3.8, identify and write down the learning goal each item or exercise assesses. Note the number of points each item is worth. By doing this you are creating a simple assessment blueprint.

FIGURE 3.8   Assessment blueprint

Name of assessment: _____

PROBLEM #	LEARNING GOAL	# OF POINTS

(Continued)

(Continued)

2. *Question your assessment blueprint. Is this a representative sample of what you taught and what you expected students to learn?*

   - Are some learning goals overrepresented? If so, which one(s)?
   - Are some learning goals underrepresented? If so, which one(s)?
   - Are some of the important learning goals you taught left out? If so, which one(s)?
   - Does the number of points for each learning goal represent its relative importance within the whole? If not, which ones are out of balance?
   - Does the number of points for each learning goal represent the amount of time you spent on it relative to the whole? If not, which ones are out of balance?

3. *Adjust your assessment blueprint as needed.*

   - Add or delete learning goals to reflect what you taught.
   - Adjust the numbers in the "# of points" column to reflect each learning goal's relative importance to the content as a whole as well as the amount of time you spent teaching it.

4. *Revise the items on your assessment to reflect your adjusted assessment blueprint.*

   - Find or create items or exercises to add to your assessment.
   - Delete those you have decided are unnecessary or inaccurate.

Closure

Discuss your assessment with a partner or with the group.

- Was it difficult to identify the learning goal represented by any of your assessment's items or exercises? If so, why?

- What did you learn from this process? Were there any surprises?

On which assessments might you use this process next?

Optional Closure Activity

Pass out index cards, and ask participants to complete either of these two sentence starters with whatever comes to mind:

- Without clear learning goals . . .

- Without knowing what each question on a test measures, we can't . . .

Give them a few minutes to write down their thoughts; then, collect the index cards, and read them aloud (using no names) to end the session. Here are some possible responses. (You can mention them if they don't come up.)

Without clear learning goals, or without knowing what each question on a test measures, we can't . . .

- know if the assessment adequately covers and samples what we taught.

- correctly identify what students know and don't know and their level of achievement.

- plan the next steps in instruction.

- give detailed, descriptive feedback to students.

- have students self-assess or set goals likely to help them learn more.

- keep track of student learning target by target or standard by standard.

- complete a standards-based report card.

Activity 3.4
Practicing With Target-Method Match

Learning Target for the Activity

- Know how to help teachers determine the appropriate assessment method(s) for the types of learning goals taught.

Purpose

Educators often have a preference for one specific assessment method, sometimes to the exclusion of the others. Yet if their curriculum contains learning goals of all types, it is not likely that all valued learning goals will be assessed or, if they are, that the results will yield accurate information. This activity is designed to help participants make decisions about which assessment method to use based on guidelines for accuracy.

Time

45–60 minutes

Materials Needed

- The learning goals for a short unit that participants have taught or will be teaching

- The assessments that accompany the unit, if available

- Electronic or paper copies of the blank target-method match chart shown in Figure 3.9

(Continued)

(Continued)

FIGURE 3.9 Target-method match planning chart

LEARNING GOAL	LEARNING GOAL TYPE				ASSESSMENT METHOD			
	K	R	PS	P	SR	CR	PA	PC

Note: K, knowledge; R, reasoning; PS, performance skill; P, product; SR, selected response; CR, constructed response; PA, performance assessment; PC, personal communication.

Suggested Room Setup

Tables and chairs for small groups (content or grade-level teachers may prefer to work together)

Directions

Working in small groups, complete each step in the order below:

1. Use the form in Figure 3.9 to list the learning goals that are the focus of your unit of study.

2. Using the information from Chapter 2, classify each learning goal as knowledge (K), reasoning (R), performance skill (PS), or product (P).

3. Using the information from Figure 2.2 in Chapter 2, select an appropriate assessment method to use for each learning goal: selected response (SR), constructed response (CR), performance assessment (PA), or personal communication (PC).

4. Compare the appropriate method choices with your current assessments. Discuss as a group: do they agree with the recommended matches? If not, what adjustments will you make?

Closure

Ask participants to discuss the following questions:

*   What new thoughts has this activity triggered?

*   What changes to your assessment practices might you make as a result?

Activity 3.5
Auditing an Assessment for Quality

Learning Target for the Activity

*   Know how to help teachers audit an assessment for quality.

Purpose

This activity is designed to give school leaders and teachers practice at using the method-specific quality guidelines described in this chapter. For a deeper understanding of the craft knowledge necessary to create items, exercises, tasks, and scoring guides, we refer you to Chapters 5 through 8 of Chappuis and Stiggins (2020).

(Continued)

(Continued)

Time

One to two hours

Materials Needed

- A classroom assessment, along with its answer key, scoring guide, or rubric
- A statement of the learning goal(s) represented on the assessment

Suggested Room Setup

Tables and chairs for small groups (content or grade-level teachers may prefer to work together)

Directions

Working in small groups, complete each step in the order below:

1. Ask participants to select one assessment method—selected response, written response, or performance assessment—to learn more about. It is suggested that participants work in teams of two or three, determined by the method they choose. Join one group, and complete the activity with them.

   (If you are conducting a deeper study of creating assessments using Chappuis and Stiggins [2020], give participants a week or two to read the relevant chapter. Those studying selected-response methodology will read Chapter 5, "Designing and Using a Selected Response Assessment," pp. 131–163. Those studying constructed-response methodology will read Chapter 6, "Designing and Using a Written Response Assessment," pp. 179–209. Those studying performance assessment will read Chapter 7, "Designing and Using a Performance Assessment," pp. 201–261, and those studying personal communication will read Chapter 8, "Using Personal Communication as an Assessment Method," pp. 272–299.)

2. Have participants work in method-specific teams to audit one of their assessments for quality.

   - The selected-response group will use the selected response test quality checklist shown in Figure 3.2 to conduct their evaluations.

   - The constructed-response group will use the quality guidelines for a constructed-response assessment given in Figure 3.3 to conduct their evaluations.

   - The performance assessment group will use the characteristics of a high-quality performance task shown in Figure 3.4 and the characteristics of a high-quality rubric shown in Figure 3.5 to conduct their evaluations.

Closure

After conducting their evaluations, each group will either make the revisions necessary to improve quality or write a revision plan for what they see needs to be done.

Activity 3.6
Auditing an Assessment for Bias and Distortion

Learning Target for the Activity

- Know how to help the teacher identify sources of bias that can distort assessment results.

Purpose

Assessment-literate educators do not use assessment results they know to be inaccurate; yet many times the causes of these inaccuracies slip under the radar of our attention, and so we are unaware that the information is not accurate. This activity is designed to raise awareness of the myriad sources of bias, so that participants will be able to watch for them and eliminate or work to counteract them.

Time

60–90 minutes

Materials Needed

- Two or three copies of each participant's assessment they currently give to students

- A copy of Figure 3.6, "Potential Sources of Bias and Distortion Common to All Assessment Methods," for each participant

- Chart paper and markers

Suggested Room Setup

Tables and chairs for small groups (content or grade-level teachers may prefer to work together)

Directions

Ask participants to work in teams of two or three to complete this activity. Have enough copies of each participant's assessment so that each team member has one.

1. Begin with a short whole-group discussion of what the terms *bias* and *distortion* mean. Then ask for examples of causes of bias in assessment. Make a list on chart paper.

2. Ask what problems inaccurate results are likely to cause. If participants don't mention the effect on students, suggest that as a topic.

3. Hand out a copy of Figure 3.6 to each participant. Ask participants to compare what is on the checklist shown in Figure 3.6 with what is on their group list, noting similarities and differences.

(Continued)

(Continued)

4. Have participants review one of their team members' assessments as a group, then individually audit it for sources of bias and distortion using the checklist shown in Figure 3.6.

5. Each team member shares the results of their audit with their small group.

6. The team discusses possible changes to the assessment or the conditions as recommended by the audit.

7. Repeat the process for each team member's assessment.

Closure

Conduct a team discussion and then a whole-group share-out of the following questions:

- Were any sources of bias a surprise to you?

- Which of your assessments may be yielding inaccurate results for some or all students due to one or more of these factors?

Definitions

Assessment blueprint: A plan, usually in the form of a table, that specifies which learning goals will be the focus of an assessment and how much weight each goal will have (also known as a *table of test specifications*).

Bias and distortion: A factor that causes results to be inaccurate is a source of *bias*. *Distortion* refers to the effect the source of bias has on the results.

Criteria: The separate categories in an analytic rubric. Criteria represent key, independently varying elements of quality.

Rubric: A scoring guide that describes a progression of levels of quality. Well-crafted rubrics use specific terms to define features of quality at each level. A rubric can be classified as *task specific* or *general*. A task-specific rubric describes features of quality that pertain only to the assignment given. For example, a task-specific rubric for a mathematics problem-solving assessment that tested students' ability to interpret a graph would describe the top level as "Answer states that Maria rides her bike to school and Gordon walks." A *general rubric* for the same learning goal would describe the top level as "Interprets information from graph to provide correct answers." Additionally, rubrics are either *holistic* or *analytic* in structure. A holistic rubric yields only one score—all features of quality are considered together in determining the rating. An analytic rubric yields two or more separate scores—features of quality are organized into categories (called *criteria*) and are rated independently of one another.

Sample: A subset of a population.

Sampling: To select a representative portion of a domain to evaluate for the purpose of making a judgment about level of achievement in the domain as a whole.

Scoring guide: A delineation of how quality will be judged. Scoring guides can take the form of an answer key, a list of desired features or elements, or a rubric.

Validity: The degree to which the results of an assessment convey information about the learning it is intended to measure.

 This chapter's online resources are available for download from **resources.corwin.com/10GoalsLeaders**

Formative
Assessment Practices

4

Assessment Literacy Goal #4: *The leader understands formative assessment practices and works with staff to integrate student-centered assessment for learning into classroom instruction.*

In Chapter 1 we defined *formative assessment* as "a collection of formal and informal processes that teachers and students use to gather and share evidence for the purpose of guiding next steps toward learning and for helping students become self-directed learners." Formative assessment clearly does improve learning, but not all instruments and activities labeled as "formative" can yield the promised gains. Calling something "formative" does not ensure increased learning; it is the *use* we make of its information that gives it its power.

Formative assessment practices help students and teachers answer the questions "Where am I going?" "Where am I now?" and "How can I get there from here?" In this chapter we will explain the critical components of formative assessment, describe what each looks like in the classroom, and suggest actions school leaders can take to support teachers as they hone their formative assessment practices.

Chapter Learning Goals

1. Understand formative assessment practices and their role in increasing student achievement.

2. Identify effective uses of formative assessment within the context of instruction.

3. Engage in discussions with teachers to enhance and expand their use of formative assessment.

4. Analyze the current formative assessment practices in a school and plan for ways to build formative assessment capacity.

What Is Formative Assessment?

Definitions of formative assessment abound. Some are prescriptive, spelling out specific practices that must be present to qualify as formative assessment. Others, such as ours, are intended to encompass all practices by which evidence about student achievement is gathered, analyzed, and used by teachers or students to make decisions about next steps in instruction and learning. In framing our definition we concur with researcher Dylan Wiliam (2019):

> Adopting an inclusive definition matters, because discussion can then move on from the relatively unproductive boundary disputes about whether certain practices are, or are not, examples of formative assessment to the more important and substantive issues about whether and if so, by how much, and under what circumstances student achievement is increased through the use of such assessment. (p. 254)

In recent literature about formative assessment in the disciplines (e.g., Andrade et al., 2019), researchers have made the case that formative assessment should be "conceptualized as an activity that integrates process and content" (Cizek et al., 2019, p. 14). That is, formative assessment should include both generalizable processes and discipline-specific elements particular to a content domain. We see a role for each and will make that clear in the sections to come.

Six Critical Components

"What then," you might rightfully ask, "is it that I will see in the classroom?" There are differing opinions as to the critical components of formative assessment, but there is a general consensus that the following are essential (Chappuis, 2015; Heritage & Wylie, 2019; Moss & Brookhart, 2019; Wiliam, 2018):

1. Establishing clear learning goals and success criteria

2. Using classroom questioning to elicit evidence of student thinking

3. Diagnosing learning needs to inform instructional next steps

4. Offering actionable feedback

5. Engaging students in self-assessment, peer feedback, and goal setting

6. Providing opportunities for students to track their learning and self-reflect

Collectively, these six components identify the next steps for both teachers and students, motivate students to keep trying, and provide the necessary skills for self-directed learning.

The Importance of the Student as Decision Maker

When we ask teachers in our workshops which formative assessment practices they are familiar with, the list skews toward strategies they themselves use to figure out where students are in their learning: diagnostic assessments, student response systems (e.g., clickers), thumbs up/thumbs down, exit tickets, nongraded quizzes. There is no doubt that teachers acting on good information gathered during instruction can increase students' learning. Noticing problems and taking the time to address them is a key feature of formative assessment. However, if meeting teachers' informational needs is our sole purpose, we have left the student sitting on the sidelines. What do *students* need to know? Simply put, students need to know *where they are going*. What is the aim of their work—what learning are they endeavoring to master? What does it look like when it is done well? They need to know *where they are now*. What is their current status vis-à-vis the intended learning? Are they able to gauge that for themselves? And they need guidance on *how to get there from here*. What actions, in what sequence, will result in mastery of the learning goal? These three questions—"Where am I going?" "Where am I now?" and "How do I get there from here?"—are often referred to as the formative learning cycle by assessment experts and the self-regulation of learning by educational psychologists.

> "Whatever the procedures by which the assessment message is generated, it would be a mistake to regard the student as the passive recipient of a call to action." (Black & Wiliam, 1998, p. 21)

Structuring instruction to address these three questions is not a formative assessment add-on, a need to attend to if we have time. Students' knowing how to answer each question is crucial to their growth and therefore central to formative assessment. In the words of Australian researcher Royce Sadler (1989),

> The indispensable conditions for improvement are that the *student* comes to hold a concept of quality roughly similar to that held by the teacher, is able to monitor continuously the quality of what is being produced *during the act of production itself*, and has a repertoire of alternate moves or strategies from which to draw at any given point. (p. 121, emphasis in original)

Prerequisites to Effective Use of Formative Assessment Information

The effectiveness of formative assessment relies on the accuracy of the information collected, as it provides evidence on which to make judgments about what actions to take. First and foremost, the assessment instrument or task is designed so that it aligns directly with the learning goals to be mastered. All items or tasks match what has been or will be taught. Questions, items, tasks, and scoring guides adhere to the principles of sound design reviewed in Chapter 3. And teachers must be on the lookout for sources of bias that may distort the results. When, for example, the information your GPS relies on is inaccurate, the flawed information will not guide you to where you want to go; so it is imperative that teachers understand the conditions for accuracy of information explained in Chapter 3.

Second, teachers need to work with clearly articulated learning goals and criteria for success, for they are the foundation from which all formative assessment practices arise. As noted in Chapter 2, in the context of formative assessment, clear learning goals accompanied by standards of quality answer the question "Where am I going?" As classroom assessment expert Rick Stiggins (2008) states, "Students can hit any target they can see and that holds still for them" (p. 1).

Third, they need to possess robust knowledge in the domains they are teaching. Do teachers understand how learning unfolds in their discipline? Researchers have repeatedly noted that a lack of disciplinary knowledge is a stumbling block for many teachers, inhibiting their ability to decide appropriate next steps in learning based on the evidence they have gathered (Heritage et al., 2009). Well-researched learning progressions can help mitigate this problem by providing a road map for how student understanding and performance develop over time. Carefully crafted success criteria may serve the same function in some disciplines. Learning progressions and success criteria can provide answers to the question "Where am I now?" by situating student responses and performance along a continuum of learning, and they can give teachers guidance on where to go next, thus informing actions in answer to the question "How can I get there from here?"

Fourth, teachers need to believe in the centrality of formative assessment to effective instruction, to understand that the traditional model of "plan, instruct, assign, assess, and grade" does not go far enough in meeting teacher or learner information needs. We also may need to consider how we define what it means to teach well. To cause substantive, relevant learning? Certainly necessary, but perhaps not sufficient. We suggest adding a second part: *to create confident, competent learners.* When we approach formative assessment with learners' needs foremost in our minds, we can accomplish both.

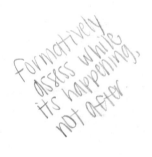

Fifth, teachers must plan time into an instructional sequence to engage in formative assessment activities and to act on the resulting information. Formative assessment opens a window into learning while it is happening that allows teachers and students to *monitor and adjust* actions, thus improving the quality of instruction. The word *adjust* is important here, for it is not enough to "give" or "do" formative assessment. If no one uses the information to take action, there is nothing formative about it. Teachers will continue to teach, some students will learn, and others will not. Although they may have insight into learning needs, without action there will be no change and therefore no gain.

1. Establishing Clear Learning Goals and Success Criteria

In addition to teachers themselves being clear about learning goals and success criteria, in Chapter 2 we discussed the importance of sharing learning targets (learning goals in student-friendly language) and success criteria with students. There is significant agreement that this practice is a good idea, and it is now an expectation in many districts throughout the United States.

Benefits to Students

We know that students who understand what they are responsible for learning have a better chance of succeeding. When students have no idea what they are supposed to learn, if the only information they have is the topic, for example, decimals, and the assignment ("Read page 78, and then do the odd-numbered problems"), few are likely to consciously recognize that the goal of their work is to learn to read decimals and put them in order. They are more likely to believe that their "target" is to finish the assignment.

Students' understanding of the learning target is a prerequisite for the following formative assessment components:

- *Understanding and acting on feedback:* Effective feedback relates to specific aspects of the learning goal, identifying strengths and offering guidance for improvement. When students aren't clear about the learning target, they are less likely to benefit from feedback.

- *Self-assessing and goal setting:* Students can't accurately self-assess without a clear vision of what they are aiming for. Learning goals and success criteria provide a standard by which to judge their current status and on which to base plans for further study.

- *Tracking, reflecting on, and sharing progress:* Students can be standards-based trackers of their own achievement when evidence is reported by learning goal. Grades without learning goals only tell them how well they have learned something, not what it is they have learned. With a direct, visible connection to the learning goal, students are better able to reflect metacognitively about their progress over time. And if they are participating in parent conferences, they will be able to speak more meaningfully about their achievement and about themselves as learners.

> "[Beyond fairness] the more important reasons for helping students develop an understanding of standards in each of the disciplines are to directly improve learning and to develop metacognitive knowledge for monitoring one's own efforts. . . . These two purposes provide students with the opportunity to get good at what the standards require."
> (Shepard, 2001, p. 1093)

Targets on the Wall Aren't Targets in the Head

Woah! Remember this!

Thinking back to Sadler's (1989) indispensable conditions for improvement, we are reminded that the purpose of sharing targets (learning goals) and criteria is to develop in students a vision of quality that aligns with that of the teacher. The aim is to help students internalize the vision of where they are headed. It is not enough to post learning goals on the wall and state them at the beginning of the lesson. Teachers can develop in students an understanding of the intended learning in several ways, depending on the type of learning goal (Chappuis, 2015).

1. Share the learning goal "as is." For example, a learning goal that requires students to find equivalent fractions may be stated as a student-friendly learning target simply by the addition of "I can": "I can find equivalent fractions." The success criterion for this target could be "I will know which operations to use and will carry them out correctly to determine if one fraction is equal to another." Teachers can ask students to write the learning target and success criterion on their assignment or in their notebook. This strategy is generally suited to knowledge-level learning goals.

2. Convert reasoning learning goals into student-friendly language. When a learning goal incorporates a pattern of reasoning, such as infer, compare, determine cause and effect, make generalizations, and so forth, the student-friendly target should include a definition of the reasoning to be carried out. For example, while a biology teacher may share the learning goal "Compare the structures of viruses and bacteria" by beginning it with "I can," students will benefit if the teacher defines what it means to "compare": to describe the similarities and differences between or among items. The resulting learning target would be "I can compare the structures of viruses and bacteria. This means I can identify basic viral and bacterial structures and then correctly identify similarities and differences between the two." Notice that by adding the definition of *compare*, the learning target now also includes the success criteria.

3. Convert the language of a rubric to student-friendly language, then introduce the rubric to students. Performance skill and product learning goals as well as some patterns of reasoning will be evaluated with a rubric. The top level of the rubric functions as the success criteria; however, the descriptors—the "goes unders" at each level—are also necessary for helping students distinguish among levels of quality. Many rubrics are written for use by adults, but with a bit of effort the language can be simplified so that it is also accessible to students. We recommend that when possible, teachers work together to translate existing rubrics into student-friendly language.

With a suitable rubric at hand, teachers are ready to introduce it to students. We don't recommend handing out a rubric without first laying the groundwork for conceptual understanding of the criteria for quality. One successful protocol for introducing the criteria that form the structure of the rubric is this:

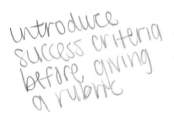

> The teacher asks students what they think the criteria should be and
> lists their responses. The teacher shares an anonymous example of the
> performance or product, asks students to add more ideas to the list, shows
> another example, and invites further ideas. (Examples are carefully chosen
> to illustrate specific strengths and sometimes typical problems.) Then the
> teacher hands out the rubric in student-friendly language and conducts a
> discussion of the criteria on the rubric that were and were not mentioned
> on the student list. Teachers can continue to share a range of anonymous
> samples with students, collaboratively using the rubric to determine the
> strengths and weaknesses of each example. This helps students internalize
> the concepts of quality represented on the rubric and also provides guided
> practice for self-assessment.

4. Co-create criteria with students. Similar to the protocol above, teachers share anonymous samples of the product or performance to be evaluated, and students draft and refine the criteria and descriptors themselves. The accuracy of co-created rubrics is dependent on the quality and range of the examples shared.

When to Share Learning Goals?

This is an interesting question. Some schools require that all lessons begin with stated learning goals or targets, but that doesn't always work well. Sometimes a "hook," an introduction to the topic, is a better place to start. Sometimes, when success criteria are in the form of a rubric, understanding of the "meat" of the learning goal develops over days or weeks. Other times, such as when engaging in inquiry lessons, the learning goal unfolds through a series of explorations. In this case it is counterproductive to share the learning goal in advance of the initial instruction. It is important that students are able to articulate the learning goal prior to engaging in sustained independent practice and certainly before the summative assessment.

Wherever in the lesson structure the learning goal is introduced, teachers should make sure that students are able to articulate what they are aiming for: "We are learning to _____" or "I am practicing being able to _____." Before engaging in a summative assessment, it is a good idea for teachers to make sure students can describe what is being evaluated: "In this assessment I am demonstrating my understanding of/ability to/proficiency with _____."

It is also advisable for teachers to check periodically for understanding of the intended learning. They might walk around the room while students are engaged in their work and ask them, "Why are you doing this activity?" An exit slip provides a more formal window into students' understanding of learning goals. At the end of class students write what they think the teacher wanted them to learn from the lesson or respond to the question "Why did we do _____ [activity] today?" Figure 4.1 suggests what to look for and what to ask within the classroom context.

FIGURE 4.1 Learning goals and success criteria: what to look for, what to ask

What to Look For

- ☐ Statements of learning targets in language students can understand
- ☐ Activities that help students understand the learning at the heart of instructional activities
- ☐ Assignments aligned directly with the stated learning goals
- ☐ Success criteria (what the learning goal looks like when it's done well) aligned directly with salient features of the learning goal
- ☐ Activities that help students understand the success criteria

What to Ask Teachers

- ☐ How do you help students understand the learning goal?
- ☐ How do you help students understand the success criteria?
- ☐ Who may not understand the intended learning? What do you do to find out?

What to Ask Students

- ☐ What is the aim of your work? Why are you doing this assignment? (If one of those questions doesn't elicit a reference to the intended learning, ask "What are you trying to learn?")
- ☐ How does this _____ [task] help you learn _____ [target]?
- ☐ What helps you understand the success criteria?
- ☐ How do learning targets help you?

2. Using Classroom Questioning to Elicit Evidence of Student Thinking

"What's in a question, you ask? Everything. It is a way of evoking stimulating response or stultifying inquiry. It is, in essence, the very core of teaching."
(Dewey, 1933, p. 266)

Classroom dialogue, where the teacher poses a question or a discussion prompt and then one or more students answer, is one of the most common instructional practices across disciplines and age-groups. Teachers ask a great number of surface-level questions whose purpose is to manage student learning ("Do you have your materials?") or check recall of prior information ("Who can tell me the definition of an isosceles triangle?") (Wiliam, 2018). However, questions designed to promote deeper thinking ("Are power and authority the same thing?"), probe students' understanding in order to plan next instructional steps ("Why do we experience night and day?"), and activate students as resources for one another ("How does your thinking differ from Javier's?") enhance learning in specific ways. In this section we will first examine the characteristics of the questions themselves and then turn to strategies that maximize participation by all students.

Promoting Deeper Thinking

Students may have been conditioned to think that answering questions is about popping out discrete bits of knowledge—a sort of verbal pop quiz. When the purpose is to promote deeper thinking, stems that elicit specific patterns of reasoning can guide students to more reflective answers (Chappuis & Stiggins, 2020).

Analyze: What familiar pattern do you notice? (e.g., in story structure or numerical sequence)

Compare/contrast: What are some characteristics that would help us discriminate (or distinguish) between _____ and _____?

Synthesize: How might you adapt or modify _____ to fit _____?

Classify: How might you sort _____ into groups or categories?

Infer/deduce: What can you conclude from the evidence or pieces of information? For example, what does that tell us about numbers that end in five or zero? (generalize)

Evaluate: Is this argument sound? What evidence supports your judgment?

Probing Student Understanding

While all types of questioning require that teachers understand their subject matter, planning questions to uncover misunderstandings and misconceptions requires well-developed pedagogical content knowledge. Misconceptions often arise from overgeneralization of a learned pattern ("Me and him went to the store" is wrong, so I should never use "me." I should say, "Give the boxes to Brad and I") or observed phenomenon (the sun comes up and the sun goes down, so night and day are caused by the movement of the sun around the earth). They involve having learned something incorrectly—students have overapplied a rule or have internalized an explanation for a phenomenon that does not fit with current best understanding. Misconceptions result in different kinds of mistakes from those that arise from incomplete understanding and, as such, require strategies to address them other than explaining what is wrong, reteaching, or assigning more practice. One teaching approach derived from research on science misconceptions is to do the following:

- Create an initial awareness of the misconception by generating cognitive dissonance in students' minds. Provide them with an experience such as a demonstration or a reading passage that runs counter to their current understanding in some way.

- Engage students in discussion to uncover the misconception and to contrast it with the correct (or accepted) interpretation.

- Have students explain what the misconception is and why it is flawed (Hattie, 2009).

The challenge is to cause conceptual change, which requires that teachers understand the likely misconceptions students will bring with them. A typical misconception in mathematics involves percent change: students are likely to understand that an increase in cost from $100 to $150 represents a 50% increase, but when asked to determine the percent decrease from $150 to $100, they are likely to say that is also 50% (Burkhardt & Schoenfeld, 2019). When teachers are aware of such problems in advance of encountering them, they are better prepared to craft questions and experiences to address them. There are many discipline-specific resources available to help with identifying preconceptions and misunderstandings. For example, Paige Keeley and colleagues have written a series of 12 books of formative assessment probes in science tailored to draw out and change common prior ideas students hold in the various content areas (e.g., Keeley et al., 2020). We refer readers to the *Handbook of Formative Assessment in the Disciplines* (Andrade et al., 2019) for a description of several other well-researched resources.

> "Teachers need research-based tools that are attuned to the very specific ways in which student understanding develops in each academic domain."
> (Shepard et al., 2017, p. 48)

Encouraging Student-to-Student Discussion

Framing a question so that students discuss one another's contributions leads to livelier thought-provoking discussions that go beyond the typical teacher-student-teacher-student volley. When teachers ask questions such as "Do you agree with_____?" or "What would you add to _____'s statement?" students learn to listen to their classmates and engage in an internal dialogue with what they are saying, even if they are not called on to respond. In this way they become learning resources for one another.

Activities such as a "line-up" discussion encourage all students to engage with one another's ideas. The teacher poses a question as a statement ("Parents should push their children to excel") and asks each student to take a position—agree or disagree. Students are given a few minutes to share their thoughts with a partner, then line up on one side of the room (agree) or the other (disagree). Students from the two lines take turns sharing their reasons, speaking to students in the opposite line rather than to the teacher. Students who change their minds move across the room to the other line.

Promoting Learning for All Students

Without careful attention to questioning protocols, classroom discussions become a spectator sport for many students. A small group of students interacts with the teacher, and the rest assume a facial expression that says, "I'm paying attention, but don't call on me." And all too often teachers comply, not wanting to embarrass students who might not know the answer. Unfortunately, without active participation, students are not likely to benefit. When teachers allow students to opt out by calling on only those whose hands are raised, they are inadvertently widening the achievement gap. Citing a study comparing the effects of discussions involving all students with traditional questioning sessions, Wiliam (2018) concludes, "Engaging in classroom discussion really does make you smarter" (p. 92).

> "Research indicates that teachers who use a range of questioning strategies to collect relevant evidence of student understanding and/or progress toward the learning goals are able to make appropriate instructional adjustments to meet the needs of more students, more often."
> (Wylie & Lyon, 2016, p. 50)

Some students always volunteer, some are listening but don't want to participate, and others tune out. Students often can't think on their feet. Students don't know the answer. These problems can be overcome by changes in the protocols for posing questions, offering "think time," calling on students, and randomizing respondents.

Posing Questions

Teachers should pose questions with their full attention, as though the answer matters, because it does. The underlying messages are "This question is important to our learning" and "I am interested in your thinking."

Offering Think Time

Often called "wait time," think time is a period of three to seven seconds between asking the question and inviting responses. We recommend renaming it because it's not *wait time* for students; it's *think time*. Without this pause, students are more likely to offer quick, right-answer responses rather than well-reasoned thoughts (Rowe, 1986). Increasing thinking time results in an increase in the length of student responses, the number of unsolicited responses, the frequency of student responses, the number of responses from lower-achieving students, student-to-student interactions, and the number of speculative responses (Akron Global Polymer Academy, 2011).

Calling on Students

All students deserve the opportunity to participate in answering instructional questions. Teachers can call on both volunteers and nonvolunteers, but the volunteer approach should be used sparingly because of the risk of developing a group of "target" students that everyone knows will carry the weight for the whole class (Walsh & Sattes, 2005). It's also important to pose the question before calling on someone, so all students understand that they could be responsible for answering.

> "Classrooms in which a small number of students get most of the 'air time' are not equitable, no matter how rich the content; all students need to be involved in meaningful ways." (Burkhardt & Schoenfeld, 2019, p. 40)

Randomizing Respondents

To keep all students engaged, we recommend that teachers use a method of randomizing respondents. One simple way to do this is to label three cups "Ready," "Responded," and "Come back to me." All students write their names on tongue depressors or popsicle sticks and put the sticks in the "Ready" cup. The teacher poses a question, gives think time, and then pulls a stick. The student responds or says, "Come back to me," and the stick goes into the corresponding cup. The teacher draws from all three cups subsequently so students don't conclude they are "one and done." To minimize "Come back to me" responses, teachers can give students a short partner talk time and then invite them to share something they said or heard when called on. Figure 4.2 suggests what to look for and what to ask within the classroom context.

Ready, Responded, Come back to me

FIGURE 4.2   Classroom questioning: what to look for, what to ask

What to Look For

☐ Key questions are planned in advance of instruction to promote deeper thinking.

☐ Teachers are aware of the misconceptions and flaws in reasoning that student work is likely to exhibit; questions are devised or selected to identify and explore them.

☐ Students respond to one another's ideas in discussions.

☐ Teachers pose questions with their full attention and offer think time before inviting responses.

☐ All students are responsible for discussing questions through participation in randomized-response activities.

(Continued)

FIGURE 4.2   (Continued)

What to Ask Teachers

❑ How many hands are in the air? Whose hand does not go up?

❑ Who is not engaged? How might you alter your questioning strategies to include all students?

❑ How often do you ask students to think and then talk to a partner, before calling on someone to answer?

What to Ask Students

❑ What's your teacher's purpose in asking questions in class?

❑ When the teacher is asking questions during class, what do you do?

❑ What do you like about classroom discussion? What do you learn from it?

❑ What don't you like about classroom discussion? What would you change if you could?

3. Diagnosing Learning Needs to Inform Instructional Next Steps

It is a universal truth that learning is unpredictable and that instructional adjustments are part of the normal flow of attaining mastery in any discipline; whether learning occurs is directly influenced by the steps teachers take during instruction in response to what students are doing (Wiliam, 2013). Australian researcher John Hattie (2009) called this the "zone of what happens next" and described it as a feedback loop. The feedback loop begins with initial instruction and student action in response. The teacher examines students' work, and then teacher and students take action based on what the students' responses reveal they did or did not learn. Teacher and students "loop back" to analyze their next efforts and adjust instruction or learning strategies until the desired level of achievement is attained. Effective diagnostic assessment is the starting block for the feedback loop, showing teachers how to keep moving forward to the point of mastery for each student.

> Learning something well requires practice with feedback and interventions. Students' not knowing something isn't a problem—it's the reason for our profession.

Sources of Information for Identifying Learning Needs

As we discussed in the previous section, teachers can discover incomplete understanding, flaws in reasoning, and misconceptions informally by eliciting explanations and asking probing questions. (*Note:* Diagnostic assessment isn't just concerned with finding problems; it can also uncover areas where students are clear on concepts, which is important for instructional adjustment in at least two ways—building on strengths when designing learning activities to address misconceptions and not spending time emphasizing concepts that, however important, are already solid for most or all students.)

Teachers can use more formal tools to provide diagnostic information as well, from curriculum documents to quizzes and tests. Learning progressions, developmental continua, and deconstructed standards all lay out learning trajectories, which when well designed can provide a detailed treatment of how learning a particular concept, procedure, or skill commonly progresses and develops. Such learning trajectories offer a rich source of information from which to build diagnostic assessments.

An assessment itself can provide diagnostic information when its results point out specific learning needs. Assessments that do this are said to have **instructional traction** (Andrade, 2013). Many assessments yield only a score, which can be used to judge the effectiveness of instruction and whether further work is needed. However, it is not enough to know that students need more help, for example, with fractions. If that's all the information an assessment provides, it is not working well enough.

Consider the following item:

Which fraction is the largest?

a. 1/3   b. 2/5   c. 7/9

This is a flawed item; most students will select answer choice "c," but for a variety of reasons: it contains the largest numbers, it has the largest denominator, and it has the largest numerator. None of these are the reason why answer choice "c" is correct. Students who understand that it is the relationship between numerator and denominator that determines size will also choose "c"; but many students are likely to get the right answer for the wrong reason, so the results will contribute to an inaccurate conclusion about students' mastery of the learning goal. Even when the distractors (wrong answer choices) are plausible, if they are not designed with typical misunderstandings, flaws in reasoning, or misconceptions in mind, the item's diagnostic value will be nil.

Now consider these answer choices:

Which fraction is the largest?

a. 2/1   b. 3/8   c. 4/3

Students who select answer choice "a" will likely get the item right for the right reason (except for random guessing), but students who believe that the denominator is the key to size will choose "b," and those who look to the numerator will select "c." This item is said to have instructional traction because the results not only differentiate between those who do and those who don't understand magnitude in fractions, they also give information about the mistakes students are making, thus giving clear direction to instructional next steps.

Let's consider rubrics as another example of instructional traction. Rubrics are easy to find on the internet. Type in "rubric for" and a topic, and you will find the good, the bad, and the ugly. Say a teacher is planning a unit on writing a research paper. One of the learning goals will be that students are able to identify relevant, credible sources. Suppose a Google search turns up the rubrics shown in Figure 4.3.

FIGURE 4.3   Rubrics for relevance and credibility of sources

Example 1

CATEGORY	POINTS
Credibility of sources: Are the sources academically credible?	____/10
Relevance: Are all sources directly related to the research question?	____/10

Example 2

Level 3: References cited are good-quality sources.

Level 2: References cited are low- or moderate-quality sources.

Level 1: References cited are of poor quality.

Example 3

Relevance

Level 3: Information from the sources relates directly to the research question.

Level 2: Some sources provide information that is relevant to the research question; others are relevant only at the topic level.

Level 1: Sources are only superficially relevant to the research topic—for example, they are chosen because they match a keyword search. They don't provide sufficient information to address the question.

Credibility

Level 3: All sources are written by authorities on the topic being researched. All authors are unbiased in their approach to the topic. Source information is current (written or updated within the past five years).

Level 2: Some sources are written by authors interested in the topic but without credentials. Some authors may have a bias toward the topic. Some source information is not current.

Level 1: Sources used are not experts on the topic. Or sources display bias in the writing about the topic. Or information is outdated.

In Example 1 the two criteria are stated as a question and are rated on a scale from 1 to 10. Although labeled a rubric, this is actually just a scoring guide—a way to assign points (as explained in Chapter 3). There is no description of levels of quality or of the features a rater should attend to in assigning points, so it is very unlikely that two raters would agree in scoring a student's paper. A student who receives a score of 7 will not know what they did well and what to improve, and the score alone will not give teachers guidance on next steps. No instructional traction here. This kind of scoring guide can be easy to write and fairly quick to use in evaluating papers, but it is highly unlikely to result in accurate information about the student's ability to select relevant and credible sources.

In Example 2 raters could arrive at the same judgments on one student's papers if they all agree on the definition of what it means for a source to be of high, medium, and low quality. However, again, this rubric doesn't tell teachers or students what the criteria are for relevance or credibility, so it provides no actionable information.

Example 3 shows a more complex rubric. It can be tempting for teachers to avoid lengthier rubrics, and a case should be made for being as concise as possible with rubric language. However, if the rubric itself is to carry the diagnostic load, then its descriptors must flesh out what contributes to quality. In this example, *relevance* refers to the degree to which the information from the source helps answer the research question, while author's expertise, author's lack of bias, and currency of information are the defining features of *credibility* (Deane & Sparks, 2019). Notice that relevance and credibility are separated in this rubric. When teaching evaluation of sources, experts recommend beginning with relevance and then moving to credibility (Dean & Sparks, 2019). The separation allows for feedback targeted to each component in turn as they are taught. Teachers can use a rubric such as the one in Example 3 to determine a student's strengths and areas of need (e.g., sources are written by authorities but the student hasn't correctly identified bias in them) by highlighting the phrases that describe the student's work. Rubrics designed to illuminate levels of quality have instructional traction for both teachers and students.

Assessments of all types can be designed to yield actionable diagnostic information. This is part of the craft knowledge of an assessment-literate teacher described in Chapter 3. Without it teachers are not able to intentionally design or select assessments for formative use.

Making Time to Address Learning Needs

One roadblock to using diagnostic assessment information is time—time to analyze it and time to act on it. A robust curriculum poses challenges. Is there more to be taught than can be learned in the given time? Pacing guides are often developed to help teachers make sure they cover all the content they are responsible for. Yet we know that covering is not the same as teaching. If the pacing guides your teachers use are built on the "plan, instruct, assign, assess" model, chances are there is not sufficient time to address learning needs as they crop up, in which case the required pacing ensures that low achievers will remain low achievers. Or if teachers are using common assessments as diagnostic tools, are the results available in time to take action with them? As stated earlier, no action, no gain. Figure 4.4 suggests what to look for and what to ask within the classroom context.

FIGURE 4.4   Diagnosing learning needs: what to look for, what to ask

What to Look For

☐ Teachers prepare or select instruments and activities that have instructional traction.

☐ Teachers plan time in their instructional sequence to gather diagnostic information and to act on it.

What to Ask Teachers

☐ How do you diagnose student learning needs? What instruments or activities do you use? How well do they work?

☐ How do you make time to address learning needs as you uncover them?

---

4. Offering Actionable Feedback

Effective feedback can be defined as information provided to students that causes an improvement in learning directly attributable to the actions they take on its basis. Researchers and those interpreting their studies consistently agree that the mechanisms by which feedback works or doesn't work are complex and variable. We do know that feedback will not improve learning if students don't act on the information. Beyond that some researchers suggest that it is the degree of mindfulness triggered by feedback that determines its effectiveness (Wiliam, 2018). *Mindfulness* refers to the response the student has to the feedback: to what extent does the student reexamine the work, think deeply about it, and engage in productive struggle to improve it? No one formula for feedback has emerged from the literature, but there is convergence on several characteristics that will maximize the chances that students will take action on the basis of feedback and that their action will lead to greater learning (Figure 4.5).

> "Formative assessment *does* make a difference, and it is the quality, not just the quantity of feedback that merits our closest attention." (Sadler, 1998, p. 84, emphasis in the original)

FIGURE 4.5   Characteristics of effective feedback

Effective feedback

1. occurs during the learning, with time given to act on it;

2. focuses on salient features of the learning goal, pointing out strengths and offering information to guide next steps;

3. addresses partial understanding;

4. does not do the thinking for the student; and

5. limits guidance to the amount of advice students can act on in the given time.

Source: Adapted from Chappuis, J. *Seven Strategies of Assessment for Learning*, 2nd Edition (Figure 3.1 p. 95) © 2015. Reprinted by permission of Pearson Education, Inc.

Timing of the Feedback

Effective feedback occurs during the learning, while there is still time to act on it, *before* the graded event. In an often cited study Israeli researcher Ruth Butler (1988) found that providing comments along with grades did not generate further learning. This makes sense—a grade signifies, "You're done." There is no use in revising based on the feedback because the window for learning has closed. If indeed the window for learning is still open, there is no point in grading it because students aren't "done."

Saving Feedback for "the End"

A major problem with feedback offered only at the close of instruction is that students are not receiving comments to guide their work while they are practicing, risking the chance that their practice work will lead to them "learning it wrong." Think of how athletic coaches function. They are not leaving student athletes alone to run the practice drills—they are watching and deciding when to intercede, with whom, and about what. They are demonstrating, or having other students demonstrate, what the skill looks like when done well. If coaches reserved their feedback for the close of the match or game, athletes would learn little from them.

Grading Too Soon

Figuring scores on practice work into the final grade is not recommended. As a high school student claimed at the close of the first week of freshman English, "I'm doomed in this class. All of my mistakes count against me." When practice work counts toward the end-of-term grade, mistakes do "count against" the student—those who are not already close to proficient at the start of instruction do receive lower grades, even though they may have mastered the learning goals by the end of the marking period. How do teachers show students that it's not only okay to make mistakes, but when they occur, they are to be welcomed as information about where to go next? To cultivate a growth-oriented mindset and encourage students to view mistakes as a natural part of the path to excellence, rather than hits to their grade, teachers must plan time for students to take the action suggested by feedback before assessing their learning for summative purposes. The question here is "Where's the practice?" That is an optimal place for feedback, rather than grades.

Practice is the optimal place for feedback

Everything counts for learning.
Some things count for a grade.

Directing Attention to the Intended Learning

Several other characteristics of effective feedback surface in research studies and meta-analyses, the most important of which is that the feedback directs attention to the intended learning, pointing out strengths and offering specific information to guide improvement. In their meta-analysis of more than 130 studies on feedback, researchers Avraham Kluger and Angelo DeNisi (1996) reported that feedback caused significant learning gains consistently in only one-third of the studies. Feedback actually worsened subsequent performance in about one-third of the studies and made no measurable difference in the other third.

In examining these results researcher Lorrie Shepard (2008) suggests that a significant factor differentiating feedback that led to increased achievement from feedback that worsened achievement was whether the content of the feedback focused students' attention on

"Feedback is effective when it consists of information about progress and/or about how to proceed." (Hattie & Timperley, 2007, p. 89)

features salient to the learning goal or on the self. Self-focused feedback can be thought of as feedback that moves students into an ego state, containing judgments about attributes of the students themselves: "Your work shows how smart you are" or "You are not trying hard enough." It's hard to think of how feedback could make learning worse. As Sadler (1998) reminds us, feedback's power comes from its "catalytic and coaching value and its ability to inspire confidence and hope" (p. 84). If feedback causes students to quit trying, it has catalyzed action in the wrong direction.

On the other hand, learning-oriented feedback focuses on pertinent features of the work or of the processes used. It can be thought of as having three parts: strength, point of intervention, and next step. *Strength* feedback identifies what was done correctly, describes a feature of quality present in the work, or highlights effective use of a strategy or process. *Point of intervention* feedback locates the area(s) of focus for continued learning by identifying a mistake, describing a feature of quality needing work, or highlighting a problem with a strategy or process. *Next-step feedback* offers a reminder, asks a question, or makes a specific suggestion for action to take (Figure 4.6; Chappuis, 2015).

FIGURE 4.6   Strength, intervention, and next-step feedback: mathematics problem-solving example

Strength: *Your strategy worked well for part of the problem.*

Point of intervention: *However, it didn't lead to a correct solution because it fell apart right here.*

Next step: *What other strategy could you use to deal with this remaining group of people who will be without water if you don't do something?*

"Formative assessment requires that pupils have a central part in it. . . . Unless they come to understand their strengths and weaknesses, and how they might deal with them, they will not make progress." (Harlen & James, 1997, p. 372).

A note about praise: Although many students enjoy praise, statements praising characteristics of the *learner* tend to move students into an ego orientation, or in Carol Dweck's mindset theory, they reinforce a fixed mindset. That is, praise for learner characteristics like intelligence—"Look how smart you are!"—reinforces a belief that intelligence is a fixed quantity; how much they have of it is outside their control. When comments link their successes to their intelligence, students tend to see their failures as indications they're not so smart and tend to believe there's nothing they can do to get better (Blackwell et al., 2007). If the goal of feedback is to keep learning moving forward, strength feedback should center on the content of the learning—"The table you drew really helped solve the problem."

Addressing Partial Understanding

Feedback is most effective when student work demonstrates at least partial understanding of the learning goal, and therefore, it is not always the best choice for an instructional intervention. If the student's work doesn't demonstrate even partial mastery, offering further instruction is a better course of action. When students are lost in understanding the content of the feedback, they are not likely to know what to do with it; it may even cause them to feel as though they have failed twice: "I don't know how to do this, and I don't understand what my teacher's telling me to do about it." When there is little to nothing of substance that could be used as the basis for success comments, trying to teach by means of feedback is generally ineffective. When they don't get it, don't give feedback—reteach. This is a time-saver for teachers.

> "Corrective feedback can be ignored if . . . the student's knowledge is insufficient to accommodate additional feedback information." (Hattie & Timperley, 2007, p. 100)

Not Doing the Thinking for Students

You will notice that of the three options for next-step feedback, none say "Do the work for the student." Sometimes feedback overscaffolds the task, giving so much guidance that students can appear to have mastered a learning goal when all they have done is follow directions given as feedback. The trick with next-step feedback is to offer enough guidance so that the student is pointed in the right direction without removing the cognitive challenge from the task. If the student needs explicit directions, a better choice is to continue instruction. This is also a time-saver for teachers.

Limiting Guidance to What Students Can Act On

The final characteristic of effective feedback is that it limits guidance to the amount of advice the student can act on in the time allowed. Strong-performing students often receive a small amount of corrective feedback, and struggling students more often receive a lot. How many pieces of advice can the student be reasonably expected to act on in the time provided for revision? More information than that is counterproductive. Pointing out every problem along with suggestions for how to fix each may be overwhelming, especially for novice or struggling students. Say you are just learning to play golf. If your instructor comments on everything that needs improving, you are likely to be a one-lesson pupil. This recommendation does not ask that teachers underestimate students' capacity for taking action; some students can respond to lots of corrective direction without giving up. It does suggest, however, that when a student's work exhibits a daunting number of problems, the teacher may want to limit the focus of feedback to one or a few areas at a time. Figure 4.7 suggests what to look for and what to ask within the classroom context.

FIGURE 4.7   Effective feedback: what to look for, what to ask

What to Look For

☐ Students receive feedback during the course of instruction, before the graded event.

☐ Feedback focuses on salient features of the work with respect to the learning goal, pointing out strengths and offering guidance on next steps.

☐ Students use the feedback to improve their work.

What to Ask Teachers

☐ When do you give feedback to students?

☐ What do they do with the feedback you give?

☐ Have you noticed gains in learning caused by your feedback?

What to Ask Students

☐ How do you use the feedback your teacher gives you?

☐ What kinds of feedback are most helpful to you?

☐ What have you learned from feedback?

5. Engaging Students in Self-Assessment, Peer Feedback, and Goal Setting

With this component of formative assessment, we move from teacher-centered to student-centered decision-making. Studies repeatedly confirm that achievement improves when students are required to think about their own learning, articulate what they understand or do well, and identify what they still need to learn (Black & Wiliam, 1998; Hattie, 2009; White & Frederiksen, 1998). Additionally, self-assessment helps students develop a sense of self-efficacy—the belief that their efforts can make a difference in how well they learn. When students learn to evaluate their own work against standards of quality and adjust learning strategies as needed, they develop self-monitoring habits and skills that will be invaluable throughout their lives.

Student Self-Assessment

The ultimate goal of self-assessment is to equip students to develop sufficient insight into their own work to improve it (Wiliam, 2018). Self-assessment answers the question "Where am I now?" To answer it accurately, students start with a clear vision of the intended learning and the success criteria. They next practice evaluating a range of work samples, using the language of the success criteria to justify their judgments, mirroring the thinking they will be doing when they evaluate their own work. Their teachers then offer descriptive feedback that models the kind of thinking students are to engage in when they self-assess. Without these prerequisites many students won't be prepared to judge their status accurately, in which case self-assessment is not likely to be of benefit. The power is in the preparation.

Another factor influencing accuracy is that of psychological safety (Brown & Harris, 2013). Do students feel safe enough to assess their work honestly? Teachers encourage a sense of emotional safety, first, by explaining to students what self-assessment is, why they are doing it, and who will see the information; second, by structuring feedback so that it doesn't label mistakes as failures but rather as a way to figure out what is next to learn; and, third, by helping students attribute their current status to a mixture of what they have already learned and what they have yet to learn (Chappuis, 2015). When student work demonstrates little to no progress, self-assessment is not generally recommended.

"The primary purpose of maintaining a classroom environment that is warm, trustworthy, and empathetic is to allow learning to thrive on error. An essential element of classroom management, then, is to establish and enforce ground rules that create a 'safe harbor for welcoming error and thence learning.'" (Hattie, 2012, p. 165)

Self-assessment activities can range from informal to formal. Figure 4.8 shows an example of a self-assessment exit slip that students complete at the close of a lesson. Figure 4.9 shows an example of a form students use to determine strengths and areas for further work on the basis of quiz results. Students review their corrected quiz, then mark on the form whether they got each question right or wrong. They examine their wrong answers and decide whether they know how to correct the mistake or they don't. Then they summarize their strengths and areas for further study.

FIGURE 4.8   Self-assessment exit slip

Name: _____

Today's learning target: _____

_____

_____

I'm good at this: _____

_____

_____

I still need to work on this: _____

_____

_____

FIGURE 4.9   Self-assessment with a quiz

QUESTION	LEARNING TARGET	RIGHT	WRONG	I SEE THE MISTAKE	I DON'T GET IT
1	Identify elements of a story: plot.				
2	Describe a character's actions based on textual evidence.				
3	Describe a character's actions based on textual evidence.				
4	Explain the meaning of simple similes in context.				
5	Explain the meaning of simple similes in context.				

(Continued)

FIGURE 4.9   (Continued)

I'm good at these!

Learning targets I got right: _____

_____

_____

I'm pretty good at these but need some review.

Learning targets I got wrong because of a mistake I see: _____

_____

_____

What I can do to keep this from happening again: _____

_____

_____

I need to keep learning these.

Learning targets I got wrong and I'm not sure what to do to correct them: _____

_____

_____

What I can do to get better at them: _____

_____

_____

Source: Chappuis, J. *Seven Strategies of Assessment for Learning,* 2nd Edition (Figure 4.10 and 4.11, pp. 164–165) © 2015. Reprinted by permission of Pearson Education, Inc.

Peer Feedback

The intent of peer feedback is to describe strengths and needs in the work of others. Giving students opportunities to examine and comment on one another's work confers a number of benefits. First, it deepens understanding of quality for the student who is providing the feedback. Second, it allows for all students to receive comments on their work in a relatively short period of time, thereby increasing feedback opportunities for all. Third, some students are more apt to be open to feedback from a peer, which may be seen as less evaluative than that from a teacher. Fourth, students can often come up with suggestions for next steps because they are encountering the same issues. Fifth, after giving someone else feedback, students are better able to view their own work through another's eyes, spurring new thoughts and insights useful in revising their own work (Chappuis, in press).

These benefits accrue only if students are able to accurately identify strengths and needs vis-à-vis the learning goal; the prerequisites for accurate peer feedback are the same as those for accurate self-assessment. It is also helpful to give students practice with giving feedback in a controlled setting, engaging them in activities such as the one shown in Figure 4.10.

FIGURE 4.10   Preparing students to offer peer feedback

1. The teacher selects an anonymous sample of student work exhibiting both strengths and areas needing improvement.

2. Students work in pairs, with one assuming the role of "student" and the other that of "teacher." Each separately examines the sample and uses the success criteria or rubric to identify strengths and areas of need.

3. Then they meet in a simulated three-minute feedback conference. The "student" shares their thoughts first, and the "teacher" follows up with anything the "student" might have overlooked or with which the "teacher" disagrees. While the "teacher" talks, the "student" takes notes.

4. At the end of the three minutes, the classroom teacher conducts a group debrief of the simulation, asking students what was easy and what was difficult about offering or receiving feedback. The class brainstorms solutions to potential problems.

5. The students switch roles and engage in another round of the simulation with a different anonymous example.

Source: Chappuis, J. (Forthcoming). Student Involvement in Assessment. In S. Brookhart (Ed.), Assessment Section; D. Fisher (Ed.), *Routledge Encyclopedia of Education* (Online). Taylor & Francis: New York.

Goal Setting

Goal setting is a logical companion to self-assessment, moving from "Where am I now?" to "How can I get there from here?" Goals that have the greatest impact on increasing achievement are challenging rather than easy. In summarizing decades of research on goal-setting theory, Edwin Locke and Gary Latham (2002) describe four mechanisms by which specific and challenging goals increase achievement:

1. They focus attention on key actions that will lead to accomplishment of the goal and divert attention from less productive activities.

2. They trigger greater effort than low-challenge goals.

3. They prolong effort—people who have challenging goals demonstrate greater levels of persistence.

4. They cause people to tap into knowledge and strategies they already have and also to look for ways to increase their knowledge and strategy repertoire to accomplish the goal. (pp. 706–707)

Elements of Effective Goals

The elements of goals that lead to productive action mirror the three questions "Where am I going?" "Where am I now?" and "How can I get there from here?" In formulating a goal students begin with a clear statement of the intended learning and a description of their current status. Then they create an action plan that specifies the steps they will take; when and where they will do the work; who, if anyone, they will work with; and what materials they will need. They may also include a reference to work they will use as their pictures of "before I met my goal" and "after I met my goal."

The requirements to specify "where" and "when" may be surprising. Social psychologist Heidi Grant Halvorson (2012) found that identifying when and where a person will accomplish a goal increased commitment to follow-through, in one study doubling the rate of goal attainment.

Figure 4.11 shows an example of a goal and action frame.

FIGURE 4.11   Goal and action frame

Name: Juan   Date: 2/20

Learning target: Explain how the immune system works

Current level of achievement: I can't explain how a neutrophil fights infection

Evidence: Quiz on communicable diseases 2/19

My goal—what I need to learn: Explain what a neutrophil does at chemotaxis, phagocytosis, and apoptosis

Plan of action

What: Study the pages on pathogens and the immune system. Practice drawing the life cycle of a neutrophil, with all stages explained.

Where: At home

When: After dinner, Tues. & Wed.

Help & materials needed: No help. Book and paper

Evidence of achieving my goal: Test on 2/26

Figure 4.12 suggests what to look for and what to ask within the classroom context.

FIGURE 4.12   Self-assessment, peer feedback, and goal setting: what to look for, what to ask

What to Look For

❑ Activities in which students practice evaluating a range of work samples as rehearsal for self-assessment

❑ Activities in which students practice offering feedback in simulated settings as rehearsal for giving feedback to one another

❑ Student use of success criteria/rubrics when self-evaluating and offering peer feedback

❑ Opportunities for students to set goals for further learning based on peer feedback and self-assessment

❑ Goal statements that include the elements of effective goals

What to Ask Teachers

❑ How do you prepare students to engage in self-assessment?

❑ How do you prepare students to offer one another feedback?

❑ What types of goal-setting activities do the students in your class engage in?

❑ How do students keep in touch with their progress in meeting their goals?

What to Ask Students

❑ How do you know what to say when you self-assess/give peer feedback?

❑ What does self-assessment help you do?

❑ What does giving feedback to/receiving feedback from classmates help you with?

❑ What goals have you set for yourself?

❑ What helps you meet your goals? How are you doing on meeting them?

6. Providing Opportunities for Students to Track Their Learning and Self-Reflect

Student involvement in assessment extends beyond participation during instruction. When they track and reflect on their progress, looking back over time to notice changes, they become increasingly efficacious. Recording assignment and assessment information by learning target and collecting evidence in a portfolio are common methods teachers use for students to track their achievement trajectory. Portfolios can be assembled to document growth, learning throughout a project, goal attainment, current level of achievement, or targeted aspects of learning. The main purpose of tracking learning over time is to collect evidence on which to reflect; without the metacognitive act of reflection, the evidence itself will not prompt deeper learning or self-knowledge.

Student self-reflection involves drawing conclusions about what they have learned, how they have learned it, what worked and what didn't, what they would do differently, and how far they have come. Figure 4.13 shows examples of prompts that elicit reflective thinking.

FIGURE 4.13   Prompts to elicit reflective thinking

TOPIC	PROMPT
Reflecting on growth	I have become better at ____. I used to ____, but now I _____.
Reflecting on learning from a project	What skills did I develop as a result of doing this project?
Reflecting on goal attainment	What helped me attain the goals I set? What problems did I encounter? How did I overcome them?
Reflecting on achievement	What did I learn? How did I learn it? What would I change about what I did?
Reflecting on self as a learner	What helps me as a learner? What gets in the way? What used to be difficult that is easier now? What did I do to make that happen?

The final step in student involvement is to share their reflections with an audience: parents, other significant adults, other students, or teachers. Student-involved or student-led conferences are well suited to this kind of discussion. They can occur at home or at school, during the school day or after. Any artifact or collection of artifacts—a quiz accompanied by feedback or self-evaluation, a record of progress the student has kept, a learning journal, a portfolio—can be the focus of the conversation. Figure 4.14 suggests what to look for and what to ask within the classroom context.

FIGURE 4.14 Student tracking and self-reflection: what to look for, what to ask

What to Look For

❑ Opportunities for students to track their progress

❑ Periodic opportunities for students to reflect on one or more aspects of learning

❑ Opportunities for students to share thoughts, conclusions, reflections, and evidence with others

What to Ask Teachers

❑ In what ways do students track their learning progress or achievement in your class?

❑ What aspects of learning do you ask students to reflect on?

❑ What opportunities do students have to share their reflections with others?

What to Ask Students

❑ How does tracking your progress help you?

❑ How do you know when you are learning?

❑ When you look at a collection of your work, what do you notice?

❑ How does sharing your thoughts about your learning help you learn better?

Leader Support for Formative Assessment

Leadership support is crucial to the implementation of formative assessment in a school or district, for it requires a shift to a formative culture (Moss et al., 2013). Supporting teachers as they build formative assessment practices into their instruction rests on the foundation of encouraging and thereby valuing learning by all members of the school organization.

The six critical components collectively define the vision of what formative assessment looks like when it is done well. While reading this chapter, you may have recognized some practices that are thriving in your school and perhaps some that are not yet a part of your school's culture or way of doing things. A significant component of successful leadership in formative assessment is your ability to identify where you are now with respect to this vision of quality and to plan for the appropriate next steps.

As a school leader you can foster successful implementation of formative assessment practices through the following actions:

1. Deepen your own understanding of what formative assessment is and how it improves learning.

2. Learn along with teachers. This act telegraphs that you believe formative assessment to be of high priority, a skill set worthy of all educators' time. Ask teachers to invite you into their classes when they are engaged in a formative assessment activity. Model learner behavior. Consciously adopt a "learner stance," as one who is interested in growing, rather than an "expert persona," one who already knows.

3. Learn from teachers. Know what they are doing to make learning explicit, to understand what their students know, and to promote learning autonomy. Watch what their students are doing in response.

4. Build commitment to the vision among teachers. Promote a shift from teacher-centered to learner-centered assessment beliefs and practices. Encourage them to experiment and take risks.

5. Marshal time, expertise, and money to support effective schoolwide practice. Provide professional development opportunities and resources. Release teachers to plan together and observe one another.

6. Help teachers notice changes in students attributable to changes in assessment practices. This, more than anything, is reward for the hard work of changing practice.

7. Identify a "concept of the week." Co-plan with teachers to highlight it at a staff meeting through examples, an activity, or student work.

8. Be quick to notice success. If someone tells you, "I tried this out, and it really worked," respond—ask or email a question, or make a comment. Recognize small wins.

> "When administrators see formative leadership as their target, they also see themselves as the leading learners in their schools, view teachers as learners, and enter into meaningful learning partnerships with teachers and students." (Moss et al., 2013, p. 216)

Summary

Formative assessment practices answer three questions about student learning: "Where am I going?" "Where am I now?" and "How can I get there from here?" In this chapter we have explained six components that define the domain of formative assessment practice. We have emphasized the importance of the student as decision maker, whose information needs must be met through active participation in the assessment process. We described five prerequisites to effective implementation and concluded with a discussion of actions school leaders can take to build formative assessment capacity in their schools and districts. Student-centered assessment for learning is the closest we will come to a silver bullet for creating substantive, relevant learning and competent, confident learners.

Success Indicators for Assessment Literacy Goal #4

The school leader

- can describe the six critical components of formative assessment;

- can offer a compelling rationale for the importance of the student as informed decision maker;

- knows what to look for in the classroom for each of the six critical components;

- has a repertoire of questions to ask of teachers and students to deepen their understanding of the application of formative assessment practices; and

- establishes a baseline for formative assessment practices in the school from which to build formative assessment capacity.

 Study Guide Questions

1. Think back over your study of formative assessment practices. What did you find most interesting? What was new information for you? Did anything surprise you? If so, why?

2. One overarching theme of this chapter is the importance of student involvement in the assessment process. Identify two or three recommendations in the chapter that put students' information needs at the center. Think of a learning or motivation problem you have seen or experienced that could be attributed to overlooking each recommendation. Then compose a compelling reason to attend to the recommendation.

3. Which of the six critical components of formative assessment do you see as done well throughout your school? Which do you think may need a "course correction"? Which do you believe are not yet in place in some or many classes?

 Personal Portfolio Entry Suggestions

- Written responses to the study guide questions

- A description of professional development offerings in formative assessment

- Staff formative assessment activities

- Faculty discussions and/or meeting agendas for which formative assessment is the topic

- A personal formative assessment learning log

- Artifacts created in the chapter activities

Activity 4.1
Identifying Talking Points for Critical Components of Formative Assessment

Learning Target for the Activity

- Be able to discuss the six critical components of formative assessment and how each contributes to increasing student achievement.

Purpose

This activity is designed to deepen your own understanding of the six critical components of formative assessment as described in this chapter:

1. Establishing clear learning goals and success criteria

2. Using classroom questioning to elicit evidence of student thinking

3. Diagnosing learning needs to inform instructional next steps

4. Offering actionable feedback

5. Engaging students in self-assessment, peer feedback, and goal setting

6. Providing opportunities for students to track their learning and self-reflect

Completing the activity will prepare you to engage in conversations with teachers about their formative assessment practices in each area.

Time

Variable

Materials Needed

- The sections in the chapter describing each of the six critical components of formative assessment

- Paper and pen/pencil, computer, or tablet

- Chart paper and markers if doing the activity with a group

- Electronic or blank copies of the note-taking form shown in Figure 4.15

(Continued)

FIGURE 4.15   Note-taking form for Activity 4.1

COMPONENT	KEY IDEAS	CONNECTION TO STUDENT ACHIEVEMENT
1. Establishing clear learning goals and success criteria		
2. Using classroom questioning to elicit evidence of student thinking		
3. Diagnosing learning needs to inform instructional next steps		
4. Offering actionable feedback		
5. Engaging students in self-assessment, peer feedback, and goal setting		
6. Providing opportunities for students to track learning and self-reflect		

Suggested Room Setup

Tables and chairs for small-group work

Directions

Review the chapter text one component at a time, noting key ideas that could form the basis of a conversation with teachers. Also, note benefits to student achievement attributable to each component. You may wish to do this activity with a small team of school leaders, first doing the work independently and then discussing your thoughts with the group. You may wish to create a consensus list for each component either on chart paper or electronically, or both.

Closure

Have each participant refer back to the learning target for this activity and also to this chapter's Learning Goal #1. Then have them perform a self-evaluation: Am I closer to this learning goal now than before the activity? Participants can share out briefly what they have learned that brought them closer to their assessment literacy goal of understanding formative assessment practices.

Additionally, participants may reflect on the following questions:

- What insights into formative assessment did you gain by completing the activity?
- What questions do you have?
- With whom might you share your insights and questions?

Activity 4.2
Looking for Evidence of Effective Formative Assessment Practices in the Classroom

Learning Target for the Activity

- Be able to identify formative assessment practices as they are used in daily instruction.

Purpose

This activity gives practice with looking for evidence of each of the six critical components of formative assessment while observing lessons.

Time

Variable

(Continued)

(Continued)

Materials Needed

- An electronic or paper copy of the form "Evidence of Formative Assessment Practices," available for download from **resources.corwin.com/10GoalsLeaders** (The form is simply a list of what to look for in each of the six formative assessment critical components.)

- An electronic or paper copy of the form "What to Ask of Teachers," available for download from **resources.corwin.com/10GoalsLeaders**

- Your notes from Activity 4.1

Suggested Room Setup

Not applicable

Directions

For this activity you will be observing in a classroom, looking for evidence of each of the six formative assessment critical components. We recommend that you ask teachers to volunteer to be observed in order to assist you in more deeply understanding how formative assessment practices are carried out in the classroom. Your notes from Activity 4.1 will help you in talking about each component prior to an observation.

1. Review with a teacher volunteer the six formative assessment components described in this chapter. Review the "look fors" listed for each component on the form "Evidence of Formative Assessment Practices" (available for download from **resources.corwin.com/10GoalsLeaders** and also presented at the end of each component section in the text). Together, identify one component that you will observe for in an upcoming lesson.

2. Observe the lesson, noting what you see and hear as evidence of each of the "look fors" for the component in question.

3. In a post-observation conference share your evidence with the teacher, asking also for their input regarding evidence that you might have missed. Use the form "What to Ask Teachers" to frame discussion questions as appropriate. (These questions could also be used in a pre-observation conference.) Discuss what each of you has learned from the observation and the post-observation conference, as well as any questions each of you has.

4. Repeat the process with a different teacher and a different component until you have observed lessons for all six formative assessment components.

Closure

Write a short summary of what you have learned about the components you have observed for. What strengths did you notice? What areas of further learning might be called for? What actions might be indicated?

Activity 4.3
Discussing Formative Assessment Practices With Students

Learning Target for the Activity

- Know how to gather evidence of effective use of formative assessment practices from students.

Purpose

At the beginning of the chapter we made a case for the importance of meeting students' information needs. In this activity you ask students to share the ways in which they are involved in the assessment of their own learning and the impact that involvement has on them as learners. You can do it formally as a series of focus groups with a small number of students or more informally as part of a classroom observation or walk-through.

Time

Variable

Materials Needed

- Your notes from Activity 4.1

- An electronic or paper copy of the form "What to Ask Students," available for download from **resources.corwin.com/10GoalsLeaders**

- The chapter section "Using Classroom Questioning to Elicit Evidence of Student Thinking"

Suggested Room Setup

If you will be conducting this activity with a focus group, set up chairs and tables so everyone can see one another. A U shape or a circle will work best.

Directions

Complete each step in the order below:

1. Determine whether you will conduct the activity formally, with a group (or several groups) of students, or as part of a classroom observation.

2. Review your notes from Activity 4.1. If you have done Activity 4.2, review your notes from that activity too.

3. Read through the questions on the form "What to Ask Students." Add or modify questions as appropriate.

4. Decide which of the six components (or perhaps all of them if working with older students) you will inquire about.

(Continued)

(Continued)

5. Pose questions to students, using the recommendations in the chapter section "Using Classroom Questioning to Elicit Evidence of Student Thinking." If conducting a focus group, encourage student-to-student dialogue.

Closure

Write a short summary of what you have learned about the components you discussed with students. What patterns did you notice? Which components seemed to be working well for them? Which components were they less familiar with? Were any areas problematic for them? If so, what actions might be indicated?

Activity 4.4
Establishing a School Baseline

Learning Target for the Activity

- Know how to determine the current status of formative assessment practices in your school.

Purpose

In this activity you will examine evidence from a range of sources to understand where your school is now with respect to implementing formative assessment effectively. You will use this information to prioritize steps in building formative assessment capacity. We recommend that you conduct this activity with a leadership team.

Time

Ongoing

Materials Needed

- Answers to Study Guide question 3

- Notes from Activities 4.2 and 4.3

- See "Directions" for a list of resources to consult.

- Electronic or paper copies of the note-taking form shown in Figure 4.16

FIGURE 4.16   Note-taking form for Activity 4.4

Name of Artifact/Document: _____

Components of Formative Assessment Addressed (check all that apply)

❑ Establishing clear learning goals and success criteria

❑ Using classroom questioning to elicit evidence of student thinking

❑ Diagnosing learning needs to inform instructional next steps

❑ Offering actionable feedback

❑ Engaging students in self-assessment, peer feedback, and goal setting

❑ Providing opportunities for students to track learning and self-reflect

Accuracy of Representation

_____

_____

_____

Completeness of Coverage

_____

_____

_____

Suggested Room Setup

Not applicable

Directions

Complete each step in the order below:

1. Collect documents and artifacts that relate to the use of formative assessment at the school and district levels. Some suggestions:

    • School board policies on assessment, grading, and homework

    • School-level policies on assessment, grading, and homework

    • Faculty handbook

    • Teacher evaluation criteria

    • School and district professional development offerings and priorities

    • Formative assessment professional development materials in use in classrooms

    • Formative assessment instructional resources in use in classrooms

    • Data on implementation (e.g., which practices are observed most frequently)

(Continued)

(Continued)

- Communications to parents regarding formative assessment practices

- Grading programs or software that incorporate recordkeeping for formative assessment results

- Any instrument in use across classrooms labeled as "formative"

2. For each document or artifact you examine, determine which of the six components of formative assessment it addresses. Check all boxes that apply.

3. Determine the extent to which it accurately reflects the intent of the practice(s). Note any issues. Is it accurate? What steps will you take to correct inaccuracies or misconceptions (if any)? Who else might need to be involved?

4. Determine the extent to which it includes all important elements of the practice(s) that are germane to the purpose of the document/artifact. Note any issues. Is it complete? What steps will you take to address what is missing (if anything)? Who else might need to be involved?

Closure

Make a plan for next steps.

Definition

Instructional traction: An attribute of an assessment. An assessment is said to have *instructional traction* when its results identify what the learning difficulty is.

 This chapter's online resources are available for download from **resources.corwin.com/10GoalsLeaders**

Grading Practices

5

Assessment Literacy Goal #5: *The leader understands sound grading practices and works with staff to ensure that all students receive meaningful, accurate grades.*

K–12 schools in the United States have been using grades of some sort as a way of communicating about students' learning since at least the mid-19th century. Grades and grading practices have been questioned for most of that time, and grading remains a controversial topic. This chapter presents principles for sound grading practices that allow meaningful and accurate communication about student learning, even as it takes the position that all grading policies and practices involve trade-offs and none is perfect.

Chapter Learning Goals

1. Understand the principles of sound grading practices.

2. Lead teachers and others in implementing sound grading practices.

3. Communicate grading policies and practices to students, parents, and community members.

Grades are the symbols assigned to individual pieces of classroom work (e.g., a test or performance assessment) and to composite measures of these individual assessments that are intended for report cards. Most K–12 educators use the terms *grades* and *grading* to refer to both, and we will do the same in this chapter. Grading is classroom summative assessment, which means it is assessment designed to summarize or report students' achievement of intended learning outcomes. Formative assessment (see Chapter 4) takes place during the learning, while summative assessment takes place after learning has been completed, or at least completed up to a point of taking stock.

Where Do Grades Come From?

There is some evidence of the use of grades in the U.S. common school as early as the mid-1800s. Grading in K–12 schools, especially high schools, mimicked university grading practices, which developed much earlier. Historically, there have been long-standing debates on several issues regarding grading practices (Brookhart, 2009). We discuss four issues in particular over which differences of opinion have been ongoing for years and are, in some places, still unresolved: (1) the purpose of grades, (2) the referencing scheme most useful for grades, (3) the relationship of grades to ability, and (4) the reliability or accuracy of grades.

Purpose: Grading to Communicate Versus Grading to Motivate

Beliefs about the central purpose of grading are related to more general beliefs about teaching and learning. One position holds that grades should communicate the current status on the learning goals students were asked to demonstrate, whether for an individual assessment or for the composite report card grade. This view is associated with a more constructivist view of learning, where the motivational aspect of grades comes from students using them as part of the monitoring aspect of the self-regulation of learning. The purpose of grades is to let parents, students, and others know where students are in their learning journey.

Another position holds that grades should function as "pay" that students earn for work done, which means that points can be added to grades for any behavior for which the teacher seeks compliance. This view is associated with a more behaviorist view of learning, where the external reward (grades or points) serves as the motivator for students, which is why this position is sometimes called "grading to motivate." These two views have been held resolutely and debated fiercely for over a hundred years (Brookhart et al., 2016; Crooks, 1933). Some teachers hold both positions simultaneously; that is, they will say both that grades show how students are learning and that grades are what students earn for their work (Brookhart, 1993), without realizing that the two positions are contradictory.

For reasons already reviewed in Chapter 4 we take the position that the primary purpose of grades is to communicate students' current status on intended learning goals. Support for this position is growing because it accords with modern theory about how students learn and self-regulate and because it aligns with the current standards-based approach to education. However, there are still many teachers who see grades as students' pay for work done, and emotions can run high when this view is challenged. This view of grades is usually closely tied with teachers' classroom management practices. School leaders who wish to lead grading reform in their building/district need to be aware of this. Some teachers will not be able to move to grades-as-communication until they have put in place successful classroom management strategies to replace grades-as-pay.

Norm- Versus Criterion-Referencing Schemes

There are several ways grades could communicate student achievement. One way would be to compare students with one another (norm referencing). Another would be to compare student performance against a description of intended performance (called criterion referencing). A third would be to compare students' current performance with their own past performance or against expectations for current performance (called self-referencing). Chapter 9 describes referencing frameworks in more detail.

Historically, arguments about which referencing framework to use have been mostly between norm and criterion referencing. Actually, Robert Glaser in 1963 coined the term *criterion referencing*, but in the field of grading the debate had been ongoing long before that. Proponents of what would come to be called criterion referencing called it "grading on absolute standards" (Crooks, 1933), using "standards" to mean a level of achievement on content to be learned, not *standards* as we use the term today. This has long been the preferred method reported in the grading literature (Brookhart et al., 2016), but norm-referenced practices like "grading on the curve" or adjusting scores based on class performance still persist in some places.

We take the position that students' performance should be graded with reference to descriptions of performance on intended learning goals, a criterion-referenced approach, because that corresponds to a view of instruction and assessment based on clear standards (see Chapter 2). The logic is clear: identify the standards as intended learning goals, base instruction on those intended learning goals, and then report level of proficiency or mastery with reference to those intended learning goals.

The Difference Between Achievement and Ability

At the beginning of the 20th century, educators and researchers both thought that grades reflected natural ability, a now outdated idea (Brookhart, 2015). We now know that much of what has been measured in the name of "intelligence" is learned in school. Therefore, early 20th century studies looked at the relationship between intelligence tests and grades. By mid-20th century, research had moved to studying the relationship between grades and standardized achievement tests, again expecting them to be highly related because they were thought to measure the same thing. What was found was that grades and tested achievement correlate moderately (at around .50) and have consistently demonstrated this level of relationship for 100 years—meaning that they don't measure the same thing. Other factors, including one that has been called the "success in school" factor (Bowers, 2011), plus error, make up the rest of the variance in grades. Recently, one study suggested that student self-regulation of learning may be related to the success in school factor (Galla et al., 2019). You can find more details and a readable summary of grading research over the past century in Thomas Guskey and Susan Brookhart's *What We Know About Grading* (2019).

Despite the fact that much is still to be learned about the precise interrelationships of grades with other constructs, there is solid evidence that grades measure a kind of learning contextualized to the school and the classroom rather than simply reflecting the kind of decontextualized achievement measured by standardized achievement tests. When teachers improve their grading practices to focus only on students' current status on intended learning goals, the relationship of grades to standardized tests increases, but it never gets close to a level that would indicate that grades and standardized achievement tests measure the same thing (Brookhart et al., 2016). We take the position that grades should be based on the principles for sound grading discussed in the next section and that school leaders should be aware that done well, these practices lead to grades that are measures of school learning, related to standardized achievement but also related to the classroom learning context. We agree with Alex Bowers (2011) in seeing that as a good thing. If grades were redundant to standardized test scores, we would not need both. If they aren't, they each give us different information and together provide a richer picture of student learning.

Grading Reliability

Some of the earliest grading research was motivated by scholars' observation that teachers' grading practices were variable and unreliable, which compromised the accuracy of their information and potentially could harm students (Guskey & Brookhart, 2019). For example, some researchers asked different teachers to grade the same student examination papers and reported the large variation in the grades they assigned. Other studies sought to distinguish different sources of error in grading, including the quality of students' work, teacher severity or leniency, differing understandings of what was important in the work, the nature of the grading scale, and random error (chance).

Early studies suffered from the assumption that teachers could just intuitively write questions and gauge student answers and that ought to somehow be sufficient. These assumptions predate today's interest in assessment literacy and provide a kind of cautionary tale in support of it. Some of these studies offered student work on exams or exam questions that would be considered poor prompts today. None of them specified the criteria by which students' performance was to be evaluated, which is part of the source of teachers' differing understandings of what was important in the work. Both of these would be considered poor practice today (see Chapters 2 and 3).

Even with advances in assessment literacy, more contemporary studies of teachers' grading practices give evidence that teachers' grading can still be unreliable because grading is influenced by a different mixture of achievement, ability, effort, and other factors for different teachers. However, it is now clear at least that achievement is the largest factor in grades, even unreliable ones (Brookhart et al., 2016), which allows us room for hope. If assessment-literate school leaders build grading reforms on teachers' current understanding that instruction and assessment should be based on clear learning goals (see Chapter 2), there is hope that grading reforms can lead to grading improvement.

Studies on grading reliability have several implications for current grading practices. First, be clear about criteria. Chapters 2 and 3 have already emphasized this point. Second, be consistent. Ways to do this are detailed in Chapter 3. For example, use a scoring guide (e.g., a rubric), so you address the same criteria to each student's work, bracket other features of the work that are not among the criteria (e.g., neatness), grade anonymously when you can, and so on. Third, use simple scales with few categories (e.g., ABCDF or proficiency levels as opposed to percentages), because there is less opportunity for error when there are fewer choices to make.

In the next section we organize the takeaways from the grading research and what we know about student learning, instruction, and measurement, and distill them into a set of sound grading practices. Assessment-literate school leaders should know about these practices, recognize them when they see them, and help colleagues reform practices that run counter to these principles.

Sound Grading Practices

Sound grading practices result in reporting students' status on intended learning goals and follow the assessment principles for any sound assessment: start with clear learning goals and criteria, use **multiple measures**, minimize bias and distortion, and so on. Figure 5.1 presents a list of these practices based on the more detailed recommendations the authors have presented elsewhere (Brookhart, 2017; Chappuis & Stiggins, 2020; Guskey & Brookhart, 2019).

FIGURE 5.1   Grading practices that communicate meaningful, accurate information about student learning

- Report achievement of learning goals separately from behavior, citizenship, learning skills, and progress.
- Start with clear learning goals.
- Use grades to report students' current status on the learning goals.
- Give students formative feedback regarding the learning goals during their learning.
- Attend to the accuracy of grades.

We discuss each practice in Figure 5.1 in turn. In our other work, and in other authors' work, lists of recommended grading practices are more or less detailed, but the general concepts remain the same. School leaders and teachers who follow these recommendations are more likely to produce grades that support student learning by providing meaningful, accurate estimates of student achievement of intended learning goals.

Report Achievement Separately

We subscribe to the principle that academic grades should reflect students' current status on academic learning goals and other criteria should be reported separately (Brookhart, 2017; Chappuis & Stiggins, 2020; Guskey, 2015). It is common to have a separate scale on a report card for reporting what Guskey called process criteria, learning-enabling skills and dispositions such as effort and participation. The important thing is to not mix the report of those skills with academic grades. If you do, you risk reporting grades with muddled meaning. For example, one student might get a B because they did C-level work but tried very hard, another student might get a B because they did A-level work but turned it in late, and yet another student might get a B for B-level work. The three Bs make it seem like all three students have achieved at about the same level on the intended learning goals, when this is not the case.

We are not suggesting you don't assess effort—of course, you do! The most appropriate response to a student who is not exerting effort is to find out why, give the student some feedback, and address the problem. Waiting until report card time to report lack of effort or other learning skills is too long. We could say the same about other learning-enabling skills, like being prompt and prepared, doing homework regularly, and so on. These characteristics can be reported—separately from academic grades—on the report card, but we would not advise waiting until report card time to work with a student or communicate with a parent on any of these.

Clear Learning Goals

Without clear learning goals it is impossible to tell what achievement grades are intended to report. As for any assessment (see Chapter 2), articulating the learning goals for students, parents, and others who will review students' grades is an important first step. This is true whether your building/district uses standards-based report cards, which report achievement by standards, or traditional report cards, which report achievement by subject area. Even with traditional report cards, it is still important to specify what learning goals have been taught and assessed during the report period.

This principle is a foundational one. Assessment-literate school leaders work to get clarity on what the goals of instruction are and on the fact that grades should be based on these goals, before proceeding with any other aspect of grading reform. Even if all that is needed in your building/district is a fine-tuning of grading practices and not outright reform, clarity on the goals of instruction and agreement that the purpose of grades is to communicate about achievement of those goals is a first principle. Without this firm foundation grading will founder.

Report Current Status

Most grading experts suggest that grades should communicate students' current status on intended learning goals. However, some argue that grades should reflect growth (how far students have come). And some suggest that effort or other nonacademic factors should be included in grades as well. Here we give a brief summary of the argument that academic grades should report current status as opposed to growth or effort.

Current status is straightforward to measure and communicate and, importantly, means the same thing for every student. For example, if two students are both graded Proficient on a standard, it should be true that they both know and can do what the standard describes. In a traditional grading context, if two students each are graded B in a subject, it should be true that they are both at about the same level of accomplishment in that subject for this report period. In addition, current status gives the most actionable information to students and parents. Students' next steps in learning start with where they are, not how far they've come.

Growth is an interesting aspect of learning, but it's best measured with standardized assessments, not classroom grades. There are several reasons for that. First, there usually isn't a reliable classroom beginning measure for where students start when teachers begin a unit or series of lessons. Even if you give a pretest, many if not most of the students will score at chance level (e.g., 25% correct if your pretest uses four-choice multiple-choice questions). Thus, there's no reliable and comparable baseline against which to compute growth with classroom assessment. Second, growth will be larger for students who start with less knowledge in the domain of a particular learning goal, and smaller for those who already know some things to begin with. Thus, grading on "growth" might result in a student who hasn't reached a learning goal getting a better grade than a student who has—or has even gone beyond—but knew something to begin with. Such grades imply that the lower-achieving student has achieved more than the higher-achieving one. In other words, "growth" grades are at the least noncomparable among students and at worst mismeasures of student learning.

Sometimes you may hear people refer to report cards as *progress reports*. That's a somewhat dated term in education, although it's frequently used in business project management. Old-fashioned "progress reports" reported student grades in various subjects, usually reporting students' current achievement status. The "progress" just meant "how students are currently getting on in school."

In today's climate, with the current interest in growth (see Chapters 8 and 9), the term *progress* has come to mean "growth." For example, Guskey (Guskey, 2015; Guskey & Brookhart, 2019) distinguishes between product, progress, and process criteria. In his terminology *product criteria* describe what students know and can produce in their assessments at a given point in time—in other words, their current status on learning goals, the basis for academic grades. *Process criteria* describe effort, participation, responsibility, work habits, and other learning-enabling qualities that help students reach their learning goals—in other words, qualities that may be reported on a learning skills or classroom citizenship scale. *Progress criteria* describe growth or gain, by reporting change on a score scale or in categories (e.g., "much improvement," "some improvement," and so on).

This discussion has unpacked the reasons why we recommend that academic grades should reflect students' current status on intended learning goals. This produces the most meaningful and useful communication with students and parents. In the remainder of this section we describe four things that are important for reporting current status:

- Base grades on clear learning goals.

- Use recent, high-quality assessment evidence.

- Keep standards-based records.

- Involve students.

Base grades on clear learning goals. Grades that reflect achievement status are criterion referenced; that is, they report students' level of achievement against defined learning standards. Therefore, it is important that those standards are clear and that both students and teachers understand them. This clarity should permeate all levels of learning goals, from state standards down to classroom learning targets. Chapter 2 shows that clear learning goals are the foundation for all high-quality assessment, not just grades.

Use recent, high-quality assessment evidence. When you report current status, where students were at the start of a learning sequence doesn't matter, nor does how quickly they caught on or how many times they stumbled. What matters is what they have learned after instruction. Therefore, recent evidence should take priority for assigning report card grades, and practice work should not be graded. The section below on attending to accuracy when combining grades describes some ways to do this.

The quality of evidence of learning is important too (see Chapter 3). This includes both the quality of assessment tests or tasks and the scoring scheme or rubrics used to grade them. This is an example of the "garbage in–garbage out" principle. If the assessments students do are not a spot-on match with the learning goals, they won't yield meaningful evidence of students' actual achievement of those learning goals.

A word about "group grades" is in order. When students do collaborative learning, sometimes called group work, often teachers are tempted to grade the resulting group project and assign the same grade to all students. We strongly recommend you do not use group grades; instead, assign grades that reflect individual achievement. Many students perceive group grades as unfair (Forsell et al., 2020). This practice also fails under the principle "Use high-quality evidence" because the quality of the group outcome does not necessarily reflect the learning of the individual student (Strijbos, 2016). Well-designed collaborative learning tasks feature positive interdependence, meaning that each student's performance is dependent on the performance of the others in the group. Well-designed assessment of collaborative learning features individual accountability, meaning that each student is assessed and held accountable for their own learning. Group grades violate these principles of collaborative learning as well. For ideas about how to assess individuals' learning from group work, see Brookhart (2013).

Keep standards-based records. For traditional grading by subject, teachers organized their records by subject (English, mathematics, etc.). This still works if your school uses traditional grading and reporting methods. But for standards-based grading, records must be organized by standard in order to aggregate and report achievement by standard. Most grading software has the ability to do this, although you may need to adjust some settings to your needs.

Note that the organization of the gradebook is by reporting standard—that is, the standard as used on the report card—even it has been slightly edited from the state standards. And as Chapter 2 showed, most standards will have several smaller-grain-sized learning goals under it; you do not need to keep separate lists for each of them. Organize your summative records according to the standards to which you will aggregate evidence for the report card.

Occasionally, you may find that you need to record evidence from an assessment in more than one place. This is really not a new idea. For example, decades ago, the authors remember receiving back reports in traditional high school English classes with two grades, one for content and one for mechanics. If an assessment really reflects two standards, you can record two grades from it. Or if part of an assessment reflects one standard (e.g., items 1–10 on a test or a few criteria in a rubric) and another part reflects another standard (e.g., items 11–20 on a test or other criteria in a rubric), you can record the relevant part scores under the respective standards.

Involve students. Earlier we contrasted grading to communicate, the position we advocate, with grading to motivate—meaning to "motivate" students by using grades as external rewards. It turns out that grading to communicate learning can support motivation to learn by providing information students can use to monitor and adjust their learning. In other words grading to communicate supports self-regulation of learning and internal motivation. If your grades communicate—as opposed to reward and punish—they support motivation to learn as well. All of this is more likely to happen when students are involved in the assessment and grading process.

One way that students can be involved in the grading process is to keep track of their own progress. Some teachers have students keep records of their work, make charts or graphs, or even keep the work itself in a folder, and then periodically ask them to look for patterns in their work. This helps them make decisions about how to address learning issues before the final report card grade.

Another way that students can be involved in the grading process is to be totally involved in the formative assessment process that precedes it (see Chapter 4). When students understand their learning targets and criteria and use them to self-assess, when they receive and act on formative feedback, they learn to use criteria, to match their work with the criteria, and to use their insights to improve their work by revising drafts, redoing problems, and so on. They participate in the formative learning cycle. This means that their grades are not a mystery; students know where they stand in relation to shared learning goals. During the formative learning process, students may say things like "I'm on track to master this learning goal" or "I am almost where I need to be," meaning where they need to be for the final summative assessment.

A third way students can be involved in the grading process is an extension of the first. Teachers may allow retakes or revisions of graded work, under certain conditions and subject to certain procedures. This gives students some power to control their level of

[handwritten margin notes: higher students = they like it; lower students = harder; more of a student voice; Portfolio; Sketchbooks]

achievement. Whether the second try at a graded assessment is a retake or a revision depends on the nature of the assessment items or tasks. For tests that have right/wrong answers, students need to retake a different test that is made to the same blueprint (i.e., addresses the same learning targets with the same number of points assigned to each target) as the first. A graded test shows students which answers were incorrect. Retaking the test would not be a good representation of student achievement because students would know which answers to change. For written work and other complex products, where there is not one "right" answer, students may revise the work they have started to demonstrate their achievement.

Retakes and revisions need to be handled carefully, however. We suggest you have a policy about allowable reasons for retakes or revisions of graded work and how to approach the teacher to request a retake. Students can be involved in making these policies at the classroom level. We know of a teacher, for example, who allows students to retake an exam or revise written work or projects, but the resubmission needs to include an explanation of what the student has done to make up the learning deficit exhibited in the first exam or project before trying again. Enough time (a day or several days) needs to have elapsed for the student to have done further learning. It should not be a matter of a student running successive tries past a teacher to see which one is good enough (or wears the teacher down sufficiently). If a student does retake an exam, use the second score for the final grade because it is the most recent evidence of learning. Don't average it with the first as a "punishment" for having two tries, or you mix behavior in with the grade. Some of these policies may be noted in school or district grading policies, and some may be classroom specific.

The Relationship Between Formative Feedback and Grades

In the previous section we made the point that deep involvement in the formative assessment process is a major way students can be involved in the grading process as well. In this section we make some additional points about the relationship between formative and summative assessment.

Formative assessment, sometimes called assessment for learning, takes place during the learning. Students and teachers both use formative assessment information for improvement. Summative assessment is assessment of learning. It occurs after an episode of learning, and its purpose is to measure and report what has been learned. Grading is classroom summative assessment.

There are two approaches to classroom summative assessment: checking up and summing up. *Checking up* refers to administering a final assessment—for example, a unit test or a final project—designed to represent the current achievement status for a standard. *Summing up* refers to the process of accumulating a series of grades on assessments of aspects of a learning goal and then summarizing them into one grade—one judgment of the current achievement status for that standard. Either approach can work.

Formative assessment opportunities help make summative assessment fair to students by providing them opportunities to practice, monitor, and adjust their learning. The formative opportunities set up the summative report to be a meaningful representation of current status on learning goals. Chapter 4 discussed feedback and other formative assessment strategies and provided rationales for using them based in learning theory and the formative learning cycle. Chapter 7 discusses opportunity to learn as a fairness issue as well. Whether you look at grading through the lens of learning (Chapter 4) or fairness (Chapter 7), or both, you arrive at the conclusion that students must have formative assessment opportunities that will help them develop their learning before summative assessment (grading) gives students a fair chance to show what they know.

What connects the two are the learning goals and criteria. The same learning goals and criteria that form the basis for formative feedback during learning are the basis for summative assessment or grading after the learning has taken place. This principle involves more than just having formative assessment in place during instruction and learning. It also involves connecting the learning goals and criteria used during formative assessment with those used for grading. Sometimes they will be exactly the same. Other times, formative assessment will be based on smaller-grained learning goals and criteria that are smaller in scope, and the case must be made that these smaller-grained goals and criteria roll up to the goals and criteria represented in the standard used for grading.

Attend to the Accuracy of Grades

Basing grades on high-quality assessments matched to intended learning goals reflects a concern about the meaning of the information grades communicate. Even if you are sure that your grades reflect "the right stuff," however, it is still necessary to ensure they reflect that information accurately. Here we discuss attention to accuracy in two respects: (1) in the number of grading categories used, to support more reliable decision-making, and (2) in the way you combine grades, so the combinatory methods do not mask or muddle the meaning.

Use Scales With Few Categories

Regarding number of grading categories, for reporting we recommend shorter scales—for example, the proficiency levels associated with standards-based grading or the ABCDF scale, associated with traditional grading—over longer scales—for example the 0–100 percentage scale. This recommendation is a direct result of the grading research that shows higher teacher agreement on what grade should be given when there are fewer distinctions to make (Brookhart et al., 2016; Guskey & Brookhart, 2019). However, the grading scale used on report cards is a matter of district policy, so if reform is necessary, you will have to work with the district administration and the school board.

Combining Grades

Determining a final grade from a set of grades on individual assessments requires some method of summarizing a body of evidence into a decision about performance or proficiency level. Combine grades in a way that preserves meaning about achievement of standards. In general, base a report card grade on more than one measure. This helps with validity, because multiple assessments together sample more of the learning domain than one assessment, and with reliability, because you have several samples of students' achievement. While this principle is important, the term *multiple measures* has caused some confusion. It doesn't necessarily mean using more than one method (e.g., a test and a performance assessment), although it can, depending on the standard you are measuring. Decisions about what assessment method to use should be based on the target-method match described in Chapters 2 and 3. And the misconception that there should be three measures is based on an overly literal interpretation of the word *triangulation*. "Multiple measures" means more than one; how many and what kind of assessments best represent students' achievement depends on the content to be assessed.

However, it is not helpful to go overboard. We know some teachers who "take a grade" every day and have 30 or more grades to combine at the end of a report period! That is not only more than necessary for a reliable decision, it is likely that some of those "grades" reflect formative assessment—intended for practice—that should have received feedback instead of a grade. Use as many individual assessments as you need to cover the learning domain the standard represents, and secure multiple measures on important aspects of the domain. For some standards, that may be as few as 3 or 4 individual grades; for others, it may be 8 or 10.

It is possible to have a set of meaningful grades on individual assessments but combine them in such a way as to muddle their meaning. For example, suppose you are combining a test that was graded in percentage points (0–100) and a report that was graded with four levels of proficiency (say, 4 = Exemplary, 3 = Proficient, 2 = Nearing Proficiency, and 1 = Not Yet). If you simply take the arithmetic average, a student's performance on the test will swamp the performance on the report, and the resulting report card grade will essentially communicate the same information as the test score, eclipsing any information from the report, because the scale is so much longer. So put all individual grades on the same scale before you combine them.

A note is in order here about the use of percentage scores. Make sure that the percentage reflects performance on the assessment and not some characteristic unrelated to the learning goal. For example, a missing assignment is not a zero; it's simply missing, no matter what the reason. Assigning a zero for absence, misbehavior, or cheating means the grade reflects behavior, not learning. In fact, avoid giving a zero on the percentage scale at all, because the zero will pull down an average and make it unrepresentative of the body of evidence. The reason for this is the skewed nature of the percentage scale, where all of the passing scores are squeezed together in the 60–100 range or thereabouts while the range for failing scores is much larger (0–59; Chappuis & Stiggins, 2020). A second problem is that each of the passing grades assigned to a percentage scale represents approximately 10 points whereas a grade of F represents 50 percentage points. One solution to the problem of unequal intervals, advocated by Guskey (2015), is to establish a minimum percentage of 50, so the F range is 50% to 59%. This doesn't mean that a student who has scored 34% has been awarded 16 extra percentage points; it simply indicates that the score is at the bottom of the F range. The **mean** of a set of percentages is a truer representative of overall level of achievement when the minimum score is set to 50%, because the 60 percentage scores on a 0–100 scale unfairly weight failing scores more heavily. For a deeper treatment of setting a minimum-percentage policy, see Thomas Guskey's (2015) *On Your Mark: Challenging the Conventions of Grading and Reporting.*

There are many defensible ways to combine grades on individual assessments in order to arrive at a meaningful composite grade. Figure 5.2 presents four of them. (For complete worked examples of these, see Brookhart, 2017; Chappuis & Stiggins, 2020.) There are other methods as well. Figure 5.2 presents what we recommend as the most straightforward methods. If applied properly, any of these methods can be explained to parents and students and can lead to defensible, fair, meaningful grades. Some grading software uses more complicated quantitative methods—for example, decaying averages—but these are harder to explain and do not, in our opinion, result in more accurate grades.

FIGURE 5.2   Methods of combining individual grades into a composite report card grade

METHOD	DESCRIPTION
Mean	This traditional method is appropriate if all the individual grades are on the percentage (0–100) scale (or, as we recommend, on a shortened percentage scale, e.g., 50–100) and you want to use a quantitative method to summarize them. Use the weighted mean, weighting assignments more if they cover a larger portion of the learning domain or in some other way should make a larger contribution to the final grade. The resulting weighted mean will be on the percentage scale and may be converted to ABCDF or some other scale for reporting.[a]
Median	This method is appropriate if all the individual grades are on a quality scale and you want to use a quantitative method to summarize them. Typically, this is a proficiency scale or ABCDF. Weight individual grades first (e.g., count the grades from important assessments twice), and then take the median. The resulting weighted median will be on the same quality scale.[a]
Logic rule	This method works best with individual grades on a proficiency scale. Instead of a quantitative summary, the logic rule method results in a logical summary. For example, students may be determined Exemplary if three out of four major assignments are Exemplary and the remaining major assignment, plus a majority of any minor assignments, are at least Proficient. These rules are usually summarized in a chart.
Pattern of learning	This method works only with standards-based grading. (In traditional grading, where different standards within a subject are combined for a final grade, looking for a learning curve pattern does not make sense. Earlier assessments may have reflected different learning goals from more recent assessments.) If you are using standards-based grading and have kept records by standard, you can privilege recent evidence by examining the scores, looking for a learning curve, and selecting the grades from when students "level off" at a specific proficiency level, to use in any of the methods above. If grades are erratic and do not show a pattern of learning, use all of them (also, try to figure out why the grades are erratic and work with the student accordingly).

[a]Convert all individual grades to the same scale before using any combining method.

No matter what combinatory method you use, you will occasionally end up with borderline grades, where a student falls right on the line—either numerically or descriptively, depending on the method you are using—between two grades. When that happens, use additional, recent evidence of student learning on the relevant learning goal (and not effort or other factors) to determine the grade.

Sometimes it's helpful to know what not to do as well (or what to avoid in grading software options). Avoid computing a grade by taking a simple arithmetic average across individual grades on different scales. Avoid taking an average of any kind (mean or **median**) without attending to weighting those grades that should count more heavily in the report card grade. Avoid norm-referenced grading or "grading on the curve"—assigning grades based on where students fall in relation to their classmates. In standards-based grading avoid giving early grades the same weight as more recent grades on the same standard.

School leaders should understand different methods of combining individual grades into a report card grade, not just the ones they themselves used as teachers. They should understand how the combinatory method affects the meaning of the final grade and should be prepared to work with teachers toward the goal of reporting meaningful, accurate grades for students.

Grading Students With Special Needs

Thirty years ago, Kathleen Donohoe and Naomi Zigmond (1990) found that a sample of urban secondary special education students in regular classes received low or failing grades, typically about a D, on a par with low-achieving students without special needs. This situation can be expected to provoke a "why try" approach among many special education students.

The standards-based method of grading we have been advocating suggests a different approach. This approach turns on understanding the difference between **accommodations** and **modifications** in standards-based assessment and instruction. Chapter 7 presents more detail about accommodations and modifications. We define them briefly here. Accommodations are changes in the conditions or materials of assessment that allow students with disabilities and special needs to be assessed on the same learning goals as other students. Modifications are changes in the conditions or materials of assessment that do change the construct—the learning goal—being measured. The meaning of assessment results changes accordingly.

The idea is that students who receive accommodations have access to demonstrating the same learning goals as other students. Therefore, they are graded on the same learning goals but may be expected to do better than the D level Donohoe and Zigmond (1990) found, because the accommodations address their learning and assessment needs.

However, students who have modifications to their learning goals are assessed on those modified learning goals, and again they are expected to be able to be successful because the goals have been modified for them. When these students' grades are reported, the report should note that the standard has been modified.

Figure 5.3 presents this graphically in Lee Ann Jung's (2017) DiAGraM model. More detail about this model is available at https://www.leadinclusion.org/single-post/2017/05/17/Differentiated-Assessment-and-Grading-Model-DiAGraM.

In short, sound grading practices for students with special needs are the same as for other students: start with clear learning goals and criteria, use multiple high-quality measures, and minimize bias and distortion. It's just that you make sure that the learning goals and criteria are appropriate for the students' needs and that they have the accommodations they need to access them.

Grading Policies

Grading policies are official district-level statements about the purpose of report cards and their dates and format, the meaning of grades, how the district uses grades, the scales that must be used, calculation of grade-point average, and so on. Buildings must work within these policies. Sometimes buildings have additional policies (e.g., about parent conferences, policies for borderline review [may also be a district policy]). Earlier, we recommended that classroom teachers also have policies for classroom-level grading issues (e.g., how to request a conference with the teacher if you want help or have a question about your grade) and, for intermediate through high school, involve students in making them.

Many district grading policies simply define the symbol system to be used on report cards, specify how frequently report cards will be distributed—for example, every six weeks—and describe the rules for calculating high school grade-point averages. More robust grading policies also capture one or more of the following issues (based on Brookhart, 2017):

- The purpose of grading (e.g., to communicate) and the role of grading in the district's assessment system

- What grades are intended to communicate (e.g., current status on intended learning goals) and the rationale for it

- Primary intended audience(s) for grades and a description of district use(s) of grades

- Policy and rationale for not grading formative work

- As appropriate, accepted methods of combining grades for reporting, borderline review, methods of handling nonsubmission of work, methods of handling resubmissions of work, and so on

FIGURE 5.3 Differentiated Assessment and Grading Model (DiAGraM)

Support Needed	Expectation Used	Assessment Strategy	Reporting Procedure
Accommodation	Use the grade-level criterion.	Assess the student's performance using the accommodation with no additional changes.	No change is needed to the report card or the transcript grades.
Modification	Determine a modified, achievable, comparably rigorous expectation.	Determine the intervention and specific scale of measure for use on classroom assessment tasks. Everyone on the team uses the same intervention and scale of measure for this skill.	Grades reflect performance on the modified expectation. Note the grade was based on a modified expectation on report card and transcript.

Source: Lee Ann Jung, https://www.leadinclusion.org/single-post/2017/05/17/Differentiated-Assessment-and-Grading-Model-DiAGraM

A robust grading policy makes communicating about grades with parents and community members easier. The policy can reside on the school website, perhaps even accompanied by a video, and it can be referenced in official school communications.

Summary

We have presented a set of recommended, sound grading practices that, if followed, will result in meaningful and accurate grades reflecting students' current achievement of intended learning goals. Assessment-literate school leaders can lead teachers and others in implementing these practices. District leadership is critical because without district leadership in the form of an overall grading policy, individual buildings and principals are left on their own when it comes to grading reform, which makes things difficult. School leaders gently monitor grading practices and facilitate improvement when needed. Grading policies and practices must also be communicated with parents and community members. Both communications should include explanation—the rationales behind the policy and practice choices—to result in grades that convey meaningful, accurate information.

 Success Indicators for Assessment Literacy Goal #5

The school leader

- can explain to students, parents, and other educators the purpose and meaning of grades in their building/district;

- can recognize the sound and unsound grading practices in use in their building/district and can work with colleagues to improve them as needed; and

- can articulate their district's official grading policies and explain why they are sound and/or can work with colleagues to improve them as needed.

 Study Guide Questions

1. In your school/district are grades used to communicate students' current status on intended learning goals? Are they used as external motivators (as "pay" for the work students do)? Some of each, depending on the classroom? Diagnose the grading purposes in play in your school/district, and draft a response you might make.

2. Did it surprise you to learn that school grades and standardized test scores do not, never have, and probably never will correlate highly? Speculate on why that might be. Make sure to include in your speculation considerations beyond the reliability of grades.

3. Describe the grading practices you followed when you were a teacher. How do they accord with the grading practices recommended in this chapter?

4. Does your school/district do standards-based grading, or is it in the process of moving to standards-based grading? What are the reasons for that, and how do they fit with what you have learned from this chapter?

5. Does your school/district have an official grading policy? What does it say? After reading this chapter, would you suggest any revisions, additions, or deletions?

 Personal Portfolio Entry Suggestions

- Copy of my district's official grading policy, critiqued according to the recommendations in this chapter

- School newsletter article or website blog that addresses issues of grading purpose, policy, and/or practices

- Copies of report cards, either report cards I issued as a teacher or report cards from my building where I had a role in assisting the teacher with grading practices, critiqued according to the recommendations in this chapter

- Video of myself explaining the purpose of grades in my district and my district's official grading policies and sanctioned practices, suitable for a school district website

---

Activity 5.1
Grading Stories

Learning Target for the Activity

- Be able to recognize when the principles of sound grading practices are not followed.

Purpose

The purpose of this activity is to practice applying the principles of sound grading practices by recognizing them in the breach. Everyone has at least one "grading story" in their background, either as a student or as an educator, when something went awry. These stories are often accompanied by painful memories or other negative emotions. In this activity we'll use those stories for the good, helping to illustrate why the principles of sound grading practices are, in fact, sound. Such stories can make good cautionary tales that can be useful to school leaders as well.

Time

45 minutes

Materials Needed

- A copy of Figure 5.1 or this book opened to Figure 5.1

- Five pieces of chart paper. Prepare each paper by writing one of the five grading practices from Figure 5.1 at the top, then hang it up.

- Large-size sticky notes (approximately 4 in. × 6 in.)

- Instead of the chart paper and sticky notes, a bulletin board app like Padlet may be used.

Suggested Room Setup

This is a small-group activity. Arrange chairs for comfortable speaking, first in pairs and then all together.

Directions

Complete each step in the order below:

1. In pairs, share a story from your past experience with grading, either as a student yourself or as an educator, when something went wrong, felt unfair, or had unintended bad effects. Each pair should have at least two stories (one from each partner), but see if you can come up with four per pair. For each grading story discuss what was intended, what went wrong, and what the consequences were.

2. Summarize each story using bullet points on a sticky note. Use one note per story.

3. Place each story on the chart paper that identifies the grading principle that was violated in the story. If a story matches more than one principle, put it on the chart that names the principle whose violation was the most to blame for the incident. Alternatively, do this part of the exercise in the bulletin board app.

4. Reconvene as a whole group. Look at the charts. Ask any clarifying questions that arise about the stories. What conclusions can you draw from the whole display? Are there any patterns in these stories? Do they cluster around one principle, or are they spread among several or all of them? Do these "sad stories" give you any insights into grading practices that you may want to be on the lookout for as a school leader? Do they give you any insights about grading beliefs or practices that may be resistant to reform?

Closure

The group reaches closure by facilitating a discussion based on these questions: What did I learn from this exercise that will be important for me to know in my role as a school leader? What questions do I have? What actions might I take?

Activity 5.2
Grading Policies and Practices in My District

Learning Targets for the Activity

- Be able to describe the official grading policies and practices in my district.

- Be able to evaluate the official grading policies and practices in my district for completeness and for conformity to the principles of sound grading practices.

Purpose

The purpose of this activity is to become aware of the official grading practices and policies in your district and appraise them in terms of the principles for sound grading that you learned in this chapter.

Time

45 minutes

Materials Needed

- Grading policy from your district (and from your building if there is an official school grading policy and you are a school-level leader)

- If the policy is on paper, colored highlighters

Suggested Room Setup

This is a small-group activity. Set chairs around a table so the group can work together.

Directions

Working in small groups, complete each step in the order below:

1. Read the district (and building if applicable) grading policy.

2. Highlight in green the aspects of the policy that reflect sound, recommended practices. Highlight in yellow the aspects of the policy that you want to question. Note what those questions are. Also, check the completeness of the policy. Does the grading policy state the purpose of grading in the district and describe the role of grading in the district's assessment system? Would you recommend any additions to the policy, and if so, why?

3. [Optional] If you are reviewing both building and district policies, compare and contrast them. What grading policy elements are in each, and why? Which elements are more specific?

Closure

Summarize what you have learned about your district's/building's grading policy from this discussion. Are there any follow-up conversations you wish to plan with other district leaders? What did you learn from this exercise that will be important for you to know in your role as a school leader? What questions do you have? What actions might you take?

Activity 5.3
Grading in Classrooms and Courses

Learning Target for the Activity

- I can describe the grading practices in one classroom.

Purpose

The purpose of this activity is to understand the grading practices in one classroom. The purpose is *not* to evaluate the teacher or to suggest changes to their grading practices. It is simply to understand how building and district grading policies and teacher classroom assessment practices work themselves out in one classroom context. The classroom you study may or may not be representative of others in the building/district.

Time

45 minutes

Materials Needed

- Interview questions (see Figure 5.4)

FIGURE 5.4   Questions about classroom grading

Thank you for sharing some information about grading in your classroom. If you teach more than one subject or grade level, select one as the focus for answering these questions.

1. What meaning do you want your grades to communicate?

2. What kinds of individual graded assessments do you use to determine report card grades? Are there other kinds of student work that do not factor into the report card grade?

3. Describe the way you keep records and summarize individual grades for a report card grade. Be as specific as you can. For example, what do you record in the gradebook (ABCDF, proficiency scales, percentages, etc.)? Do you weight some grades more heavily than others? What method do you (or does the grading software) use to determine the report card grade?

4. What do you do when a student's grade is just below the borderline or cutoff for a grading category?

5. What do you do when a student's grade is just above the borderline or cutoff for a grading category?

6. Do you have a classroom policy about retakes or revisions of graded work? If so, please describe it.

7. How do you communicate with students and parents about grading in your classroom?

8. What do your students say about your grading practices?

9. Is there anything else you want to share about your grading practices?

Suggested Room Setup

This is an activity for one school leader and one classroom teacher. Alternatively, two school leaders can do this activity together if one of them teaches a class and is responsible for grading. Use a quiet, private space for a one-on-one interview.

(Continued)

(Continued)

Directions

Complete each step in the order below:

1. Identify a teacher who is willing to share information about how they approach grading.

2. Begin by thanking the teacher (or the other school leader) for being willing to share approaches to grading. Assure the teacher that you are interested in a descriptive example of grading in one classroom and are not evaluating them. Ask the interview questions, one at a time. You may follow any of the questions with "Can you tell me more about that?" or "Can you give me an example?" or other similar questions. Be careful to phrase any follow-up questions in value-neutral language.

3. Make notes during the interview to help you process the information and reflect on its value to you as a school leader.

Closure

Both the school leader and the teacher should end this activity with individual self-reflection. Questions for the school leader include the following: What did I learn from this exercise that will be important for me to know in my role as a school leader? What questions do I have? What actions might I take? Questions for the teacher include the following: What did I learn from this exercise in sharing my grading practices? Are there any practices I might want to consider revising?

Definitions

Accommodations: Changes in the conditions or materials of an assessment to allow students with disabilities access to the same assessment as regular students, without changing the construct being measured or the meaning of the assessment results.

Grades: Symbols assigned to individual pieces of classroom work (e.g., a test or performance assessment) and to composite measures of these individual assessments that are intended for report cards. They can be letters, numbers, names of performance levels, or figures.

Mean: An average score arrived at by adding up a set of scores and dividing by their number; also known as the *arithmetic mean*.

Median: An average score arrived at by identifying the score in a set of scores that has 50% of the other scores above it and 50% of the other scores below it.

Modifications: Changes in the conditions or materials of assessment for students with disabilities that change the construct being measured and the meaning of the assessment results.

Multiple measures: In the context of grading, the use of more than one assessment to determine a student's grade. Multiple measures can also mean using different kinds of measures for any educational decision (e.g., using grades, attendance, work habits, and test scores in a decision to recommend a student for a special program).

 This chapter's online resources are available for download from
resources.corwin.com/10GoalsLeaders

Effective Communication

6

〰〰

Assessment Literacy Goal #6: *The leader communicates effectively with all members of the school community about student assessment.*

Research over more than 30 years is consistent: students benefit when parents are involved in their schooling. Among other benefits of parent involvement, students attend school more regularly, receive higher grades and scores on tests, have better behavior and social skills, and on graduation go on to postsecondary education (Leithwood & Louis, 2012). There is growing evidence that family engagement can also lead to higher student achievement and that family engagement can be strengthened by school-to-home communication.

What does this have to do with assessment literacy? Surveys show the school-to-home communications most valued by parents are those pertaining to individual student achievement (Brenner & Quirk, 2020). Report cards, progress reports, test scores, and the papers stuffed in a backpack or folder are all the products or results of assessment. A common element in all of them is that what to do next is often unclear to students and parents; the form and content of the communication allow for little or no action to be taken by parents in support of their student. Just as teachers unpack curriculum standards, helping parents and community members unpack what is underneath a single score or grade, and what they can do to assist their student is at the heart of what this assessment literacy goal is about.

In a balanced assessment system a school leader has communication responsibilities for all five assessment levels (see Figure 1.1). Communications from the school regarding classroom and common assessments, grading and report cards, district benchmarks, standardized assessments, and the state accountability assessment programs all default to the school leader. In this chapter we will focus on the school and classroom levels of assessment and the communication opportunities each presents. Although we are mindful of the many communication responsibilities a school leader has, it is the classroom teacher who in our view carries the heaviest load in communicating with parents about assessment and student progress. To that end, our hope is to help school leaders assist classroom teachers in planning and delivering effective, two-way communication, which has been shown to make a difference in student learning.

Chapter Learning Goals

1. Understand the differences between parent involvement and family/parent engagement.

2. Become familiar with teacher-to-home communications that can promote family engagement.

3. Understand which assessment topics may be of most interest to parents at both the building and the classroom level and consider communication strategies for potential use.

Parent Engagement, Communication to Families, and Student Learning

For a long time school test results have been reported out like box scores from a baseball game. Charts and graphs are displayed in the local newspaper; this year's results are compared with last year's results and with results from neighboring schools and districts. Districts and schools similarly send home newsletters and reports with group and individual student results, accompanied by an explanation of how to interpret the scores and how to decode the various symbols and numbers. However, the primary vehicle parents rely on to gauge how well their student is doing is not the score from a large-scale assessment but the school report card (Learning Heroes, 2018). Report cards traditionally have also been like baseball box scores in form, and everything from weekly allowance to weekend restriction, praise to scorn, reinforcement to punishment hangs in the report card balance once the student brings it home. (Activity 6.1 explores other information parents could receive that would give them a fuller understanding of student progress beyond the report card.)

This scoreboard mode of display has been changing in the era of standards, and it continues to fade as schools find more meaningful ways and, just as important, new reasons to communicate more regularly about student progress. The reasons for this shift in practice are many and include the following:

- The number and types of assessments administered in schools today exceed what parents experienced when they were students. Lack of familiarity with the different ways student learning is currently assessed requires more varied communication strategies.

- Standards-based assessment stands in opposition to the bell curve approach to grading, which compares students with one another, thereby imposing an artificial limit on how many students can succeed. Instead, the emphasis in standards-based assessment is on comparing an individual's performance with a preset standard, thus offering equity in opportunity to succeed. Often criteria for success are used to report progress and award promotion or credit in formats that are unfamiliar to some parents.

- Technology has eased the limitations for teachers and schools on how to communicate about student learning, and it has not just increased the frequency of school-to-home communication but also enabled it to be two-way, as in a phone call. Just as your dentist might text you a reminder of your upcoming appointment, schools now leverage technology by texting parents about things like student attendance, project due dates, and testing schedules, and some systems can even do so in parents' preferred language. We'll examine this topic further later in this chapter.

- Parents are more involved in schooling than ever before (MetLife, 2012). Car washes and fund-raising drives still happen with parent support, but more parents are now present on site councils, on leadership teams and working committees, in volunteer activities in the classroom, and in advisory roles in matters of policy, discipline, and school finance. Their support and involvement come with curiosity and a desire to learn about schooling today, how the school gauges success, and the many nuances of teaching, learning, and assessment that go beyond a single test score. Simply put, parents seem no longer satisfied with the level of communication that was the norm a generation earlier, characterized by an annual parent-teacher conference, phone calls as needed, and report cards. In a study examining how technology can change teacher-to-parent communication, parents' proactive use of the technology application provided suggested a high demand for more information from teachers and schools (Kraft & Bolves, 2019).

- The emerging shift from **parent involvement** to **parent engagement** (used here interchangeably with "family engagement") helps create a new mindset among educators about reporting student progress and is fundamental to our discussion in this chapter about communication and assessment. This transition from *involving* parents in schooling and school activities to *engaging* parents in learning requires deploying specialized communications from the school and providing families the information, skills, and resources needed to support students academically at home.

- Certain aspects of assessment, such as changes in grading practices, can be difficult to explain and may require an adjustment period for some parents. Unless the change is put in context prior to implementation with a rationale and a description of how the change will benefit student learning, confusion and, in the worst case, a backlash can result. When this happens, concerns and suspicions can arise about other aspects of school assessment. The best antidote to this dilemma is to follow the "no surprises" rule, being in front of changes as much as possible with information and education and, when possible, engaging parents and community members as partners in the change process.

An additional factor influences schools in teacher- and school-to-parent communication practices: research. Educational research has shown the value of family engagement, and now there is also evidence that teacher-to-parent communication can strengthen both the student and family engagement. Below are summaries from a sample of studies that help show why this body of knowledge is important for all school leaders to learn more about:

- Researchers combined a low-cost communication technology (texting) with school information systems to automate the collecting of information and sending of weekly academic progress reports to parents of middle and high school students. Automated alerts were sent to parents about missed assignments, grades, and class absences. The alerts reduced course failures by 28%, increased class attendance by 12%, and increased student retention, though there was no impact on state test scores. There were larger effects for below-median GPA students and for high school students (Bergman & Chan, 2019).

- A high school mathematics instructor sent regular notifications home to parents in two of his four classes regarding daily homework and test scores. Students whose parents received the notifications had better test scores and higher grades than students in the other classes, despite student abilities in the four classes being similar prior to the experimental study (Sirvani, 2007).

- Another study found that frequent teacher-family communication immediately increased student engagement as measured by homework completion rates, on-task behavior, and class participation (Kraft & Dougherty, 2013).

- Teachers' sending parents text messages when their child was missing assignments resulted in significant gains in GPA, test scores, and measures of student engagement (Bergman, 2021).

- When parents of preschool students received weekly text messages with literacy tips they could use at home with their children, they were more likely to act on the tips and students showed learning gains in some areas of early literacy (York & Loeb, 2014). The authors also speak of texting as an attractive, low-cost, and scalable approach to parent communication.

Teacher-to-parent communication has been described as having "underutilized potential" (Kraft & Rogers, 2014). Increasing the frequency and quality of school-to-home communications, especially when the message content is related to student progress and assessment, can also promote the assessment literacy of parents.

Assessment Literacy and School-to-Parent Communication

One common evaluation standard for school principals centers on communication with parents and the broader community regarding assessment, often with wording such as this:

Assessment results and information are shared in a timely and relevant manner with students, teachers, parents, and the larger school community.

It would be ideal if all parents and the broader community were assessment literate or if schools had the capacity to educate parents and community members to a literate level. Then, sharing information from the classroom would result in parent understanding. Efforts to inform and educate parents and others about assessment are well-placed, add value, and should be included as part of a broader, comprehensive assessment plan. However, given the school's resources and priorities, and a noncaptive audience, it's not realistic to expect all parents and community members to be assessment literate. Therefore, school leaders and classroom teachers must make choices about which assessment topics are most important for parents to understand, and then communicate about those topics in ways that engage parents and invite them to partner with the school to help support their children.

Communication About Large-Scale Assessment

We'll go into only brief detail on the practical approaches that many educators already use to communicate about large-scale assessment results. Helpful strategies can be found on state department of education websites and also with test publishers, and we suggest calling first on those with state or district assessment contracts to take advantage of the local context. Some test publishers provide professional development for teachers on communicating with parents, sample letters to parents, parent portals, and other online features that allow parents to access scores and a host of resources to interpret scores and help their students.

Other tools and strategies include the following:

- Posting an assessment Q&A on the school or district website for parents to access

- Providing assessment overviews at open house or parent evenings

- Sending out assessment newsletters from the school or district (these typically include the purpose of the assessment, how the results are reported and will be used, how they do or do not fit into the report card grade, etc.)

- Describing to parents how teachers communicate with students before assessments are given and how parents can help communicate the same message at home.

Strategies of this sort are typically utilized in conjunction with large-scale assessments from the state or district and involve for the most part one-way communication. Yet they are necessary to help parents interpret the results and are proactive in that they try to follow the no-surprises rule. An ongoing effort to provide information for families new to the district or school is important, and so the offerings should repeat during the school year or a version should be made available online.

Communication From the School About Classroom Assessment

The closer communication is to day-to-day classroom assessment, the more likely it is to be relevant for the parent. The suggestions below start with strategies to develop understanding of classroom practices, so that teacher-to-parent communications can be understood in context and also be actionable when appropriate. One successful strategy to use with small or large groups of parents is to *compare and contrast*, noting the similarities and differences of two items in question. Some of the suggestions below could be delivered as in-person presentations, via recorded video presentations or webinars, on slide decks posted on the school website, or in a regular newsletter devoted entirely to assessment.

- Compare and contrast a traditional A–F letter grade report card (with and/or without separate reports for effort, participation, etc.) with a standards-based report card. Identify both similarities and differences, such as the characteristics of each, their philosophical foundations, pros and cons, and the use of coded symbols versus descriptive language. If your school uses an online grading program, this activity is a good opportunity to display and explain the program to parents not familiar with how it works. Refer to Chapter 5 for ideas on what points to include.

- Compare and contrast a norm-referenced standardized assessment, such as a test of basic skill, with a standards-based assessment. Explain the differences in how scores are derived and what each is used for. This can also include a comparison of the types of assessment methods typically used. Chapter 9 can provide specific guidance in this area.

- Compare a formative assessment process or tool with a summative assessment tool. You could also compare a formative use of assessment results with a summative use of assessment results.

- Compare how to keep track of formative assessment information and summative assessment data. This topic can also help explain to parents how to help their children keep track of each and why formative results are typically not part of the summative gradebook or final grade calculation. Chapters 4 and 5 are good resources for this activity.

- Compare a teacher's traditional gradebook with a standards-driven online gradebook.

- Compare a rubric to score a project or written essay with a subjective judgment. You can do the same with a rubric for effort or participation for reporting purposes, if your school uses one.

Other suggestions that may not fit a "compare-and-contrast" presentation include the following:

- Demonstrate sharing anonymous student work samples with parents to show the range of quality in what students produce. Post and annotate work samples online to help parents understand the expectations for current projects and assignments.

- Show parents how students can use a scoring guide to self-assess and how they can assist their student in doing so.

Teacher-to-Parent Communication and Family Engagement

Parent involvement—getting parents into the school for meetings, presentations, student activities, tutoring, and volunteering—is one thing proven valuable in and of itself. Family engagement—giving parents the skills, incentive, information, and resources they need to support their child's learning at home—is another. And the difference is not insignificant: the research findings summarized at the beginning of this chapter on the impact on student learning illustrate why. Parent engagement has gained traction in schools and districts, and it does not have to be at the expense of parent involvement programs.

So what types of teacher-to-family communications encourage family engagement? The form (phone call, text, email, web chat, etc.) of the messages sent home can vary, as does the content of messages.

- The content of the message can convey information about what the student has done well.

- The message can be an improvement message, sharing what steps the student can take to improve.

- The message can be about an in-class issue: test scores, work habits, participation, and so on.

- The message can be about an issue outside of class: homework, preparation for a test, staying current with assignments, and so on. This type of message more often includes suggestions for action to be taken at home.

- The message can be "scripted" for a specific topic and then used over and over (e.g., a project due date missed, reminder of an upcoming assessment); it can be sent out to an individual student, a subset of the class, or the entire class.

- The message can be personalized, communicating a specific problem and how to help address it (Kraft & Rogers, 2014).

In all cases the message focuses on some manageable aspect of student learning. "Great job this week" provides praise and affirmation of sorts, but it is likely to be unclear to students and parents what was great and why. Messages can be short; a weekly one-sentence message focused on student schoolwork can be enough to influence academic success. Messages that specify what students need to do to improve have the largest effects (Kraft & Rogers, 2014). Plus, actionable messages deliver what parent surveys indicate they value: information to help with early intervention when a problem arises. Examples of improvement messages that are actionable are given below:

- Anne shows difficulty with decimal placement; her quiz score from last Friday was 4 out of 10 correct. I'm hoping you can practice with her using the brief tutorial and worksheet posted on our website. Please follow the link below.

- Charlie's writing shows end-of-sentence punctuation problems. For example, sometimes he ends a sentence with a comma. Please work with him on periods, question marks, and exclamation points.

- We are learning different land forms and features in geography. I have attached a brief slide deck and encourage you to review it with Martin prior to the test on Friday.

- Sasha's algebra in-class and homework assignments are always on time and completed accurately. However, her quiz and test scores seem lower than they should be. I'm trying to diagnose this problem and am hoping you can discuss this with her and get back to me with any ideas on how we can improve the match between the two.

The examples above are short, convey small steps, and provide the necessary resource as appropriate. In a way these types of messages constitute a form of feedback, but it is delivered through an intermediary, the parent, who then helps the student take action. That is the essence of family engagement.

Using Technology for Communication and Family Engagement

The use of technology can help support high-quality teacher-to-parent communication, increase its frequency, and assist in promoting family engagement. Phone calls remain high-value but must be completed during the teacher and/or the parent work day. Text messages or email can be automated, sent to groups or individualized, and still offer opportunities for dialogue. The choice of messaging and communication products, online services, and apps is rich and varied, beyond standard smartphone applications. Among many others, they include Edmodo, ClassDojo, Google Classroom, Remind, Class Messenger, and Pupil Path. Other strategies involving technology that teachers are using successfully include the following:

- Classroom websites can be created (usually via a district/school platform) to post resources, syllabi, schedules, class assignments, and corresponding activities for parents.

- Skype, Zoom, Microsoft Teams, Face Time, or similar tools are used to conference with parents virtually; some of these also allow schoolwork to be displayed and shared.

- Online survey tools can be used to invite parents to share information about their student (special interests, health concerns, academic strengths, etc.) for future reference. Teachers can also ask about communication preferences and contact information.

- Some online gradebook programs allow parents to access student progress, exchange messages with the teacher, view homework schedules and upcoming assessments, and so on.

- Online calendars can be used to keep parents informed of the class instruction and assessment schedule, as well as for reminders and due dates. Parents can also sign up online for meetings, volunteering, field trips, and so on.

- Online portfolios document and keep track of student progress, which can also be a part of student-led conferences.

Barriers to Implementation

Some states have added "family engagement" to their principal evaluation criteria. Figure 6.1 shows one example.

FIGURE 6.1   The AWSP Leadership Framework for school leader evaluation

Criterion 7.1

ELEMENT	UNSATISFACTORY	BASIC	PROFICIENT	DISTINGUISHED
Engages families	Demonstrates no effort to engage families in school activities that promote student learning	Encourages and supports involvement of families in some school activities that support student learning	Encourages and supports consistent and ongoing family engagement in school activities that support student learning	Engaged families support student learning, led by staff who value and encourage these partnerships

Source: *The AWSP Leadership Framework for School Leader Evaluation* Version 3.0, 2020 Criterion 7: Engaging Families and Communities, Association of Washington School Principals.

Some districts also fund family engagement specialists and budget resources for program support. What we have described above can be daunting to conceptualize and then organize into a schoolwide concerted effort, one that usually falls on the already busy school leader to deliver. But strong support from the principal is needed to (a) understand and value parental engagement, (b) inform parents how the school can partner with them to benefit student learning, and (c) support teachers in implementing a school-to-home communication strategy.

Other barriers include the following:

ex: Lunch Buddies Program

- School leaders are already called on and expected to do so much to help involve families and school communities. Establishing community partnerships and volunteering in local service organizations are just two examples of expectations that school leaders be visible in the community, also frequently called out in principal evaluation frameworks. With a fixed amount of time in the day and calendar, choices have to be made, often heavily influenced by initiatives and priorities set outside of the school.

Schoolwide Dojo innitiative this yr

- Technology itself can act as a barrier; the lack of tools and/or connectivity is a common problem for some families. Many schools still rely on phone calls and letters sent home with students as the primary methods of communication. And mixed-technology platforms and different apps used by teachers can confuse parents and unnecessarily fragment a school's effort. An organizational plan that communicates expectations, relies on a single platform, and provides technology support and dedicated time for teachers to use the technology is a necessary consideration (Kraft & Bolves, 2019).

- Teachers report some hesitation around communicating with parents, and this is true particularly for novice teachers, who count it as their biggest challenge (MetLife, 2012). High school and middle school teachers are more likely to report reluctance than elementary teachers. Part of that hesitation stems from a belief that parents will hold them responsible if their student is encountering difficulty. In one survey 71% of teachers thought that parents blame the teacher when the student does not perform at grade level, and 51% thought that parents will believe and side with the student if the information contrasts with what the parent sees at home (Learning Heroes, 2018).

- Teacher time is limited, and a resistance to add more duties can naturally follow, particularly if the duties fall outside the school day. Technology can contribute to that resistance in that sending a text or email frequently necessitates a reply. Teachers need dedicated time to communicate with parents and time for sharing effective communication strategies with one another (Kraft & Bolves, 2019).

- As the student gets older, both parents and teachers agree that the communication responsibility shifts from the school/teacher to the student. This means that in the upper-grade levels, teachers may tend to communicate with parents less frequently.

- Cultural differences can cause communication challenges, signaling a need for professional development and increased understanding of the uniqueness and value systems of different cultures (Graham-Clay, 2005).

- As anything else teachers are asked to do, support in the form of time to learn and time to implement is key. Professional development for teachers in family engagement and teacher-to-home communication is essential, and resources are available that can assist teachers and principals in their learning (Graham-Clay, 2005).

Students as Communicators

This chapter has examined the actions school leaders and teachers can take in communicating with parents about student assessment and the benefits to student learning that can result. Yet we shouldn't overlook students themselves as communicators about their learning. One especially significant benefit of students talking with their parents about their work and their progress is the impact these conversations have on parents' developing higher expectations for their children. In an analysis of studies on the influence of home-related factors on achievement, researcher John Hattie (2009) found that parents' hopes and expectations for their students' level of achievement contributed significantly more to level of achievement than other factors such as family structure, amount of supervision, or homework and study rules. In fact, they were the most powerful contributing factor to high achievement *across all home variables*.

Students' discussions with parents about their learning when they have made progress strengthen their parents' beliefs about their capabilities and therefore contribute to increased achievement. One of the most successful methods of encouraging this communication is to institute student-involved or student-led conferences.

In a student-involved parent conference the teacher is also present. The student may lead the conference, or the teacher may do so. In a student-led parent conference the student is in charge of the conference. Figure 6.2 summarizes four types of student-led conferences that can involve both parents and students. It shows how topics, types of evidence, and participants can be configured to create options that meet different information and learning needs. Note that these conferences can occur at school or at home.

In student-involved and student-led conferences, students may be making a claim about improvement, presenting an explanation of their level of achievement at a point in time (often at the end of a grading period), or sharing achievement or behavior goals they have

FIGURE 6.2   Student-led conference options

DISCUSSION TOPIC	EVIDENCE	PARTICIPANTS	LOCATION
Improvement on one learning target	• Tracking form • Two or more dated work samples showing progress over time or project portfolio • Student reflection on growth	• Student and parent • Student and other adult • Two or more students • Student and teacher	• Home • School
Improvement in a subject overall	• Tracking form • Dialogue journal • Learning log • Growth portfolio • Project portfolio	• Student and parent • Student and other adult • Two or more students • Student and teacher	• Home • School

(Continued)

FIGURE 6.2 (Continued)

DISCUSSION TOPIC	EVIDENCE	PARTICIPANTS	LOCATION
Current level of achievement in a subject	• Tracking form • Dialogue journal • Learning log • Growth portfolio • Project portfolio	• Student and parent • Student and other adult • Student and teacher	• Home • School
Attainment of goals	• Short- or long-term goals and evidence of progress or goal attainment	• Student and parent • Student and other adult • Two or more students • Student and teacher	• Home • School

Source: Chappuis, J. *Seven Strategies of Assessment for Learning,* 2nd Edition (page 295) © 2015. Reprinted by permission of Pearson Education, Inc.

set, along with evidence of having attained their goals. Student prerequisites for successful conferences include the following:

- A clear vision of the intended learning
- A clear understanding of their status on each learning goal.
- A hand in selecting the evidence they will present
- Opportunity to practice and rehearse engaging in dialogue about the conference topic

(For more detailed information about preparing for, conducting, and debriefing student-involved and student-led conferences, see Chappuis, 2015.)

There are many other ways in which students can share their learning with parents, including a note or letter sent home (e.g., What's working well? What are my next steps? What do I need help with?), a family message journal, a weekly calendar of the learning targets in progress and/or mastered, and self-assessments and reflections on progress, growth ("before" and "after" descriptions), what the student learned from a project, current level of achievement, or self as a learner (Chappuis, 2015).

If you already have student-to home communication in place in your district or school, you may want to look for ways to increase the frequency or depth of the conversations. If you do not yet have student-to-home communication embedded in your culture, we recommend that you begin an exploration of the topic with teachers and colleagues.

 Success Indicators for Assessment Literacy Goal #6

The school leader

- can share agendas, memos, professional development descriptions, or other documentations that reflect the effort by the school leader to help teachers understand the benefits to student learning of school-to-home communications and/or show opportunities provided for teachers to learn and practice strategies that support that effort;

- understands the value of a school culture that honors and encourages parent engagement, with consistent communication to families;

- is aware of the difficulties and barriers that exist that can impede a shift from parent involvement to parent engagement; and

- can point to multiple sources of evidence of student learning beyond the traditional report card.

 ## Study Guide Questions

1. Explain, aloud or in writing, the difference between parent involvement and parent engagement. What are the contributions each makes? How well is the difference understood in your school?

2. What school-to-parent and teacher-to-parent communication strategies and tools are in use in your school/district currently? What would you change or add to that list?

3. What have you found to be the most challenging assessment topic about which to communicate with parents? What makes it that way, and what might be done to make it less problematic?

 ## Personal Portfolio Entry Suggestions

- Written protocols for student-led conferences that specify the discussion topic and evidence included

- Copies of parent newsletters focused on assessment issues

- Evidence of the use of multiple methods to communicate to parents and the broader community

- School and community partnerships/agreements, including mentorships, guest speakers, and scholarships

- List of community members on school-based committees or projects and their expertise

- Personal volunteer record or community leadership role(s)

- Memos or communications with staff regarding parent engagement and parent assessment literacy outreach

- Professional development provided to staff re: parent communication strategies or assessment literacy

Activity 6.1
Beyond the Report Card

Learning Target for the Activity

- Understand the different information sources that can be used to inform parents about student learning, other than report cards and progress reports.

Purpose

Nine out of 10 parents believe their student is performing at grade level, and yet data show that the number of students performing at grade level is much lower. Parents report that they believe the school report card is the best source of information about how their student is progressing and is in part how they determine if their student is at grade level. A majority of teachers, however, know that much can go into the consideration of a report card grade that is not directly tied to what the student knows and can do, or that the grade is not an indication of the most current status but often is a mix of past and current scores. They understand that good grades do not always equate to being at grade level (Learning Heroes, 2018).

The purpose of this activity is to consider what other sources of information a school or teacher could provide that would give parents a more complete and therefore accurate picture of how their student is doing.

Time

45 minutes

Materials Needed

None

Suggested Room Setup

Tables and chairs

Directions

Working in small groups, complete each step in the order below:

1. Consider your current school/district report card. What information does it provide parents? What other specific information do parents get during the course of the year that informs them about their student's achievement level? Make a list of what you include.

2. Using the list, what other data points exist in the school or classroom that could be provided? What is already provided but might be amplified or provided more regularly?

3. What else might be done to lessen the disconnect between a report card and a fuller picture of individual student achievement?

Closure

When the activity is completed, it may be helpful to display the results on a simple spreadsheet. If more than one school or district team participates, each spreadsheet can be used to combine the results into a single document. Some entries may be calendar driven, others might be a school responsibility or task, while other entries may be classroom or teacher specific. Other areas to categorize might include the communication method or form, what additional information on context/setting might be included to help parents understand the data, and how each source of data is used at the school or district level.

Definitions

Parent engagement: Parents contributing to their child's learning at home.

Parent involvement: The participation of parents in the life of the school, such as academic programs, volunteering, student activities, and volunteering opportunities.

 This chapter's online resources are available for download from **resources.corwin.com/10GoalsLeaders**

Ethical and Appropriate Assessment Use

7

Assessment Literacy Goal #7: *The leader understands the conditions required for the ethical and appropriate use of student assessment and protects students and staff from potential misuse.*

Ethical and appropriate use of assessment information is a part of educators' professional responsibility, and school leaders are central to ensuring it. School leaders need to understand and actively support appropriate assessment practices and processes and at the same time protect students and staff from misuse of assessment information.

Chapter Learning Goals

1. Understand the rationale for ethical and appropriate use of student assessment.

2. Be familiar with professional standards for the use of both large-scale and classroom assessment.

3. Understand the following concepts in assessment use and be able to lead others in their ethical and appropriate use: fairness, opportunity to learn, accommodations and modifications, confidentiality, test preparation.

The quality of assessment information (see Chapter 3) and the way it is used (see Chapters 4–6) affect the decisions that are made in classrooms and schools. Whether the decisions are small in scope, like deciding on what feedback to give a student on a 10-minute exercise, or large in scope, like deciding whether or not a student receives credit for a course, over time they can have huge consequences for students and their learning. The accumulation of effects of educational decisions over a school career directly affects students' learning, for example, by determining instructional time, materials, and activities, and affects students personally by helping determine students' views of themselves as learners. An important way to improve educational decisions is to use high-quality assessment information. Educational decisions based on high-quality assessment information are more likely to be sound, and those based on poor-quality assessment information are more likely to be unsound.

In addition to supporting the best possible educational decisions and their effects on students and learning, there are legal and ethical reasons to use assessment appropriately.

Ethical and appropriate uses of assessment give students and other users of assessment information the respect they deserve and the legal requirements to which they are entitled.

Professional Standards

Professional standards exist in the field of assessment. Many of these standards reiterate assessment literacy concepts, underscoring the point that it is important to provide high-quality assessment information to students, so important that it is unethical and unprofessional not to do so. As a school leader you may find yourself in a situation where it would be helpful to reference published, professional standards.

The *Standards for Educational and Psychological Testing*, published by the American Educational Research Association (AERA), American Psychological Association (APA), and National Council on Measurement in Education (NCME) in 2014, is the professional standards document most relevant to large-scale testing and assessment. For school leaders this document is important because it should be the main source of guidelines for ethical actions by developers and users of state accountability tests, interim and benchmark assessments, and any other large-scale assessments in use in the district. These standards should also be the foundation for any school or district policy related to large-scale test use in the district.

In terms of the pyramid model of a balanced and comprehensive assessment system presented in Chapter 1, the *Standards for Educational and Psychological Testing* (AERA, APA, & NCME, 2014) presents criteria for the ethical development and use of the top two layers of the pyramid: state accountability and district summative assessment and interim and benchmark assessment. Any assessment vendor should be able to describe how their products comply with these standards. With the help of material from the vendor and the state, school leaders should be able to describe how their uses of the assessment comply with these standards.

Some educational professional organizations also have standards that include the ethical use of assessment. For example, the American Counseling Association's *2014 ACA Code of Ethics* has a section devoted to evaluation, assessment, and interpretation. *The Professional Standards of the National Association of School Psychologists* (2020) has a section titled "Responsible Assessment and Intervention Practices." The National Center on Educational Outcomes, in collaboration with the Council of Chief State School Officers and the National Association of State Directors of Special Education, has published *Principles and Characteristics of Inclusive Assessment Systems in a Changing Assessment Landscape* (Thurlow et al., 2016). However, the document that comes closest to describing the sorts of ethical actions you might take at the school and classroom levels, in some detail, is *The Classroom Assessment Standards* (Klinger et al., 2015).

The Classroom Assessment Standards

In 2015 the Joint Committee on Standards for Educational Evaluation (jcsee.org) revised their student evaluation standards to reflect the needs of school-based educators (the previous student evaluation standards had been more focused on the needs of external evaluators). The result was *The Classroom Assessment Standards* (Klinger et al., 2015), a document that contains statements describing ways to ensure that assessment information collected via classroom assessment is valid, reliable, and fair and therefore likely to benefit students and their learning. The document states that "the support of student learning is the key purpose of classroom assessment," and this stated assumption forms the basis on which the specific standards rest. In terms of the pyramid model of a balanced and comprehensive assessment system, presented in Chapter 1, *The Classroom Assessment Standards* (Klinger et al., 2015) presents criteria for ethical and appropriate development and use of the bottom three layers of the pyramid: common assessment, classroom summative assessment, and classroom formative assessment.

These standards are organized into statements in three broad areas of assessment: foundations, use, and quality. Each statement is then expanded into a brief section explaining the statement and providing guidelines on how to meet it. Figure 7.1 shows these statements.

FIGURE 7.1   Outline of *The Classroom Assessment Standards*

Foundations

F1 Assessment Purpose

Classroom assessment practices should have a clear purpose that supports teaching and learning.

F2 Learning Expectations

Learning expectations should form the foundation for aligning classroom assessment practice with appropriate instruction and learning opportunities for each student.

F3 Assessment Design

The types and methods of classroom assessment used should clearly allow students to demonstrate their learning.

F4 Student Engagement in Assessment

Students should be meaningfully engaged in the assessment process and use of the assessment evidence to enhance their learning.

F5 Assessment Preparation

Adequate teacher and student preparation in terms of resources, time, and learning opportunities should be part of classroom assessment practices.

F6 Informed Students and Parents/Guardians

The purposes and uses of classroom assessment should be communicated to students and, when appropriate, parents/guardians.

(Continued)

FIGURE 7.1   (Continued)

Use

U1 Analysis of Student Performance

The methods for analyzing evidence of student learning should be appropriate for the assessment purpose and practice.

U2 Effective Feedback

Classroom assessment practices should provide timely and useful feedback to improve student learning.

U3 Instructional Follow-Up

Analysis of student performance should inform instructional planning and next steps to support ongoing student learning.

U4 Grades and Summary Comments

Summative grades and comments should reflect student achievement of the learning expectations.

U5 Reporting

Assessment reports should be based on a sufficient body of evidence and provide a summary of a student's learning in a clear, timely, accurate, and useful manner.

Quality

Q1 Cultural and Linguistic Diversity

Classroom assessment practices should be responsive to and respectful of the cultural and linguistic diversity of students and their communities.

Q2 Exceptionality and Special Education

Classroom assessment practices should be appropriately differentiated to meet the specific educational needs of all students.

Q3 Unbiased and Fair Assessment

Classroom assessment practices and subsequent decisions should be free from all factors unrelated to the intended purposes of the assessment.

Q4 Reliability and Validity

Classroom assessment practices should provide consistent, dependable, and appropriate information that supports sound interpretations and decisions about each student's knowledge and skills.

Q5 Reflection

Classroom assessment practices should be monitored and revised to improve their overall quality.

Source: Klinger, D.A., McDivitt, P.R., Howard, B.B., Munoz, M.A., Rogers, W.T., & Wylie, E.C. (2015). *The Classroom Assessment Standards for PreK–12 Teachers.* Joint Committee on Standards for Educational Evaluation; Kindle Direct Press.

Notice that these statements align very well with the 10 assessment literacy goals in this book. In fact, some readers might wonder why these topics resurface in a chapter about ethics. *The Classroom Assessment Standards* (Klinger et al., 2015) are very clear in their stance that knowing and implementing effective and appropriate assessment practices *is* the ethical thing to do and not to do so is unethical. Because of their weighty effects on students and their learning, and the potential harm that can come from inappropriate assessment use, there is a kind of moral imperative attached to "doing it (assessment) right." In other words, all of these standards, even the ones that are covered in other chapters in this book, relate to assessment literacy goal #7, about ethical and appropriate assessment use.

The standards in Table 7.1 and their associated explanations and guidelines summarize ethical and appropriate conduct in classroom assessment. In schools where these standards are met you are likely to find an assessment-literate school leader (or leaders!) who not only understands the standards but also promotes a school assessment culture that develops assessment-literate teachers and students.

In this chapter we will not repeat information about how to create high-quality assessments and employ high-quality assessment practices, which is covered in other chapters, beyond making the point that these are professional responsibilities and ethical practices as well. However, we will briefly expand on some elements of ethical and appropriate use of student assessment about which school leaders may wish to have more information: **fairness**, **opportunity to learn** (OTL), accommodations, **confidentiality**, and preparation for standardized tests.

Fairness

The *Standards for Educational and Psychological Testing* (AERA, APA, & NCME, 2014, p. 219) defines *fairness* as "the validity of test score interpretations for intended use(s) for individuals from all relevant subgroups" and goes on to explain that this can be best accomplished by minimizing irrelevant factors that might contribute to score differences for some individuals for reasons other than the achievement or other construct one intends to measure. The measurement term that describes how factors unrelated to what is to be assessed can differentially affect the assessment of different individuals is **construct-irrelevant variance**. In Chapter 3 we called this "bias and distortion." An informal term sometimes used for this situation is "score pollution" (the idea being that the "pure" score is "polluted" if extraneous factors are included—similar to how air and water are polluted when substances are added that are not supposed to be there).

For large-scale assessment this means things like making sure that scenario-based problems do not have contexts that some students would be more familiar with than others (e.g., a math word problem about a polo match might privilege wealthy students over poorer students and affect their scores accordingly). The *Standards for Educational and Psychological Testing* (AERA, APA, & NCME, 2014) devotes a whole chapter and 21 standards to removing barriers to valid score interpretations and uses for all students for whom an assessment is intended. Although it is difficult to achieve, fairness in standardized assessment has an agreed-on definition and associated procedures for fair test design, validation, development, administration, scoring, interpretation, and use.

The waters muddy a bit when the discussion moves to fairness in classroom assessment. Different students, teachers, and parents have different ideas about what is "fair" in classroom assessment. Because classroom assessment is integrated with teaching and is affected by teacher expectations (Wang et al., 2018) and sociocultural factors in classrooms, because classroom assessment encompasses a wide range of formal and informal assessment techniques, and because students are not only "examinees" but also active learners in the classroom assessment process, scholars have not yet converged on one definition of fairness in classroom assessment (Rasooli et al., 2018).

Amirhossein Rasooli and colleagues (2018) analyzed 150 studies on fairness with a focus on classroom assessment. Results revealed that "fairness" in classroom assessment encompasses four elements: teaching, learning, classroom interactions, and assessment. That is, classroom assessment cannot be judged "fair" or "unfair" without some understanding of the teaching and learning context in which it takes place.

Fairness within the assessment setting included (1) opportunity to learn (OTL) and access to demonstrate learning; (2) transparency, consistency, and justification of the criteria used for feedback and grading; (3) appropriate use of accommodations; (4) the "do no harm" principle and a constructive classroom environment; (5) avoiding "score pollution" (bias and distortion) or construct-irrelevant variance; and (6) considerations related to group work and peer assessment. These six issues, plus issues underlying teaching, learning, and classroom interactions, have all been found to contribute to one's concept of fairness in classroom assessment.

Simply being aware of what the issues are may benefit school leaders, even though the research on classroom assessment fairness has not yet converged on one definition. This awareness will give focus to discussions with teachers, students, and parents and suggest areas for policy and practice decisions within schools. Notice that among the six issues, #5 (avoiding construct-irrelevant variance) is the same as the underlying principle for fairness in standardized testing, ensuring valid results for all students. Two more of these classroom assessment fairness issues (#1, OTL, and #3, appropriate use of accommodations) are relevant to standardized testing as well as classroom assessment. We have some more to say about these in the next two sections. The other three issues (#2, transparency of criteria; #4, a constructive classroom environment; and #6, considerations of group work and peer assessment) are more clearly related to classroom teaching and learning and in this book have already been treated in Chapters 3–5.

Opportunity to Learn

Our understanding and treatment of OTL is still evolving, as is our understanding of most of the concepts related to fairness in educational assessment. Related to the issue of OTL is the issue of equity, providing each student with the opportunities they need to learn (as compared with equality, providing every student the same opportunities to learn). Teachers are the first line of defense for equity in classroom learning; a classic and consistent finding is that teachers who believe they can make a difference with all children are the ones who do, in fact, make a difference (McLaughlin & Marsh, 1978).

One of the first OTL theorists was John Carroll, who famously derived "Carroll's model" of instruction, in his article "A Model of School Learning" (Carroll, 1963), which specified that the degree of a student's learning is a function of the time actually spent learning something compared with (divided by) the time needed to learn it. This article marked the beginning of a field of study that has led to our current understanding of OTL as a function of three factors: instructional time, the content of instruction, and instructional quality (Elliott & Bartlett, 2018).

Each of these aspects can be further understood. For example, discussions of instructional time can consider how much time is allocated, how much is actually spent, how much of the time students spend on a topic is engaged time, and so on. Instructional content can include the enacted curriculum (what is actually taught) and the cognitive processes invoked—whether students merely memorize or whether they must apply their learning. Instructional quality includes teacher clarity and pedagogy, the quality of materials and resources used, the nature of instructional grouping, and so on.

Two aspects of OTL are central to ethical and appropriate assessment. First, students should have had sufficient OTL—including sufficient opportunity to practice, receive feedback, and act on it—before any assessment for which they will be held accountable. Second, this principle should apply across all demographic or other relevant categories. OTL is a basic aspect of effective teaching and fair assessment regardless of a student's gender, ethnicity, cultural background, socioeconomic status, or disability status.

Accommodations and Modifications

Students may have disabilities or special needs that affect their performance on assessments. Accommodations are changes in the conditions or materials of assessment that allow students with disabilities and special needs to be assessed on the same learning goals as all other students. The accommodation is not expected to change the construct (the learning goal) that is assessed. So, for example, questions on a geometry test might be read to a student with a reading disability. Since the test is intended to assess knowledge outcomes in geometry, the reading is irrelevant, and the assessment results—in this case, percentage of problems answered correctly—are interpreted as an indicator of the student's geometry knowledge. Ethical and appropriate use of assessment includes providing assessment accommodations to students who need them.

Modifications are changes in the conditions or materials of assessment that do change the construct—the learning goal—being measured. The meaning of assessment results changes accordingly. Ethical and appropriate use of assessment includes providing assessment modifications to students who need them. Students first qualify for, and are given, modified learning goals, typically via an Individualized Education Program or a 504 plan, and then the assessments are altered accordingly. That is, modified assessments are provided for students who have modified learning goals. Modifying an assessment as an afterthought, for example, because a teacher realizes a student did not learn what the teacher intended, is unethical and harmful to students. The ethical course of action in this case is to use the assessment information to plan further learning opportunities.

Accommodations and modifications are possible at all levels of the assessment system. The student should have access to the same or similar accommodations at all levels of the system. So, for example, a student who gets extra time for classroom assessments should qualify for extra time on a standardized test.

Confidentiality

Confidentiality refers to students' right to the privacy of test results, grades, and other information. Confidentiality does not mean secrecy. People with a legitimate need to know may access students' records—for example, the student's teacher or a building or district administrator. Official school records are protected by the legal right to privacy described in the Family Educational Rights and Privacy Act. Parents or guardians may sign written authorization forms when students' records need to be transferred, for example, when a student moves to another school.

Unofficial school records, for example, students' grades on one classroom test, are not protected by the Family Educational Rights and Privacy Act, but it still may be unethical to share them because it may cause the student discomfort or may contribute to a low-quality learning environment. Posting student test scores on a classroom wall chart, for example, is not illegal, but it is unethical.

Sometimes researchers request access to student information for research purposes. Students who are 18 years old may sign informed consent documents, which typically inform them of what information is sought, how it will be used, and what the anticipated consequences are and solicit the students' permission for their information to be shared. For children under 18, parents or guardians sign the informed consent documents.

Access to written records without permission is not the only, or in some cases the most egregious, violation of students' right to confidentiality of information. In many school settings confidentiality is violated by overhearing people speaking. Teachers' lounge conversations can violate students' confidentiality rights. Parent conferences in crowded settings, where one family is waiting for their conference within earshot of another conference in progress, can violate students' confidentiality rights.

Preparation for Standardized Tests

All students should have the opportunity to be prepared for the assessments they are to take. (Yes, that means that "pop quizzes" are unethical.) This holds true at all levels of the assessment system. For classroom summative assessment and common assessment, preparation usually takes the form of informing students when and how they will be assessed—giving enough time for students to study—and how the results will be used. This means, for example, that you would let students know what learning goals will be assessed (e.g., understanding of *Hamlet* in its literary and historical contexts), in what form (e.g., essay test), and with what consequences (e.g., the test grade will make up one-fifth of the report card grade). This approach preserves the sampling aspect of the essay test questions. Students do not know exactly which questions about *Hamlet*, out of all possible questions, they should be ready for, so they will be studying in the whole domain of the learning goal. Yet their study is focused on their understanding of *Hamlet* and not on other things they may have learned during this report period. Because they know how the results will be used, they can judge how much time and energy they will invest in studying. In short, informed students can prepare appropriately for the essay test they will take, and if the test is well constructed, their score will be an accurate representation of their achievement on the whole learning goal.

Students can also be taught how to study, how to approach different kinds of assessment questions and tasks, and so on. For classroom formative assessment, preparation usually takes the form of sharing learning targets and success criteria with students so they know what they are looking for, and creating a classroom culture of learning where students know they will be able to use the assessment results to improve.

Ethical and appropriate preparation to take standardized tests is similar, whether the standardized test is a state accountability assessment or an interim assessment. Students should know when and how they will be assessed, how the results will be used, and anything else relevant to their testing experience (e.g., if they will need to go to a different room).

Ethical and appropriate test preparation practices ensure that the test items remain a sample of the intended learning domain (e.g., a reading standard measured by an end-of-year state accountability test in reading). As a general principle test preparation that helps students learn in the domain (here, the state reading standards), but does not narrow the domain so that the test no longer measures what is intended but some smaller subset, is ethical.

An analogy may help. Suppose a restaurant critic eats at a restaurant, sampling menu items to make a judgment about food quality. The critic cannot eat everything but can come in a few times and try different menu items. If the critic were to tell the restaurant which items they were going to order in advance, they would no longer have a representative sample of the quality of the food because the restaurant would make sure those items were top of the line.

Similarly, test preparation that narrows students' learning experiences to the items on the test, thus narrowing the learning domain, is unethical. It "pollutes" the test scores, which now no longer mean what they were intended to mean. It also shortchanges students because it denies them opportunities to learn some important content.

For example, if a teacher knows that the state reading test will include an essay question on characterization (intended as a sample of all the reading questions that could possibly be asked) but not setting in narrative text, and therefore teaches about characterization but not setting, the teacher is narrowing what the students learn about reading to what will be tested and depriving them of knowledge they are meant to develop according to their curriculum and state standards.

But the devil is in the details, and people have disagreed especially on what it is appropriate to say and do with students to communicate how they will be assessed.

For example, giving students a practice test using the same questions that will be on the standardized test is considered unethical. That narrows the domain of learning that the test will assess and changes the meaning of the results. This is the same principle we illustrated with the *Hamlet* example above.

Some standardized testing programs (e.g., the Advanced Placement Program) release previous questions with sample student responses and scores. Students can practice with questions that are *like* the questions on the exam they will be taking but not the same. Some states release previous items from state accountability tests or provide practice tests. For example, the Smarter Balanced Assessment Consortium has practice tests for member states (http://www.smarterbalanced.org/assessments/samples/).

But how close can test preparation come to the actual test before it becomes unethical? For example, is it ethical to not teach a learning goal that you know will not be covered on the standardized test in order to spend more time on a learning goal that will be tested? Is it ethical to only give students classroom assessments in the same format as the one used on the standardized test? Our position is that school leaders should know where to draw the line between ethical and unethical test preparation by applying criteria that indicate fair and valid assessment, should be able to explain their reasoning, and should be able to lead others accordingly. Activity 7.4 will help you reach this goal.

Success Indicators for Assessment Literacy Goal #7

The school leader

- can explain how ethical and appropriate use of student assessment supports students and their learning;

- can reference relevant professional standards in assessment when dealing with assessment issues in school leadership;

- can create a school climate in which fairness and OTL are the hallmarks of student assessment;

- can ensure that students in their school receive assessment accommodations as needed; and

- can lead teachers and others to provide ethical and appropriate test preparation.

Study Guide Questions

1. Why is it important to use student assessment appropriately and ethically?

2. Before reading this chapter, were you aware that there are professional standards for student assessment? If so, in what ways have you used professional standards

in your previous work? If not, how will knowing there are such standards affect your future work?

3. Fairness and OTL are two concepts that are particularly important currently, and interest in them is growing. What have you learned in this chapter that will help you deal with questions of fairness and OTL in your school?

4. Have you ever been involved in requesting or selecting accommodations for students? What was that experience like? What were your takeaways for school leadership?

5. The testing landscape is changing. For example, more testing is being done online, for reasons of efficiency and cost as well as in response to the recent pandemic of 2020. How do you imagine preparing students for standardized tests will change with this?

 ## Personal Portfolio Entry Suggestions

- Copy of school or classroom policies regarding assessment practices in general, fairness, OTL, accommodations and modifications, confidentiality, and test preparation, critiqued using information from this chapter

- Video describing assessment policies in general, fairness, OTL, accommodations and modifications, confidentiality, and/or test preparation that is suitable for posting on a school website or showing at a meeting (e.g., a school board meeting, parent-teacher organization meeting, or school open house)

Activity 7.1
Recognizing the Ethical and Appropriate Use of Student Assessment

Learning Target for the Activity

- I can identify ethical and appropriate student assessment use and explain my reasoning.

Purpose

The purpose of this activity is to give school leaders an opportunity to analyze common student assessment scenarios according to whether they comply with assessment standards and principles of ethics and fairness. The activity also gives school leaders a chance to practice describing and explaining what is ethical and appropriate (or not) in a given situation in order to better prepare them for work with colleagues, teachers, students, and parents.

(Continued)

(Continued)

Time

45 minutes

Materials Needed

- Copies (paper or electronic) of the handout "Recognizing the Ethical and Appropriate Use of Student Assessment" (see Figure 7.2)

FIGURE 7.2   Recognizing the ethical and appropriate use of student assessment

Scenario 1. A high school English teacher has been teaching students how to write argumentative (persuasive) text by stating a clear thesis and using several different kinds of support. Students have written essays on their opinions about the importance of the electoral process in the United States. The teacher provided written feedback on each student's essay, handed them back today, and told the students to take their papers home.

a. Is this practice ethical/appropriate?

b. Why did you make this choice? Include your reasoning and evidence from the text of Chapter 7.

Scenario 2. On March 14 (3.14) all of the mathematics teachers in a building celebrate "Pi Day." Students were told they will receive bonus points on their report card grade if they bring a pie to class for the Pi Day party. The mother of one student made a homemade chocolate cream pie and sent it to school with the student, who received 10 bonus points.

a. Is this practice ethical/appropriate?

b. Why did you make this choice? Include your reasoning and evidence from the text of Chapter 7.

Scenario 3. In one fourth-grade class students are learning to multiply a fraction by a whole number. Today, they are doing practice work that will be used for formative assessment. Most of the students are working on a problem set with 10 problems. One student is allowed to use a multiplication chart because they have not memorized the multiplication facts through 10.

a. Is this practice ethical/appropriate?

b. Why did you make this choice? Include your reasoning and evidence from the text of Chapter 7.

Scenario 4. A middle school teacher has found that student test, homework, and classwork papers often are turned in without proper identification (name, date, period number). To address this problem, the teacher gives students 5 points (out of 100) for having their identification information in the upper-right-hand corner of each paper.

a. Is this practice ethical/appropriate?

b. Why did you make this choice? Include your reasoning and evidence from the text of Chapter 7.

Scenario 5. A 10th-grade student is taking a biology class that includes many performance assessments and other project-based work. The student dislikes projects because they take a long time and has asked the teacher to "just give me a test." The student asked if they could substitute the unit tests that came with the biology textbook for their project-based performance assessment. The teacher refused to allow this and said the student had to complete the performance assessments and other project-based work.

a. Is this practice ethical/appropriate?

b. Why did you make this choice? Include your reasoning and evidence from the text of Chapter 7.

Scenario 6. A high school student was absent from school for a week because of illness. On the day the student returned, the class was given a writing assignment that would count toward their report card grade. The teacher gave the student the directions for the assignment and said, "Just do your best."

a. Is this practice ethical/appropriate?

b. Why did you make this choice? Include your reasoning and evidence from the text of Chapter 7.

Scenario 7. A high school history teacher assigned students to read four chapters in their textbook for a unit on early civilizations. The chapters described the rise of civilization in Ancient Egypt, Mesopotamia, Ancient India, and Ancient China. During class time, the teacher gave lectures on these four civilizations that mirrored the material in the chapters. For a unit test the teacher gave the students an open-book test composed of 25 fill-in-the-blank questions.

a. Is this practice ethical/appropriate?

b. Why did you make this choice? Include your reasoning and evidence from the text of Chapter 7.

Scenario 8. A middle school science teacher gave students a test on the phases of the moon. It included 15 multiple-choice questions (1 point each), 5 short-answer questions (5 points each), and 1 longer essay question (10 points). The teacher scored the test using a key, recorded the results in the gradebook, and passed back the tests. As the class was going over the test, one student brought to the teacher's attention that the key for one of the multiple-choice questions must have been wrong. The teacher checked and found that to be true and asked the students to pass the tests back and rescored them, which changed the test grade for some students.

a. Is this practice ethical/appropriate?

b. Why did you make this choice? Include your reasoning and evidence from the text of Chapter 7.

Scenario 9. In an eighth-grade foreign language (French) class, students are learning the forms of the French verb *être*, which means "to be." Toward the end of that day's lesson, they take a 10-question quiz that is intended to help them see where they still need to study. Each answer is one or two words, representing some form of the verb. After the quiz, the teacher writes the answers on the board and has students switch papers with their elbow partners. The partners grade the quiz and pass them back to their owners.

a. Is this practice ethical/appropriate?

b. Why did you make this choice? Include your reasoning and evidence from the text of Chapter 7.

Scenario 10. One student in a fifth-grade class has an Individualized Education Program and is given extra time to do classroom assessments. Other students in the class complain, saying it's not fair to give that student extra time if they can't have extra time. The teacher explains that fair does not always mean equal. The students grudgingly accept what their teacher tells them, but they are still grumpy.

a. Is this practice ethical/appropriate?

b. Why did you make this choice? Include your reasoning and evidence from the text of Chapter 7.

(Continued)

(Continued)

Suggested Room Setup

This is a small-group activity. Arrange chairs around a table suitable for both individual writing and group discussion.

Directions

Working in small groups, complete each step in the order below:

1. The school leader reviews the contents of this chapter, which they have read prior to this activity. The group should entertain any questions people have about the meaning or content of the chapter text. (5 minutes)

2. Individually (or in pairs if the group is larger than eight persons), consider each of the scenarios in the handout "Recognizing the Ethical and Appropriate Use of Student Assessment." Make sure the group members know that these scenarios were constructed to raise a variety of issues described in the chapter and that some of the scenarios may invoke several issues or standards of ethics and appropriateness. For each scenario individuals should answer two questions: (a) Is this practice ethical/appropriate? and (b) Why did you make this choice? Answers to the second question should include evidence from the text of Chapter 7 (with page and paragraph numbers) as part of the explanation and support. (15–20 minutes)

3. The group reconvenes after the individuals (or pairs) have considered the scenarios. A volunteer facilitator calls on each individual (or pair) in turn to volunteer one of the scenarios for discussion. Participants should choose a scenario that was difficult for them, raised an issue they thought was especially important to discuss, and/or resonated with something in their own experience as school leaders. They should identify the scenario they would like to discuss, explain why, and ask any specific questions they have about it. (15–20 minutes)

Closure

Participants should refer back to the learning target for this activity and also to the chapter learning goals. Each one should perform a self-evaluation: Am I closer to this learning goal now than before the activity? Participants should share out briefly what they have learned that brought them closer to their assessment literacy goal of ethical and appropriate assessment use. (5 minutes)

Some facilitators may find it useful to have an answer sheet, so we offer one here (see Figure 7.3). It should not be used to grade or score participants but only to assist in discussions where needed. It is not necessary to use this answer sheet in the activity at all, especially if discussions are lively and on point. Note that some of the scenarios are open to interpretation, and a case may be made for answers other than the authors'.

FIGURE 7.3   Suggested answers to scenario questions

Scenario 1

a. No

b. Students should have opportunity to use the feedback they receive. In the authors' view that makes this scenario at least an inappropriate assessment practice, if not unethical. We anticipate that others might offer counterarguments and expect that this scenario might prompt some heated discussion.

Scenario 2

a. No

b. Bringing pie is not a part of any math learning goal. Even if the student had made the pie, this would not be ethical and appropriate.

Scenario 3

a. Yes

b. The student who has not memorized the math facts is using an accommodation. Memory of multiplication facts is not part of the learning goal of multiplying fractions by whole numbers.

Scenario 4

a. No

b. The teacher is adding points that are not related to the respective learning goals for the classwork, homework, and tests, thereby distorting or polluting the meaning of the scores. This mismeasurement, in turn, may harm students (e.g., some students may be assessed as satisfactory on a particular goal when in fact they need additional instruction).

Scenario 5

a. Yes

b. If the teacher was using performance assessments because they were the most appropriate measures of some complex learning goals in the biology course, allowing this student to substitute test scores would result in lower-quality assessment information for him.

Scenario 6

a. No

b. This is a clear-cut case of lack of OTL.

Scenario 7

a. No

b. The test as described would measure students' looking-up abilities, not their understanding of the ancient civilizations, which was the learning goal.

Scenario 8

a. Yes

b. Once the error was discovered, rescoring the test was the ethical thing to do, because it resulted in more accurate assessment results.

Scenario 9

a. Yes

b. The students were not asked to call out scores in front of the class, just to give feedback to their partners. However, while ethical, this practice would work better in some classroom environments than in others. In a learning-focused climate, where mistakes are perceived as opportunities to learn, this could be a very formative activity. In an evaluative classroom climate, where being wrong is perceived as being judged inadequate in some way, students

(Continued)

(Continued)

might be uncomfortable doing this—and therefore should not be asked to do it until changes are made to the classroom climate. In fact, when students are acclimated to a learning-focused climate, there is no need to have them exchange papers to mark them. There is benefit in students looking at their own work during the answer review process, because it presents an opportunity for them to understand their own mistakes.

Scenario 10

a. Yes

b. The student is receiving an accommodation. This assumes that the assessments in question are power assessments, not speed assessments, meaning that all of the other students really do have the time they need (because every student should have the time they need to do an assessment).

Activity 7.2

The Classroom Assessment Standards

Learning Targets for the Activity

- I can describe the contents of *The Classroom Assessment Standards*.

- I can apply *The Classroom Assessment Standards* as an assessment leader in my school/district.

Purpose

The purpose of this activity is to familiarize school leaders with professional standards in the area of classroom assessment and provide practice in applying these standards to situations that arise in schools.

Time

45 minutes

Materials Needed

- Copy (print or electronic) of Figure 7.1 or this book opened to Figure 7.1

- (Optional) Copy of *The Classroom Assessment Standards* (available for purchase on Amazon Kindle)

- Chart paper and markers

Suggested Room Setup

Arrange tables and chairs to accommodate a small group working in pairs and then together.

Directions

Complete each step in the order below:

1. In pairs, discuss assessment issues, problems, or questions that have arisen in your school/district as a result of an event or scenario that you can share. Each pair should describe and discuss at least two events or scenarios (one from each partner) in which the issues, problems, or questions have arisen.

2. For each event or scenario draw a cartoon, line drawing, diagram, or other visual rendition of it in the center of a piece of chart paper (therefore, each pair should produce at least two drawings, on two separate pieces of paper). The purpose of the visual is to symbolize the event and spark thinking; do not worry about creating an image that is "artistic."

3. Using Figure 7.1, identify the standard(s) that you would use to analyze the issues, problems, or questions. It is likely that several standards are implicated in any one event or scenario. On each piece of chart paper, around the edges of the visual image, write the letter/number identifiers for the standards you have identified for it (F1, U4, Q3, etc.). Be prepared to explain why you have chosen the standards you did, how each standard speaks to the issues represented in the event or scenario, and what actions the standard might suggest.

4. Reconvene as a group. Each pair shares one (or both if there is time) of their scenarios and standards analysis and asks the group for their thinking. Discussion should center on why and how the standard(s) could make the assessment in the story more ethical and appropriate.

Closure

The group reaches closure by facilitating a discussion based on these questions: What did I learn from this activity that will be important for me to know in my role as a school leader? How do I envision *The Classroom Assessment Standards* helping me in my work? What questions do I have?

Activity 7.3
Assessment Accommodations

Learning Targets for the Activity

- I can describe a method for selecting, administering, and evaluating assessment accommodations for students with disabilities.

- I can identify the types and characteristics of common accommodations used in assessment.

Purpose

The purpose of this activity is to familiarize school leaders with the process for selecting and evaluating accommodations and with some common categories of accommodation

(Continued)

(Continued)

methods. The purpose is *not* to equip the school leader to decide on assessment accommodations for a particular student; that decision should be made by a team of people with the relevant expertise. Rather, the purpose is to help school leaders understand the process by which accommodations are selected and what some of those accommodations might be, in order to help school leaders facilitate the provision of appropriate accommodations for students in their charge.

Time

45 minutes

Materials Needed

- Copies (electronic preferred) of *Accommodations Manual* (Thompson et al., 2005)

- Copies (paper) of Figure 7.4: "*Accommodations Manual*, Scavenger Hunt, and Thought Questions"

Suggested Room Setup

Arrange tables and chairs to accommodate a small group working in pairs and then together.

FIGURE 7.4 *Accommodations Manual*, scavenger hunt, and thought questions

1. For whom is this manual designed (Thompson et al., 2005, p. 7)? Do you fall into any of the intended user groups?

2. What are the five steps to follow for selecting, administering, and using accommodations in assessment and instruction (p. 7)? Why do you think assessment and instruction are considered together?

3. Into what four categories are assessment accommodations typically placed (p. 14)? Without looking further into the manual, can you think of an example in each category?

4. What is the difference between accommodations and modifications (p. 15)? Why does the manual caution against using modifications unless specifically prescribed?

5. Review fact sheets 1 through 4 (pp. 25–37). For each category of accommodations (presentation, response, setting, and timing/scheduling) identify the accommodation with which you are least familiar. It may be a new idea for you, or it may be something you have heard of but never seen in practice.

6. Review fact sheet 5 (pp. 38–42). Select one or more sections (based on student characteristics), and look at the potential accommodations listed in the last column (Accommodations to Consider for Assessments). For each selected accommodation give at least one reason why that accommodation allows access to the assessment but does not change the construct (the learning domain) that is assessed.

Directions

Complete each step in the order below:

1. Divide the group into pairs. Each pair works together on the scavenger hunt. Each pair works to answer the scavenger hunt questions by navigating to the designated page in the *Accommodations Manual* (15–25 minutes), retrieving and summarizing information, and noting it on the handout. Each scavenger hunt question is followed by a thought question. Pairs should discuss their answer and summarize their thoughts on the handout. Note that just discussing, without making notes, does not count as fulfilling the scavenger hunt.

2. After 20 minutes, the group reconvenes and discusses the answers to each scavenger hunt question in turn. Any discrepancies should be discussed until a consensus of understanding is reached. Time is also available to group members to share any relevant experiences they have had as each question is answered. (15–20 minutes)

Closure

The group reaches closure by facilitating a discussion based on these questions: What did I learn from this exercise/this manual that will be important for me to know in my role as a school leader? What questions do I have? With whom might I share my insights and questions? (5–10 minutes)

Activity 7.4
Ethical and Unethical Test Preparation

Learning Target for the Activity

• I can evaluate test preparation strategies according to whether they are ethical or unethical and can explain my position.

Purpose

This activity gives school leaders practice in evaluating the ethicality of test preparation practices. In so doing, school leaders discern the line they would draw between ethical and unethical practices and get practice in articulating their reasoning.

Time

45 minutes

Materials Needed

• Chart paper and markers, pink and green sticky notes

Suggested Room Setup

This activity is designed for a small group. Arrange chairs in a circle or at a table and have available wall space for chart paper.

(Continued)

(Continued)

Directions

Complete each step in the order below:

1. Prepare a separate piece of chart paper for each of these eight statements. Put the statement at the top of the chart paper, leaving room for sticky notes or comments below. Hang the chart paper on a wall, from left to right, in the order the statements are given here. (5 minutes)

   a. Familiarize students with different test item types and test-taking strategies.

   b. Teach the curriculum as given.

   c. In teaching emphasize curriculum objectives that map to the standardized test.

   d. Give students practice tests and worksheets that use the same item formats as those on the standardized test.

   e. Give students practice on published released items or forms of the standardized test.

   f. Teach only curriculum objectives that map to the standardized test.

   g. Suspend instruction two weeks before the test, and replace it with test practice.

   h. Give students practice on the same test items that will be on the standardized test.

2. Reread the section of this chapter titled "Preparation for Standardized Tests." Use the criteria implied in that section: ethical test preparation (a) does not narrow the curriculum or pollute the test score and (b) does not shortchange students. (5 minutes)

3. Individuals use sticky notes (or write with red and green markers directly on the chart paper) to apply these criteria to the statement on each sheet of chart paper. Remember that the evaluation task for each statement is to decide what should be considered ethical or unethical, not what is currently done in a specific school. Use green sticky notes for statements judged to be ethical practice and pink sticky notes for statements judged to be unethical, and write at least one sentence on the note explaining why you have made that choice. (5 minutes)

4. After each individual has placed sticky notes on all the statements, the group may do a brief gallery walk, depending on the size and wishes of the group. (5 minutes)

5. Group members reconvene as a small group for a discussion based on the following questions: (10 minutes)

   • Which statements drew general agreement that they were ethical? Why?

   • Which statements drew general agreement that they were unethical? Why?

   • Which statements drew mixed evaluations? Why?

- Focusing on the statements that drew mixed evaluations, and assuming that they will be in the middle of the series of charts, see if you can come to a group consensus about where to draw the line between ethical and unethical test preparation practices. When you have drawn that line between two of the statements, the group should craft a one- or two-sentence rationale for the difference between ethical and unethical test preparation practices as illustrated in these statements.

6. After the group has crafted its rationale, school leaders may continue the discussion by describing test preparation practices they have observed or participated in in their schools. What is the relationship between the things you have observed and the rationale you have just crafted in this exercise? Be careful not to judge others, who may not know what you now know about test score meaning and student learning. The purpose here is to describe real scenarios that a school leader might encounter and to relate those to your growing understanding of ethical test preparation practices. (5–10 minutes)

Closure

The group reaches closure by facilitating a discussion based on these questions: What did I learn from this exercise that will be important for me to know in my role as a school leader? What questions do I have? With whom might I share my insights and questions? (5 minutes)

Definitions

Confidentiality: Students' right to have test results, grades, and other school information held private, accessed and used only by those authorized to do so, and not released outside the school without permission.

Construct-irrelevant variance: Variation in assessment scores related to factors that are not part of the achievement domain or learning goal assessed, causing bias and distortion in the scores (sometimes called "test score pollution").

Fairness: In standardized testing fairness means that assessment results have the same meaning for individuals from all relevant subgroups. In classroom assessment fairness means that the conditions of teaching, learning, classroom interactions, and assessment result in assessment tools and processes that are appropriate, accessible, and useful for learning for all students.

Opportunity to learn: The extent to which students have had a chance to learn the content on which they are assessed—currently studied as a function of instructional time (including time to practice), the content of instruction, and instructional quality.

 This chapter's online resources are available for download from
resources.corwin.com/10GoalsLeaders

Evaluation of Assessment Competencies and Providing Appropriate Professional Development

8

Assessment Literacy Goal #8: *The leader evaluates teachers' classroom assessment competencies and uses that information to present and/or secure appropriate professional development.*

Although states and districts vary in their teacher evaluation practices, there is one constant: the building principal is a part of the process. Regardless of training, preparation, or experience, it is almost always part of the job description and responsibilities. Some principals work in evaluation systems that use a mix of student growth measures, classroom observations, surveys, and other factors that when combined, yield a teacher performance rating. Other principals work in schools that require only a single, annual observation. In either case, and for all of those in between, a challenge (which is also an opportunity) is how to link the results of the teacher evaluation to effective professional development, particularly in assessment literacy, so as to make a positive difference for teachers and students.

Chapter Learning Goals

1. Understand the implications of recent teacher evaluation reforms for the evaluation of classroom assessment knowledge and skill and how that may affect professional development in assessment literacy.

2. Become familiar with various measures used for teacher evaluation and their connection to assessment literacy.

3. Understand how the evaluation process can connect to and drive the district staff development program, and why.

4. Know how to unpack teacher evaluative criteria.

As a school leader, instructional coach, district leader, or classroom teacher, you are accustomed to evaluation, particularly the type that occurs every day. During the school day someone is bound to be forming an opinion, making a judgment about how you do your job. Other administrators, other teachers, students, parents, school board members, and community members are all likely to manifest human nature and join in when opportunity is provided. This life-in-a-fishbowl aspect of being an educator causes only a shrug for most, something benign that just comes with a job that has you working in front of people all day, every day.

The actual performance evaluation, however, may now come with something considerably more than a shrug. After decades of **teacher evaluation** procedures that held little rigor or value (Kraft & Gilmour, 2016) and resulted in almost all teachers being rated above average, the past 10 years have seen evaluation reforms in three major categories, aimed at adding rigor and growth measures to the evaluation process and improving teaching practice:

1. New evaluation tools, procedures, and other standards-aligned sources of evidence to be considered in the final effectiveness rating, in addition to classroom observations

2. The use of professional teaching standards as the basis for evaluation criteria

3. Requirement for continued professional growth based on the evaluation criteria and the individual teacher effectiveness rating

These all have links to assessment literacy. We will briefly examine each of them before turning to the assessment literacy connection.

1. Evaluation procedures and factors used to judge teacher effectiveness. Prompted by NCLB and Race to the Top, recent teacher evaluation reforms have focused on decreasing the reliance on the subjective judgment of the evaluator and increasing the importance placed on reliable sources of data. In other words, evidence of good instruction collected via classroom observation must be coupled with evidence that students have learned. Consistent with a characteristic we've noted as part of a balanced assessment system, states and districts sought to include multiple measures of teacher effectiveness in the belief that they are necessary to more completely understand a teacher's knowledge and skill, to accurately evaluate performance, and to provide feedback for improvement (Cantrell & Kane, 2013; Hull, 2013). For example, more frequent classroom observations and additional observers beyond the school principal are adopted to provide increased and more immediate, meaningful feedback to the teacher. **Observation rubrics**, which allow for a greater number of possible ratings beyond a 2-point scale of "meets expectations/does not meet expectations," are widely utilized to get a fuller picture of teacher performance, both of strengths and of weaknesses (Ross & Walsh, 2019).

And student growth data, as measured by standardized tests and other assessments, are now in use as part of teacher evaluation in many states, modeling the growth models used during the NCLB era to determine adequate yearly progress. Growth models are statistically complex and numerous (see Chapter 9), but all go beyond measuring status, reported as a single, point-in-time description of student achievement. Status measurements, like the annual state accountability assessment, are mainly used in improvement models, where changes in performance are reported in a variety of ways but the group of students assessed changes from year to year. A growth model requires data from student assessments over two or more points in time, and the group of students assessed remains constant, meaning all data come from the same group (Castellano & Ho, 2013).

Weighting systems that consider the appropriate mix of **student growth measures**, observation results, student and parent surveys, and other variables described later in this section vary from state to state, but all strive to create an individual teacher profile of effectiveness, one that can then inform professional development decisions and support. We'll look at other sources of evidence used in teacher evaluation, particularly in relation to assessment literacy, later in this chapter.

An additional implementation issue warrants a bit more context, namely that the teacher evaluation process is often intended to be both summative and formative. Teacher evaluation has long been expected to serve multiple purposes: improve the quality of instruction, provide information for personnel decisions, validate the teacher selection process, and provide a basis for professional growth plans (Bolton, 1973). These purposes all require reliable measures of teacher performance, largely missing in traditional evaluation systems. In some new evaluation systems it often remains difficult to reconcile the long-standing conflict that many teachers perceive when an observer is both evaluator and coach/mentor. While there is a strong belief that teacher accountability evidence can also be used to help determine the direction of professional development, especially in the case of novice teachers (Goe et al., 2012), this may be even more problematic now that the stakes are higher for teachers in states and districts where student growth measures are factored into the final effectiveness rating. Teachers have reported difficulty focusing on the suggested improvements requiring professional development because of excessive worry over the status of their employment (Will, 2016). This push-pull problem is similar to the one described in earlier chapters related to assessment purpose, and how the identification of purpose prior to designing or conducting any assessment is critical to properly maximize the use of the results. When an assessment is called on to serve double duty, whether it can fulfill both roles equally well is usually in question.

Some of the changes in teacher evaluation we describe support a more rigorous and differentiated accountability system (a summative purpose) and are also intended to be a catalyst for professional growth (a formative purpose). Both purposes are founded on the assumption that a positive impact on student achievement will result. So far the findings are mixed. Some studies have found that specific, frequent feedback as part of an evaluation system can in fact lead to improved teacher and student performance (Garet et al., 2017; Steinberg & Sartain, 2015). But Brian Rowan and Stephen Raudenbush (2016) report that the bulk of research evidence shows that the anticipated benefits of using criterion-based measures of teacher performance for "consequential" decisions such as tenure, dismissal, and compensation have not materialized as expected. However, they also believe that under the right conditions the use of such measures, particularly in classroom observation, can affect instructional practice, a belief supported in studies by Julie Marsh et al. (2017) and Brian Stecher et al. (2016). Those conditions include frequent observations and specific, narrative feedback that is consistent and contains advice for improvement. And current evidence is limited as to whether or not the combination of summative and formative purposes for teacher evaluation systems undermines the professional development benefits (Jackson & Cowan, 2018).

Teacher evaluation reforms continue to be implemented in varying degrees and at differing rates in at least 40 of the 50 states. In 2019, 34 states required some form of student growth measure as part of the teacher effectiveness rating, 41 states required a rating scale beyond two points, and 31 states included teacher and/or parent surveys. States and districts continue to work out the structure, effectiveness, and implementation issues associated with the changes, including the following:

who does your evaluations? (P + VP)

- Training school leaders as evaluators, specifically in the use of performance rubrics for classroom observations

- Integrating differentiated approaches to evaluation that consider novice teachers differently from veteran staff

- Determining the mix of factors to consider and the weight assigned to each for the final rating

- Making staffing and budget decisions related to a coaching and mentoring model to train classroom observers and provide professional learning support for classroom teachers

- Connecting evaluation results to specific professional development that will lead to improvement

Throughout this book we have stated our belief that quality data are necessary to make quality decisions about students. When the data are flawed, a lack of assessment literacy is usually the culprit. In the evaluation of teachers the decisions being made are about teachers, not students, but the assessment literacy message is the same: good decisions require accurate data, which can only come from quality assessments.

2. Professional teaching standards and teacher evaluation criteria. The second major shift in teacher evaluation systems has involved an effort to identify effective teaching practices supported in current research and develop criteria for teacher evaluation linked to those findings. This reform is also grounded in the belief that evaluation has the potential to improve teacher performance and thereby student learning. In the absence of a nationally accepted and implemented framework for professional teacher standards, organizations that focus on teacher preparation and development, subject-area organizations, professional associations, and various consortia have developed teacher effectiveness frameworks that apply to all subject areas and grade levels. States and districts have also developed their own, sometimes adapting and combining standards from more than one source and then translating the standards into evaluation tools. Three sources commonly drawn from are the following:

- The Interstate Teacher Assessment and Support Consortium (InTASC) is a group of state education agencies and national educational organizations focused on improving the preparation, licensing, and professional development of teachers. The *InTASC Model Core Teaching Standards* (InTASC, 2021) are voluntary and intended to be used by states to guide discussion and development of teacher preparation, licensure, evaluation, and professional development policies and practices.

- The National Board for Professional Teaching Standards (https://www.nbpts.org/) was established in 1987 for the purpose of advancing the quality of teaching and learning. It is the basis for a voluntary professional certification for teachers.

- The Framework for Teaching from the Danielson Group (https://danielsongroup .org) provides a common language for instructional practice, from preservice teacher preparation through teacher leadership and beyond. When used as a foundation for professional conversations among educators and administrators, The Framework can guide a school or district's mentoring, coaching, professional development, and teacher evaluation processes, providing a common language for all activities.

For both summative and formative evaluation purposes the benefits of using a set of standards for teaching effectiveness include the use of a common language and a unifying platform from which to develop a mutual understanding about what is important. Such standards provide the vision of what teachers should know and be able to do, as well as serving as a common basis for teacher selection, teacher evaluation, and teacher professional development. They are in effect the learning goals and success criteria, the targets of professional learning for all teachers.

3. Continued professional learning and growth. One vision for human resource management in school districts is a comprehensive, integrated system in which teacher selection, teacher evaluation, and teacher professional development are all legs on the same stool supporting instruction and student learning. When professional standards for teachers and aligned observational rubrics become the foundation for evaluation, accompanied by proper observer training, the quantity and quality of feedback teachers receive can improve, and that feedback can increase accuracy in identifying professional development needs. In addition, school leaders can tailor professional development for individual and group needs identified through the evaluation process, and teachers can use the results to set personal growth goals when formative growth support systems are in place to help achieve their goals.

For schools and districts this may mean a fundamental restructuring of what professional development is offered and how it is delivered, and this has direct implications for how we assist teachers in gaining assessment literacy. The shift toward professional learning driven by data provided by an evaluation system is dependent on the following (Minnici, 2018):

- Growth goals that are connected directly to the knowledge, skills, and behaviors defined in the professional teaching standards in use

- A professional learning system that treats all learners as individuals, allowing for different forms of delivery and individualized content

- Professional learning that takes place within the daily context of teaching

Before proceeding, it may be helpful to pause and briefly reflect on your current evaluation system relative to what has been described above. Not every reader will have an evaluation system connected to a specific set of professional standards. Your system may have a different vision as its foundation, or it may be rooted in evaluation criteria or checklists from a pre-NCLB era. To help process where you are, below are a few prompts. It would be helpful to have copies of your current evaluation tools on hand as you consider these questions:

- To what extent are your evaluation instruments based on a set of professional teaching standards? On which standards are they based? If you don't know, how might you find out?

- Are you readily familiar with the section(s) of your evaluation instrument relating to student assessment? What specific criteria come to mind as you think about that section?

- Do you provide observation feedback to teachers through a performance rubric? How many rating levels are there in the rubric? Is the language tightly aligned with the professional teaching standards?

- Does the rubric itself provide enough detail to point out specific strengths and areas for improvement?

- How would you describe the connection between teacher evaluation results and the formulation of professional learning (goals and activities) provided in your current system?

- To what extent is professional learning in your school or district
  - job embedded in delivery, such as coaching, mentoring, learning team based, and so on?
  - individualized and self-paced based on evaluation results?
  - teacher-involved or driven via professional growth goal setting?

Implications for the Evaluation of Teachers' Assessment Competence and Professional Development in Promoting Assessment Literacy

To reiterate, your school or district's evaluation system may or may not reflect each of the three reforms described above and listed in Figure 8.1. And in the transition from NCLB to ESSA, states are now more in control of system design, but many have chosen to pass that responsibility back to the district level, increasing the likelihood of continued system variability.

FIGURE 8.1   Three reforms in teacher evaluation

1. Evaluation procedures and factors used to judge teacher effectiveness
2. Professional teaching standards and teacher evaluation criteria
3. Continued professional learning and growth

Variability notwithstanding, assessment literacy is a fundamental requirement for school leaders to carry out many of the functions across the three areas of evaluation reform we've described. Again, we will consider each of the three areas in turn, examining each from an assessment literacy perspective, considering what's needed, potential pitfalls, and what role the school leader can play.

1. Evaluation Procedures and Factors Considered

Here we will examine a sampling of sources sometimes used in evaluating teacher effectiveness through the lens of assessment literacy.

Lesson Plan Review

Do lesson plans indicate what will be assessed, when, how, and by whom? Does the plan specify or imply how results will be used? Any lesson plan should include multiple points at which the teacher checks for understanding—a formative assessment event. So the lesson plan may include preplanned questions or activities used for that purpose. It may also indicate points at which students receive and act on feedback or self-assess relative to clearly stated learning goals and success criteria. If the lesson spans several days, it may include multiple checks for understanding, opportunities for student involvement, as well as a summative assessment event. Reviewing lesson plans with teachers and discussing which of these elements are present can provide an accurate picture of their understanding of formative assessment practices.

Teacher Self-Assessment

Do teachers understand the elements of self-assessment well enough to offer an accurate analysis of their relative strengths and areas for further work on the criteria contained in the teacher observation rubric? Is the school culture supportive of teachers' identifying what they need to work on without being judged or marked down? Do they view self-assessment as an opportunity to identify their own professional learning needs? By discussing a self-assessment with a teacher, school leaders can assist them in setting professional learning goals and in action planning, as needed. They can also identify teachers' needs with respect to understanding self-assessment and implementing it effectively.

Student Artifacts

If student artifacts are to be considered in teacher evaluation, are the criteria for selection clear? What can be claimed on their basis? These discussions provide an opportunity for school leaders to explore their understanding of what constitutes evidence of student learning, a fundamental aspect of assessment literacy. It can also provide evidence of teacher learning—for example, looking at artifacts as evidence that the teacher is learning to ask more open-ended questions.

Student and Parent Surveys

[handwritten: how do you feel about parent surveys? wording in these is so important]

If student or parent surveys are used as evidence of teacher effectiveness, do we have confidence that the results are free from bias and distortion? Surveys have been shown to provide useful feedback to teachers regarding their classroom practice (Cantrell & Kane, 2013). But like any other form of assessment, they can be either more or less effective in terms of yielding actionable results. What opinions and information have been asked for? Have the questions been designed to elicit an accurate reflection of the respondent's knowledge or opinions? When eliciting information about the teacher's assessment practices, survey items should relate specifically to the classroom assessment experience of students. Information from parents and students about topics such as the use and frequency of formative assessment practices, student involvement opportunities, grading procedures, and communication practices can provide data for instructional conversations between teachers and school leaders as well as for self-assessment, goal setting, and action planning.

Standardized Test Results

Measuring student growth in new evaluation systems has proven to be a difficult implementation challenge (American Institutes for Research, 2019). See Chapter 9 for a fuller discussion of the nature of growth measures. For our purposes here, note that it is important not only to understand the growth model in use but also to consider whether the standardized test being used is an indicator of valued learning goals in your building/district.

Teacher Portfolios

A portfolio in itself is not an assessment. Rather, it is a collection of artifacts intentionally selected to tell a story. In the case of teacher portfolios the "story" is generally one of competence in one or more domains of teaching and assessment; the artifacts taken as a whole can be used as evidence to make a judgment on level of competence. In reviewing portfolios with teachers, school leaders can guide the discussion with the following questions: What story are your portfolio artifacts intended to tell? What competence does each illustrate? How does it show that competence? How do your artifacts as a whole demonstrate your level of competence? All of these questions serve as a catalyst for personal reflection, with the purpose of helping teachers better demonstrate their knowledge and skill through a portfolio.

Classroom Observations

The traditional direct classroom observation, accompanied with pre- and postconferences, remains the most common element of the great majority of evaluation systems. Classroom observations can accomplish multiple objectives, including the following:

- Helping teachers reflect on what students are learning in the classroom rather than exclusively documenting what the teacher is doing

- Contributing information to inform next steps in learning for the teacher

- Allowing for evidence collection about the learning environment in the classroom, interactions between teacher and students, and much more

When the postobservation conference is conducted without professional dialogue and feedback, it serves an accountability purpose only and contributes minimally to teaching and learning. When dialogue and feedback are included, the evaluation process as a whole can have a lasting, positive effect on teacher practice, and this before any professional development suggestions have been acted up (Goe et al., 2012). Some studies also show that the number of observers or feedback providers may also be related to how positively teachers view the evaluation process. And observation feedback from colleagues is valued and perceived more positively by teachers than observations made only by a building administrator (Tuma et al., 2018).

Although much that is important can be evaluated through observation, some things, such as the quality of assessments the teacher uses, must be evaluated another way. In this case examining a sample of the teacher's assessments would be informative.

Observation Rubrics

The use of observation rubrics for teacher evaluation is an example of assessment-literate thinking. Both teachers and principals have reported that the use of rubrics as an observation tool is viewed positively (Kraft, 2018).

Assessment-literate teachers know how to use a rubric as a teaching tool and understand that it is the basis for feedback and student self-assessment. They understand that without clear descriptions of learning targets relative to the intended learning goals, a rubric can be misleading. Furthermore, they are likely to continually revise rubrics after use to improve their alignment with the targets and for clear delineation among the points on the scale. Observation rubrics for teacher evaluation function in the same way. In the table below is a 4-point rubric used to evaluate classroom teachers' skill in helping students self-assess. Note how the instructional sophistication and the involvement of students increase as you read from left to right across the scale.

TABLE 8.1   Assessment for student learning: student self-assessment

UNSATISFACTORY	BASIC	PROFICIENT	DISTINGUISHED
Teacher does not provide an opportunity for students to assess their own learning in relation to the success criteria for the learning target(s).	Teacher provides an opportunity for students to assess their own learning in relation to the success criteria for the learning target(s) in ways that may not deepen student understanding of progress toward the target(s).	Teacher provides an opportunity for students to assess their own learning in relation to the success criteria for the learning target(s) in ways that deepen student understanding of progress toward the target.	Teacher provides an opportunity for students to assess their own learning in relation to the success criteria for the learning target(s) in ways that deepen student understanding of progress toward the target(s). Students use the success criteria for improvement.

Source: 5D+™ Rubric for Instructional Growth and Teacher Evaluation Center for Educational Leadership, University of Washington.

The changes or progression in this rubric defines a continuum from no opportunity for students to self-assess at the *basic* level, moving through to the *distinguished* level, where students do have the opportunity to self-assess. Doing so deepens their understanding of the learning target, and students can then use the success criteria to determine next steps in learning.

One or more of these factors described above may be included in your evaluation system. Although established instruments, protocols, and training from the state or district are essential and most likely probable, both school leaders and teachers must possess the knowledge and skill embedded in assessment literacy to carry them out effectively.

2. Professional Teaching Standards and Teacher Evaluation Criteria

A primary key to success for all learners, as we've described in Chapters 2 and 3, is the clarity of the learning goals they are expected to master. Students can hit any target that they can see and that holds still for them; this is, of course, true also for teachers. What teachers are expected to know and do in the classroom is defined by professional teaching standards, which when translated into evaluative criteria must be unambiguous and precise (see, e.g., Figure 8.1). For the school leader to evaluate the classroom assessment competence of teachers, four conditions need to be in place:

1. The evaluative criteria relating to classroom assessment practices must be clear and at a level of specificity that allows both teacher and the principal to have a similar understanding of what constitutes quality.

2. The criteria as a set must describe all of the important characteristics of high-quality classroom assessment practices.

3. The principal and other classroom observers must have sufficient assessment literacy to be able to recognize good assessment practice or the lack of it and to provide the feedback needed for validation and/or improvement.

4. Teachers must have the opportunity to learn the principles of sound assessment before they are evaluated on them. Some districts have differentiated evaluation plans in place for teachers at varying levels of instructional knowledge and skill; assessment literacy could also be treated that way in that there may be different expectations for novice teachers. What if teachers are hired into, transferred into, or simply caught in the middle of a new evaluation system but have never had the opportunity to learn the principles of sound assessment? A lack of assessment literacy for any teacher is rarely if ever initially a fault of their own.

All four of these conditions are important. Principals and teachers often have the least control over the first two conditions, although they directly influence the degree to which teacher assessment skills and knowledge are evaluated. Decisions at the state or district level about what and how much classroom assessment knowledge and skills to include in teacher evaluation criteria vary considerably. For example, an evaluation instrument that uses InTASC standards is likely to have criteria drawn from InTASC Standard #6 on student assessment, which states,

> The teacher understands and uses multiple measures of assessment to engage learners in their own growth, to monitor learner progress and to guide the teacher's and learner's decision making.

This standard unfolds into four pages of specific detail in three categories: teacher performances, essential knowledge, and critical dispositions. These are followed by the standard deconstructed into three learner progressions, which include professional learning examples. Inclusion of this entire set would constitute a program of study in assessment literacy for both a professional growth program and teacher evaluation standards. However, with so much other content required for teacher evaluation frameworks, the student assessment requirements generally are abridged, sometimes considerably, resulting in a set of criteria that may not be comprehensive. If this is the case in your school system, it means that significant portions pertaining to assessment literacy have been left out of the description of teacher effectiveness, so the evaluative criteria should be reconsidered.

Finally, if the assessment literacy elements in the teacher evaluation framework are not congruent with the assessment literacy elements in the principal evaluation framework, the disconnect will be apparent. Principal criteria related to assessment can have statements such as the following:

- The principal helps staff in analyzing data and in using data to improve instruction and make appropriate decisions about students.

- The principal monitors the assessment instruments and tools used in classrooms and assists staff in improving their quality.

- The principal assists staff in implementing effective formative assessment practices in the classroom.

Each of these expectations can be deconstructed into what actions the school leader might take when working with teachers to fulfill the requirement (see Activity 8.1 for other criteria and practices in this process). But if there are no corresponding criteria on the teacher evaluation document or observation rubric (e.g., using effective formative assessment practices), it would be analogous to assessing students on content that hasn't been introduced, let alone taught. This example of congruency between two evaluation instruments reminds us of what makes a system a system.

It is no longer a question of whether or not the principal will evaluate the assessment competence of teachers. The question now is one of degree: what and how much should be included. The answer determines to what extent assessment literacy is supported by the evaluation systems and, through that, by the professional development program in the district.

3. Continued Professional Learning and Growth

Some teachers report that they welcome the evaluation process if the focus is on improvement, instead of what is perceived by some as a "gotcha" game of finding fault. Teachers also report a favorable reaction to administrator walk-throughs, especially when the feedback is both immediate and formative (Goe et al., 2017). The downside is there is evidence that points to a lack of sufficient training for principals in supporting teachers instructionally (Curtis, 2012; Donaldson et al., 2014; Leithwood & Louis, 2012). It's one thing for all teachers to be held to the same set of professional standards but another if observers are not uniformly trained, thereby increasing the variability from one observer to another when viewing the same lesson.

Professional development has long been driven largely by district and school priorities. With the implementation of teacher evaluation reforms, school and district interests must be balanced with the professional development needs of individual teachers. Integrating the two would contribute to aligning individual needs with school/district interests; this connection can be created when teachers set goals based on the evaluation results or the evaluation criteria. Some districts use digital tools that can suggest professional development options based on teacher evaluation results, as well as ideas for individual goal setting.

As noted earlier in this chapter, the structure of a postobservation conference between teacher and observer allows for a dialogue that can focus on improvement in practice and the learning required to achieve it. Focus the reflection on adapting or revising current practices to positively affect student learning. The discussion can include sharing successes, formulating a goal, developing a plan for learning, identifying resources, and establishing a plan for implementing and measuring the new learning. In fact, in some postobservation conferences the principal may learn more than the teacher, for example, after having observed an effective assessment strategy the principal has never seen before.

Classroom walk-throughs also create the opportunity for reflection and dialogue about instruction and assessment, and goal setting for future learning. Again, models of walk-throughs vary. As with formal observations, observers can be personnel other than a school administrator; procedures can be informal or structured, are usually brief, and most often have standardized observer forms or an observer set of "look-fors" that are established in advance (Kachur et al., 2013). Some models provide for peer observation followed by reflection on practice, and others place as much emphasis on observing what the students are doing as what the teacher is doing. Imagine how beneficial this might be in a situation where the observer is "looking for" evidence of a formative assessment strategy such as one of those described in Chapter 4. The trained observer can see and hear exactly what students are doing and saying, can observe what and how well students are learning as a result, and can provide feedback to the teacher to help determine next steps in instruction and/or next steps in self-directed inquiry. In a University of Washington study, Honig et al. (2010) found that effective principals were likely to be very visible throughout the school and focused on making formative observations about learning and providing direct and timely feedback to teachers. In addition, in another study (Tuma et al., 2018), the frequency of both classroom observations and feedback was positively associated with teachers' perceptions that their evaluation system improved their practice.

Administrator and Observer Training: Assessment Literacy

One of the keys to linking evaluation and professional development is the ability of the observer(s) to interpret the results from all the sources of evidence in an evaluation and connect professional development suggestions to those results (Goe et al., 2012). In this process, the school leader gains detailed knowledge about the professional development needs of each individual teacher, something research has shown to be a specific and instructionally helpful leadership practice (Leithwood & Louis, 2012).

Below are a few hypothetical examples of evaluation observations. Each scenario illustrates one or more problems that can be solved by increasing the teacher's assessment literacy. The observer's first task is to analyze the problem to determine whether to recommend that the teacher stop a practice and replace it with something else, modify an existing practice, or add a new practice. The observer then prepares for a professional dialogue that might include determining where coaching might be desirable or offering professional development suggestions based directly on the results.

1. During a review session prior to a test, students in a fifth-grade science class seem confused about what learning will be assessed on the test and appear to be unfamiliar with some of the content being reviewed.

2. A seventh-grade language arts teacher's grading practices include providing zeros to students who did not turn in their homework, with no later opportunity provided for the students to satisfy the requirement.

3. A high school social studies teacher's assessments are all bubble sheets, and there is little evidence of any writing practice or assessment. This teacher also limits the number of A grades that can be earned in the class.

4. Students in an algebra class are completing an assignment. Some have stopped working before they are finished. The teacher is at the teacher's desk catching up on paperwork.

It is important to remember that the information from this evaluation is intended to serve multiple purposes: the summative purpose of determining overall level of competence and the formative purpose of fostering improved practice. Therefore, we suggest that the evaluator consider a few things.

First, observers might want to access or make an inventory of the available expertise, support personnel, resources, and professional development offerings in classroom assessment. External options for support could also be included. It is also possible that the observation shows that the teacher can be a resource for others.

Second, it may be necessary to guide or direct the teacher toward different or modified practices. From a teacher's perspective, if the issue is not one they have also identified for improvement, the evaluator will need to spark discussion on what the problem is and then be prepared to lead a discussion of what change is needed, why it is needed, what new practice, replacement strategy, or modification is recommended, and what resources are available to help the teacher make the change.

Third, it is a good idea to look for related building or district policy language that could contribute to the discussion of the changes needed.

Let's walk through how an observer might prepare for a conference after observing the fifth-grade science class in the first scenario, with the assumption that the district or school has a protocol for postobservation conferences that includes encouraging the teacher to reflect on the observation results.

What Is the "Assessment Literacy" Problem?

At first glance we might think that the teacher has not made the learning targets clear to the students. Before we draw that conclusion, it is a good idea to make a list of all potential problems. Here are some examples:

- Do the students have a list of learning targets for the unit of study the test will cover?

- Is the review linked to the learning targets on the list?

- Have the students had sufficient opportunity to learn and practice with all the learning targets to be assessed on the test?

- Are all items on the test directly linked to the list of learning targets?

What Change Is Needed, and Why? What New Practice, Replacement Strategy, or Modification Is Recommended?

After a discussion with the teacher to identify the problem(s) (since the answers to some of these questions will not have been apparent during the observation session itself), the observer and the teacher can then discuss what change(s) might be needed and what anticipated benefit would accrue if implemented. For example, if the problem is that students have not been aware of the learning targets for each of the unit's activities and assignments, the teacher may decide to prepare such a list for future units. Or perhaps the teacher posts targets for each lesson, but they're erased each day. The change may be to have students write the target on the assignment or tracking sheet. The observer could explain to the teacher why it is important that students understand the intended learning that underlies their work.

If the problem is that the teacher did not have enough time to teach everything that is to be on the test, an immediate change is required, either to extend the learning time or to modify the test. Why? It is not ethical to hold students accountable for mastering content they have not had sufficient opportunity to learn. Sometimes teachers need to hear that this is an option they can decide to use.

If the problem is that the content of the test does not align directly with the lessons taught during the unit, the change could be to help the teacher prepare an assessment blueprint for each test at the beginning of each unit. One reason for the change is ethics: we can't hold students accountable for content they did not have opportunity to learn. Another relates to accuracy: the resulting grade will not be an accurate representation of mastery of what was taught.

What Resources Are Available?

Resources will vary depending on the problem identified and the mutually agreed-on improvement goals. For example, in the first problem—the lack of published learning targets—the teacher may not be clear about the difference between an activity and a learning target. In this case, a discussion with colleagues who are adept at creating and sharing learning targets can function as the resource. If the problem is one of running out of time to teach before the planned test, there could be a discussion with colleagues about pacing expectations. Is there an expectation that a teacher be at a certain point in the curriculum on a certain date? Is that realistic? Will all students have sufficient opportunity to learn prior to the test? If not, the change needed may not be in the classroom but at the policy level. And if the problem is one of content validity—the test not matching what was taught—the teacher may need to learn how to prepare an assessment blueprint. So an activity such as Activity 3.3 in Chapter 3 would be an appropriate resource, especially when done with colleagues and/or an instructional coach.

Assessment-literate school leaders can themselves be a resource in coaching and mentoring teachers in their assessment practice. Some modifications in assessment practice need sustained study; others can be quickly taught and demonstrated, then practiced, and the process of discussion and reflection continues. Clearly the relationship established between evaluator and teacher is critical to this being effective. When appropriate conditions are in place, professional learning is on site, job embedded, and needs driven.

For further practice in preparing assessment literacy conversations for postobservation conferences, see Activity 8.3: Practice Linking Evaluation Results to Professional Development Recommendations at the end of this chapter.

Summary

Teacher evaluation and professional development are both changing, and whether those changes will be successful is to some extent dependent on how the two functions work together to support teacher effectiveness and student learning. There is some evidence that can happen: one large study reported that 76% of the teachers who participated reported that they made improvements to their teaching practices as a result of their evaluation system (Tuma et al., 2018). Teacher evaluation and professional development are integral components in a coherent system that also includes curriculum, instruction, and assessment. Well-designed and effectively delivered professional development supports teachers in their performance and responsibilities in the system. And when linked to individual teacher needs and interests relative to the professional teaching standards defined in evaluation criteria, professional development fulfills the purpose for which it is intended: improving teaching and learning (Darling-Hammond et al., 2017).

Success Indicators for Assessment Literacy Goal #8

The school leader

- can explain the standards of sound classroom assessment practice (Chapters 2–5) on which evaluations of teacher performance can/should be based;

- considers interview questions that relate to the classroom assessment literacy of candidates for teaching positions (see Activity 8.3);

- creates ways to observe, analyze, evaluate, and provide feedback on classroom assessment processes and instruments; and

- facilitates the conditions for effective adult learning in schools and secures professional development characterized by a long-term *process* that teaches new ideas and strategies through interaction with appropriate materials, hands-on practice, coaching, and collaboration.

 ## Study Guide Questions

1. To what extent would you say classroom assessment competence is currently addressed in your district's teacher evaluation system?

2. In your own words, describe what you see as the connection between teacher evaluation and teacher professional development currently in place in your school or district.

3. Do you think that student growth measures should be included in teacher evaluation? Why or why not? What are some conditions you would want to be in place if they are to be used?

4. Classroom walk-throughs have become a popular practice for school leaders. What conditions do you think are necessary for their success? What might be some strengths and limitations of this practice?

5. What do you think "job-embedded professional development" really means? What would be some of its characteristics?

 ## Personal Portfolio Entry Suggestions

- School or district professional development plan focused on student assessment, showing content and delivery methods

- Sample evaluative and/or formative feedback to teachers regarding student assessment (anonymous)

- Template/protocol for teacher pre- and postobservation conferences

- Personal-learning log

- Calendar/log of observations, evaluations, conferences, walk-throughs, and so on

- Sample of notes taken during observations (anonymous)

- School and/or individual collaborative goal-setting protocols

- Rubrics to evaluate classroom assessment practices developed or revised collaboratively with teachers

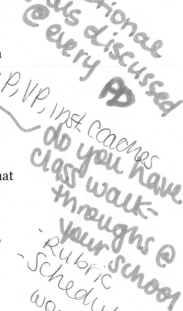
instructional goals discussed @ every PD

super, P, VP, inst coaches do you have class walk-throughs @ your school
- Rubric
- scheduled + would pick teachers

- we have the Rubrics

Activity 8.1

Practicing With Teacher and Principal Evaluative Criteria in Assessment

Learning Target for the Activity

- Understand the benefits of unpacking teacher and principal evaluative criteria.

Purpose

This activity has participants work with selected criteria from teacher and principal evaluation instruments. By "unpacking" individual criteria, participants will gain a deeper understanding of what is needed to either accurately observe or fully demonstrate a particular evaluation indicator.

Time

60–90 minutes

Materials Needed

- Flip charts, sticky notes

- Teacher or principal evaluation criteria for part 2 of the activity

Suggested Room Setup

Tables and chairs for groups of four to six participants per group

Directions

This activity has two parts. In part 1 you will follow a protocol using sample criteria to practice unpacking them. In part 2 you will follow the same protocol with your own evaluation criteria.

Part 1: Practice With the Sample Set

Working in a small group, begin by selecting one criterion from either the School Leader Criteria or the Teacher Criteria. You may have each small group work with the same criterion, let each group choose their criterion, or assign a criterion to each group.

School Leader Criteria

- The principal helps staff to use data to modify and improve classroom instruction.

- The principal assists staff in aligning classroom curriculum to district and state learning goals.

- The principal incorporates assessment knowledge into evaluation practices.

- The principal helps staff implement formative assessment practices.

- The principal assists teachers in helping students become involved partners in their own assessment.

Teacher Criteria

- The teacher uses sound grading and reporting practices.

- The teacher helps clarify learning goals for students, including the use of student-friendly language.

- The teacher shows knowledge and evidence of when and why to use different methods of assessment.

- The teacher provides students opportunities to assess their own learning in relation to the success criteria.

- The teacher has a system for keeping records of formative assessment results.

    1. Unpack the criterion with your small group by discussing answers to the following questions. Note your answers on chart paper.

       For the school leader set:

       a. What does the principal (or observer) need to know about assessment in order to satisfy this criterion?

       b. What evidence would you look for to show that the school leader is fulfilling the criterion successfully?

       For the teacher set:

       a. What would the teacher need to know and do in order to satisfy this criterion?

       b. What evidence would you look for to show that the teacher is fulfilling this criterion successfully?

       c. What specific strategies and resources might you use to help the teacher progress toward fulfilling the criterion?

    2. Have small groups share their answers with the large group. Some possible discussion activities:

       - Discuss similarities and differences if two or more groups have unpacked the same criterion.

       - Ask the groups to add their thoughts to other groups' charts.

       - Discuss what was easy and what was difficult about the activity.

    3. (Optional) Select another criterion, and follow steps 2 and 3.

Closure

Ask participants to discuss the following questions:

- What have you learned as a result of engaging in this activity?

- What new thoughts do you have?

- What questions have come to mind?

(Continued)

(Continued)

Part 2: Unpack Your Own Evaluative Criteria

1. Select one criterion related to assessment from your local principal or teacher evaluation document. Consider choosing one that has been difficult for the evaluator or the teacher to understand.

2. Unpack the criterion with a partner or a small group using the protocol in step 2 of part 1.

3. Have partners or small groups share their answers with the large group. Some possible discussion activities:

    - Discuss similarities and differences if two or more groups have unpacked the same criterion.

    - Ask the groups to add their thoughts to other groups' charts.

    - Discuss what was easy and what was difficult about the activity.

4. (Optional) Select another criterion, and follow steps 2 and 3.

Closure

Ask participants to discuss the following questions:

- What have you learned as a result of engaging in this activity?

- Did you uncover any lack of clarity in the criterion? If so, how might it be revised to communicate more clearly the desired competence?

- What actions does this activity prompt you to take?

Activity 8.2

Personal Reflection on Classroom Assessment, Teacher Evaluation, and Professional Development

Learning Target for the Activity

- Know how to unpack evaluative criteria.

Purpose

This activity can be done individually and/or used as discussion prompts in small groups. The purpose is to understand your own experience with the big ideas in this chapter.

Time

45 minutes

Materials Needed

- None

Suggested Room Setup

Small groups of four to six participants

Directions

Each of the prompts below can be processed:

1. Take a few minutes and consider each prompt individually, making notes of your thoughts as you proceed.

2. When you have finished, have each participant at the table share their thoughts.

3. When this is completed, consider and discuss the following:

   a. What commonalities are there?

   b. What stands out as noteworthy?

   c. Did any conflicts or contradictions emerge?

4. What professional development have you participated in that has truly affected your classroom practice? Other than the delivery of important and useful content, what qualities made the learning experience memorable?

5. After reading this book through Chapter 8, what goals will you set to enhance your personal learning in assessment literacy?

6. What examples have you tried where professional development was on site and embedded? How have they worked? What were the successes and difficulties?

7. If you could add any classroom assessment criteria to the evaluation form for teachers you currently use, what would they be? Why? Are there any criteria you would delete? Why?

8. If possible, describe an experience where you suggested a change in assessment literacy practice as part of a postobservation conference and the end result of that suggestion.

Closure

Processing book content can come in more ways and with more prompts than the ones listed above. If participants are curious about how others reacted to other ideas or topics in the chapter, develop you own prompts and extend the activity.

Activity 8.3
Practicing Linking Evaluation Results to Professional Development Recommendations

Learning Target for the Activity

- Understand how the evaluation process can inform the district staff development program, and why.

Purpose

This activity helps participants identify assessment literacy problems in classroom observation scenarios and prepare for postobservation conferences aimed at solving those problems.

Time

One hour

Materials Needed

- White/smart boards or flip charts and easels for capturing discussion points

Suggested Room Setup

Tables and chairs set up for ease of discussion among participants

Directions

Complete each step in the order below:

1. Select one of the classroom observation scenarios described in the section "Administrator and Observer Training: Assessment Literacy" in this chapter. If working as partners or in small groups, you can assign each group a different scenario, assign the same scenario, or let each group select which one to work with.

2. Make a list of the problems within the scenario you believe are related to assessment literacy issues. Write each problem on a separate piece of chart paper.

3. For each problem identify what assessment-related practice needs to be changed, and provide a rationale for the change. Then identify what new strategy, replacement strategy, or modification you would recommend. Transfer this to the chart paper for the problem.

4. Make a list of resources available to guide professional development for the teacher in each scenario. Also, make a list of desired resources, if any, that are not available. Put these lists on the chart paper for the problem.

5. Have the partners/small groups share their work with the large group. Some possible discussion activities:

   - Discuss similarities and differences if two or more groups have worked with the same scenario.

- Ask the groups to add their thoughts to other groups' charts. Also, ask them if they can identify other assessment-related problems within the scenario.

- Discuss what was easy and what was difficult about the activity.

6. (Optional) Have each person write a short summary of an observation they have conducted that illustrated an assessment-related problem. Then, working with a partner or a small group, have them select one summary to work with. Follow the protocol in steps 2 and 3 to analyze it and make potential recommendations for professional development. You can provide the form in Figure 8.2 to record their thoughts.

FIGURE 8.2   Form for linking observation results to professional development recommendations

Summary of the evidence from a classroom observation:

What is the "assessment literacy" problem?

What change might you discuss with the teacher, and why? What new practice, replacement strategy, or modification might you be prepared to recommend?

What resources are available?

Closure

Participants discuss the following questions:

- What have you learned as a result of engaging in this activity?

- Did you uncover any lack of resources needed to address your own or teachers' assessment literacy needs? If so, what recommendations might you make for professional development offerings or materials in your school or district?

- What actions does this activity prompt you to take?

Activity 8.4
Verifying Teachers' Content Knowledge and Assessment Competence

Teaching applicants must answer many questions, both in writing and at interviews. When building principals interview potential new hires, they often ask questions related to classroom management, instructional skill, and student discipline. Questions related to the candidate's mastery of content knowledge and the development and use of quality assessments necessary for the specific teaching assignment are sometimes overlooked. By adding in questions related to student assessment, we can identify candidates who are well prepared to carry out the assessment-related aspects of teaching.

(Continued)

(Continued)

Learning Target for the Activity

- Formulate questions for interviewing applicants for teaching positions that produce evidence of their level of assessment literacy.

Purpose

This activity asks participants to consider the teacher applicant interview:

1. What questions could be asked in an interview with prospective teachers that would help school leaders evaluate their academic preparation to teach the assigned subject(s)?

2. What questions can school leaders ask or what evidence they should seek to determine a candidate's level of assessment literacy?

Time

60–90 minutes

Materials Needed

- Interview forms and teacher evaluation forms currently in use in your district

- Your district's comprehensive assessment plan, if available

Suggested Room Setup

Tables and chairs set up for ease of discussion among participants

White/smart boards or flip charts and easels for capturing discussion points

Directions

Think about and discuss the following questions, keeping track of answers on a white board:

1. What should you reasonably expect the interview component of the overall hiring process to produce in terms of useful information about the candidate's subject matter knowledge?

2. Given that, what interview questions could you design that would help inform you about the applicant's subject matter knowledge? What is the range of acceptable answers to those questions?

3. What should you reasonably expect the interview component to produce in terms of useful information about the candidate's level of assessment literacy?

4. What interview questions could you design that would inform you about the applicant's assessment knowledge and skill? What answers would you consider acceptable for that set of questions?

5. What staff development and support do you provide for teachers who are not masters of the standards or accomplished assessors of the standards? Are they adequate? What improvements need to be made?

Closure

Whatever questions you might ask about subject matter knowledge and assessment competence, consider the following points:

- Is there a link between what questions are asked in an employment interview and teacher evaluation criteria? If not, should there be? Why or why not?

- Is there a link between those same questions, which in part act as expectations of teacher skills and knowledge, and the staff development program of your school or district? If not, should there be? What might be missing?

Definitions

Classroom walk-through: Brief, infrequent, and informal focused classroom visits by observers aimed at gathering data on classroom practices to assist in instructional improvement.

Observation rubric: A scoring tool that represents the performance expectations for classroom teachers.

Student growth measure: In teacher evaluation an analysis of student assessment data over two or more points in time.

Teacher evaluation: The process of rating the performance and effectiveness of classroom teachers.

 This chapter's online resources are available for download from **resources.corwin.com/10GoalsLeaders**

Analysis of Student Assessment Information

9

///

Assessment Literacy Goal #9: *The leader analyzes student assessment information accurately, uses that information to improve curriculum and instruction, and assists teachers in doing the same.*

Analyzing and using data for informed decision-making is widely acclaimed as a strategy for improving teaching and learning. It is baked into national initiatives like the Every Student Succeeds Act and is part of the professional responsibility of school leaders locally. Therefore, facility with analyzing and using data is a key part of assessment literacy for school leaders.

Chapter Learning Goals

1. Understand basic concepts in quantitative data analysis.

2. Understand a process for problem solving based on data.

3. Lead and support teachers in understanding and problem solving with data.

The phrase "data-based decision-making" seems to imply a simple one-two process—get data, make a decision—when in fact the reality is much more nuanced, relational, and sometimes even "micropolitical" (Leithwood & Louis, 2012, p. 160). In any interpretive and decision-making process, there are multiple stakeholders with different preferences, so educational decision-making is never just about crunching numbers. With Kenneth Leithwood and Karen Louis (2012), we take the position that "problem-solving" is a better descriptor for the process an assessment-literate school leader might lead than "decision-making." It implies a longer process of collaborating with colleagues to identify and describe teaching and learning needs, brainstorming and prioritizing potential solutions or improvements, trying out likely improvements, and monitoring their effectiveness.

Assessment literacy goal #9 has two parts: (1) the ability to analyze data, both large scale and classroom level, and (2) the ability to reason from data as part of informed decision-making about next steps in teaching and learning. These two general "literacies" imply several others as well. For example, identifying what data you want to analyze is key to raising and answering meaningful questions with data. This chapter is organized into two main sections. First, we review some basic concepts in data analysis. Second, we describe methods of using data for identifying and addressing educational problems.

Data Analysis Basics

Our purpose in this section is to go over some concepts that are basic to the kind of data analysis commonly used with measures of student achievement. We will emphasize conceptual and quantitative reasoning in our treatment of data analysis. School leaders do not need to be statisticians. They, however, *do* need to be assessment-literate conceptual and quantitative reasoners. Topics addressed in this section include referencing frameworks, **aggregation** and **disaggregation**, **unit of analysis**, **growth measures**, and attention to **error** and the compounding of error. These topics apply to both large-scale and classroom-level data, and we make some additional comments about more qualitative data analysis that can be applied to classroom-level data as well.

Referencing Framework

A raw score by itself doesn't mean much. What would you think if we told you that you got a raw score of 18 (i.e., you got 18 correct) on a test of adding mixed numbers? Hard to tell, right? For that raw score of 18 to have meaning, it has to have a referencing framework. Scores that are referenced against defined requirements are called **criterion referenced**. Scores that are referenced against the performance of others are called **norm referenced**. Scores that are referenced against state achievement standards through a standard-setting process (typically by setting cut scores for proficiency levels) are called **standards referenced**.

Thinking again about that 18 on your mixed-numbers test, suppose you knew that there were 20 questions on the test and your score of 18 meant you got 90% of them correct. To interpret that, you'd need some description of the domain from which the 20 questions were sampled. If the domain was addition problems with two addends, both of which were mixed numbers with denominators less than 10, you could claim that your score meant that you could do 90% of the problems in that domain. That kind of interpretation, using a score to describe what you can do, is criterion referenced.

Or suppose you knew that your score of 18 meant that your percentile rank was 95, that is, 95% of the others who took the test scored lower than you did. Percentile ranks are norm referenced. Wow, you might think, nicely done! But not so fast. To interpret norm-referenced scores, you need to know something about the norm group, the others who took the test. You would interpret your 95th percentile differently if the norm group was composed of fourth graders than you would if the norm group was composed of college freshmen. In fact, one of the things you should check when interpreting norm-referenced scores from large-scale test results for students in your building/district is the composition of the norm group, including how many students there were and how they were sampled. Don't assume that the norm group is representative of an appropriate population against which to compare your students' scores. For example, if your school population includes many students from an underrepresented group, check what percentage of the norm group included students with a similar background.

Or suppose you knew that a score range of 18–20 meant that students had mastered the learning standard, 14–17 meant that students were nearing the learning standard, and 13 and below meant that students had not yet met the standard. This standards referencing is often considered a kind of criterion referencing, assuming that those levels have been set thoughtfully. In fact, many standards-setting procedures also use normative data (e.g., sharing with standard-setting panelists during their deliberations information about the percentage of students who would be designated "masters" given the cut scores they were considering), so the standards referencing used in many large-scale accountability tests is a kind of hybrid referencing framework.

We hope this little thought experiment about the mixed-numbers test has helped you understand that to interpret the scores that result from measures of achievement, you need to know what referencing framework is being used. Figure 9.1 names some common kinds of criterion-referenced, norm-referenced, and standards-referenced scores.

FIGURE 9.1   Some common types of scores and their definitions

Criterion-Referenced Scores

Percentage: A number telling the percentage of maximum points earned by a student; percentages can be interpreted as criterion referenced if the assessment represents a well-defined domain of learning.

Quality level: A rating of the quality of a student's performance, typically using a rubric, rating scale, or checklist.

Speed: The time a student takes to complete a task or the number of tasks completed in a fixed time (e.g., reading 50 words per minute).

Precision: The degree of accuracy with which a student completes a task (e.g., measuring accurately to the nearest quarter inch).

Norm-Referenced Scores

Percentile rank: A score that tells the percentage of the norm group scoring lower than a particular raw score.

Stanine: A score that tells the location of a student's raw score in a normal **distribution** that has been divided into nine parts.

Standard scores: Norm-referenced scores that are transformed from the raw score by changing the mean, the standard deviation, and sometimes the shape of the distribution, to make them more easily interpretable. There are many different kinds of standard scores, depending on how the transformation is done.

Standards-Referenced Scores

Proficiency level: A designation that tells where in a series of defined levels, typically set using cut points in a score distribution, a student falls (e.g., Standard Exceeded, Standard Met, Standard Nearly Met, Standard Not Met, as is reported in the state of California); sometimes called achievement-level descriptors or by other terms.

The referencing framework helps you decide how to analyze and interpret your data. For example, some interim/benchmark tests use scale scores (one type of standard score) and suggest you chart student "progress" by graphing their pre- and posttest scores. When you know that scale scores are norm-referenced scores, you realize that those graphs can tell you whether students have gone "up" or "down" from pre- to posttest but not exactly what it is they have learned. Other than the topic area of the test or subtest (e.g., "reading comprehension"), there is no information in the scale scores to help you decide what aspects of reading comprehension students have learned or still need to learn.

Aggregation and Disaggregation

Most measures of student achievement of learning goals are administered to individual students and then aggregated to arrive at a statistic that describes achievement at the desired unit of analysis. A common way to do that is to report the mean (the arithmetic average) score for the unit, whether it's a class, school, or district. As you can imagine, when you take the mean of a group, you mask the performance of individuals. Everyone in the group is now represented by one number, even if some students' scores are much above that and some much below.

One of the successes touted for the NCLB, which has been continued in the Every Student Succeeds Act, is that it required disaggregating scores by subgroups of students, for example, by socioeconomic status, race/ethnicity, English proficiency, or disability status. Reporting disaggregated results means that the achievement of any one subgroup cannot be hidden in an overall average. State accountability test scores disaggregated by subgroup are typically available for buildings and districts, and the school leader's job is typically to interpret and use the information provided. More rarely, buildings or districts may want to conduct some inquiry of their own that requires disaggregation. A federal *Forum Guide* (National Forum on Education Statistics, 2016) gives advice on how to do that; it should be done in the context of a needs assessment and planning with stakeholders. In this chapter we focus on understanding disaggregated data that are already available in reports to stakeholders and school leaders.

Representing Groups With Measures of Central Tendency

Measures of central tendency are used to report one number to represent the performance of a group or subgroup. There are many measures of central tendency. The ones school leaders will use most, which we discuss here, are the mean and the median. The mean is what you probably called the "average" when you were in school: add up all the scores, and divide by the number of scores. Strictly speaking, there are many kinds of averages, so we'll use the term *mean* in this chapter. The median is the middle-most score, such that half of the scores in the group are above it and half are below it. Another name for the median is the *50th percentile*.

No matter what the size of the group—whether it's all students or just students in a particular subgroup—calculating a mean only makes sense for certain kinds of data. For score scales where the interval between each score is the same size, using a mean makes sense, because adding numbers on an equal-interval scale makes sense. Think of test scores as if they were inches on a yardstick or tape measure. Student A gets a 2, and student B gets a 3. Two units plus three more of the same-size units is five units; divide by 2 (the number of scores), and you have a mean of 2.5.

Most test scores have this equal-interval property. When you take the mean of the scores, remember two things. First, the mean needs to be interpreted in light of the amount of spread in the scores. In our example above, 2 and 3 are close, so the mean of 2.5 is a pretty good representation of our little group of two students. But what if the scores were 1 and 4? The mean would still be 2.5, but it would be less representative of the students in the group. You address this issue by reporting a measure of the spread of the scores whenever you report a mean, typically either a standard deviation or the range. If a mean is reported without a standard deviation or range, school leaders should know to ask about how dispersed (spread out) the scores in the group were, before interpreting and using the information. Second, the size of the group makes a big difference. The larger the group, the more representative the mean is likely to be overall. For very small groups states do not usually report means because it would be possible to reason backward and perhaps even identify the few students in that group. For very small groups thinking about "average" performance isn't very useful anyway; why not just address the individuals?

Some assessment results are reported on scales that do not have equal intervals. The most important example for school leaders is proficiency levels or any other quality-level scale, such as rubrics. Calculating a mean requires adding up scores, and adding only makes sense if all the intervals (all the units on the yardstick, to use our metaphor) are the same size. Proficiency levels are *ordinal measures*; that is, they denote rank or ordered categories. Advanced is better than Proficient, which is better than Partially Proficient, and so on; but the amount of achievement in each of those categories is not the same. The different cut points for each category are not necessarily the same number of points apart. So adding them up—for example, adding two Proficients and one Partially Proficient—doesn't make sense. It would be like adding apples and oranges. Or a better metaphor might be that it would be like adding two big things and a little thing; you'd get 3, but you wouldn't know what you had three of.

For ordinal scales like this, where the "score" is a rank or ordered category, there are two main ways to aggregate data. If you want one number to represent the group, use the median instead of the mean. Calculating a median doesn't require adding, just lining things up in order, which of course is what ordinal measures do. So, for example, if a class had two students at Advanced, five at Proficient, and one at Partially Proficient, the median performance would be Proficient. Another way commonly used to aggregate data for short scales is to describe the distribution.

Distributions

A distribution is a description of all of the scores so you can see how spread out they are, which scores are common and which are rare, and so on. Many state accountability reports use tables or bar graphs to show the distribution of students within proficiency levels. This can be done, for example, by making a bar graph showing the number or percentage of students in the Advanced category, in the Proficient category, in the Partially Proficient category, and in the Not Proficient category. You can see an example of this if you look ahead to Figure 9.3.

One caution about cut scores is in order here. Numbers of students in categories created using cut points in an underlying test score distribution can shift, or not, in ways that don't accurately reflect a shift in actual achievement. Think of it this way. A state test, for example, has a distribution of scale scores that range from very low to very high. When graphed, the distribution would be a curve—maybe a normal curve, maybe somewhat skewed, but still a curve that shows lots of students scoring in the middle and fewer toward the extremes. When cut scores occur in areas of the distribution where lots of students score, it doesn't take much of a shift in performance (in terms of an increase in scale scores) to change the percentage of students in a proficiency level. When cut scores occur in areas of the distribution where fewer students score, the same-size shift in performance will not result in many students changing proficiency levels. Therefore, depending on where the cut points are in the underlying distribution of test scores, percentages in categories can vary wildly, sometimes implying change that isn't really there or suggesting changes in the gaps between group performance that are not real (Ho, 2008). This is an important caution for school leaders, who sometimes set goals like "We will increase the number of students scoring Proficient or above in mathematics." While that's not a bad goal, to really understand the changes in proficiency, you will need to look at more than just the changes in percent-in-category. Look, as well, at the changes in students' scale score means and in other descriptive information if it's available.

Distributions can also be graphed using test scores themselves, without chopping them into categories. Those graphs will be line graphs or curves. Such graphs may give a clearer picture of the test score distribution than bar graphs of performance by category. The trade-off, of course, is that they are more complicated to interpret. In fact, it is rare to see line graphs or curves for large-scale test results in buildings or districts, probably because of the vast amounts of data. However, for classroom-level data (e.g., a set of scores on a final exam in French), where the data sets are smaller, it is quite possible to look at a line graph of class performance. A simple spreadsheet app (e.g., Excel) can make one for you.

Unit of Analysis

The unit of analysis is the entity you want to describe for some purpose. Some large-scale tests supply score reports for various units of analysis (e.g., individual, class, school), and you can also make them yourself (e.g., when your school gives a common assessment).

The unit of analysis should be appropriate for the decision you are going to make. For example, a teacher might want to know about the achievement of individual students in order to plan differentiated classroom instruction. The unit of analysis, in that case, is the individual student.

A building administrator, however, might want to know about the current achievement of students in each third-grade class in, say, mathematics according to the state test. The unit of analysis in that case is the class. The simplest way to get one score that represents each class would be to aggregate the scores of all the individual students in the class, perhaps by calculating the mean mathematics score for the students in that class. A district administrator might want to know about the current achievement of all third graders, fourth graders, and so on in the district, and in that case the unit of analysis is the grade level. Again, the simplest way to get one score that represents each grade level would be to aggregate the scores of all the individual students in a given grade level.

Scores for groups are not always arrived at by aggregation. It depends on what you want to measure. For example, if you wanted to know class size, you would just count the number of students in each class and assign that score to the class directly (23 students in this class, 24 in that one, etc.). Another class-level variable might be teacher's years of experience for each class. That number (e.g., three years, five years) applies to the whole class.

Unit of analysis is important because different decisions require data at the appropriate level (individual, group), and different analysis methods are appropriate for individual and group scores. As school leaders you may not do those analyses, but you should be very aware of what was done and how to interpret it, with awareness of the unit of analysis.

For example, one common unit-of-analysis mistake happens when building administrators want to see how their building's performance on a norm-referenced test compares with performance in other buildings in the district and around the country. Intuitively, it might seem that you would just take the average percentile rank of your students on that test and look it up in the table of norms for individuals. So if the average percentile rank of your students on a math test was 57, you might think that 57% of the schools whose students took the test did less well, overall, than your students did. This intuitive reasoning is not correct. Building norms are based on building performance (i.e., a set of scores where the building is the unit of analysis and each building is represented by its average score). The resulting norms for building averages are different from the norms for individual scores. Specifically, they are much less spread out. Building averages will not be spread from very high to very low, as individual students' scores are, because the extreme scores in a building will be averaged with all the other scores in that building. Rather, they will be closer to the middle, and a building's percentile rank—which tells how its average compares with other buildings' averages—is calculated accordingly. A building with an average individual student percentile rank of 57 would likely have a building percentile rank much higher than 57.

Growth Models

In the context of student growth models, defined in Chapter 8, *growth* means a description of student (or group) academic performance over two or more time points. Contrast this with *status*, which means academic performance at one point in time. A growth model is "a collection of definitions, calculations, or rules that summarizes student performance over two or more time points and supports interpretations about students, their classrooms, their educators, or their schools" (Castellano & Ho, 2013, p. 16).

There are many different growth models. Katherine Castellano and Andrew Ho (2013) describe seven types of them. School leaders who are interested in more details about the different models will find Castellano and Ho's paper *A Practitioner's Guide to Growth Models* very readable. School leaders should be aware of what kind of growth model, if any, is used in their district, because different growth models support different primary interpretations.

The primary interpretation supported by some growth models is to describe growth, calculating in some way how much change in student achievement has occurred from one time point to another. Intuitively, you might think of change as a gain in test score from one time to another, but there are other ways to describe growth as well—for example, average gain score among grades, the slope of a line through a plot of individual or group performance across time, or the pattern of transitions among proficiency categories (e.g., Exceeds/Meets/Nearly Meets/Does Not Meet Standard) over time.

Instead of describing growth, some growth models seek to predict future performance. Again, several different statistical models can serve this purpose. For example, some models extrapolate students' past performance into the future, some predict changes in proficiency categories given past momentum, and some predict the percentile rank expected in the future given past performance.

A third primary interpretation served by some growth models has been called "value added." This kind of growth model seeks to tease out what caused growth in achievement. Some of these models are relatively simple equations that calculate the relationships between achievement gains and classroom or school membership. Other value-added models are more complex equations or sets of equations that include estimates for the influence of teacher and/or school. The size of those estimates can be interpreted as "teacher effects" and/or "school effects" on learning. As appealing as this may sound to some, these estimates, especially those that are very high or low, have been found to be unreliable, and it is precisely the very high- or low-scoring teacher whom school leaders might wish to identify. In addition, often most teachers in a district are statistically similar; that is, their teacher scores are not significantly different from that of the average teacher in the district, all of which makes value-added scores of limited use.

We think three main take-aways about growth models are important for readers of this chapter. First, there are many different growth models, and it's important to identify which one you are dealing with, what results it produces, and what primary interpretation about growth it supports. Second, it's important to avoid making interpretations your data cannot support. For example, if you have a simple gain-score model, you may be dismayed at the low gains reported for a particular class, but the model does not allow you to conclude that the teacher of that class was the cause of the disappointing gains. Third, student growth models are just that—they are models. They are mathematical representations of changes in students' test scores over time. Thus, any conclusions about the results of the model depend on the design decisions that went into creating the model. For example, a model that does not condition growth on the socioeconomic status of the students in a class may disadvantage a teacher because it ignores a known background factor for student achievement. However, a model that does include student socioeconomic status in effect predicts different performance for students from different economic backgrounds.

Attention to Error and the Compounding of Error

Finally, in this last part of our treatment of data analysis, we want to remind you that assessments of student achievement are always prone to measurement error. "Error" in this sense means the difference between the score a student receives on any real assessment and the hypothetical "true" score that describes their actual performance level on the particular learning goal you are measuring.

Teachers are accustomed to thinking of error in measurement as students having good days and bad days, and that is true but not the whole of it. The characteristics of the test questions, performance tasks, and/or rubrics can also introduce error into student assessment, which we explained as sources of bias and distortion in Chapter 3. Just chance itself can introduce error (did you ever get a test back with a question marked wrong, causing you to wonder why in the world you answered as you did because you actually knew the correct answer?). The important point for school leaders is to treat any assessment result as an estimate, subject to verification with other information. This, by the way, is part of the argument for multiple measures. The existence of measurement error doesn't mean we should throw up our hands and give up. The assessment result you have is an estimate, true, but it is the best estimate you have at the moment.

The converse of error is **reliability**. Reliability is the degree to which scores are consistent across various factors that can lead to error in measurement. The degree to which two scorers give the same score to the same student work on an assessment is called interrater reliability. The degree to which one scorer would give the same score to the same student work if they regraded it is called intrarater reliability. The degree to which students would get the same score on a test no matter whether it was given in the morning or the afternoon is another type of reliability. In terms of our discussion of "true" score and error, reliability denotes how much of the observed score is true. If the reliability of a test score, for example, is .90, then the amount of error in that score is .10.

A metaphor can help us think of the relationship between reliability and measurement error. Think of the signal-to-noise ratio in old-time radios you had to tune with a dial. Error tells you how much white noise is in what your radio receives, and reliability tells you how much signal is there. Just as with listening to a radio, you want to select the most reliable assessment available for your purpose, so that most of the information in the score is true and only a small amount is error.

Understanding that any assessment result includes error provides a caution for interpreting the growth models described in the previous section. Think of the simple case: two scores, from a pre- and posttest (the same test given twice). Each score includes some error. If you simply subtract the pretest score from the posttest score, the result is the true score gain, which may not be very large, accompanied by two sources of error (one from the pre-test and one from the posttest) instead of one. There are more complicated explanations of compounding error and why you should proceed with caution when you interpret test scores, but this simple explanation has always been enough to persuade us to be cautious with gain scores.

The main point: scores are not absolute truth; they are estimates of true performance levels. They include error. There is no perfectly reliable educational measure. Therefore, for any decisions with big consequences, never use just one score. Even for decisions with smaller consequences, like what to say to a student after looking at the results of a 20-minute in-class exercise, always realize your assessment is an estimate subject to corroboration from other evidence.

Classroom Assessment Data

The basic concepts in quantitative data analysis described in this section apply to classroom assessment data as well as large-scale data, although you are likely to run into norm-referenced scores only in the context of large-scale data. Nevertheless, the principles regarding types of scores, aggregation, distributions, and so on apply to all quantitative data. As you will see in the second part of this chapter, on using data to make decisions, you may well want to analyze data from classroom assessments as part of your interpretive and decision-making process.

However, in contrast to large-scale assessment, where all you usually get is the data (the results), classroom assessments offer additional opportunities for analysis. For most classroom assessments you have access to the assessment instruments themselves (e.g., tests, performance tasks, rubrics) and to student work samples. So in addition to analyzing students' achievement scores, you can analyze other aspects of the classroom assessment as well. These analyses may take the form of a qualitative approach to describing a set of assessments or student work, or they may use simple quantitative methods, for example, using a rubric or rating scale to address some aspects of assignment quality.

For example, if a high school leader was helping the English department investigate students' abilities to "write arguments to support claims in an analysis of substantive topics or texts, using valid reasoning and relevant and sufficient evidence," a writing standard for high school, they could summarize student performance on writing assignments in grades 9 through 12 in any of the ways described above: aggregating to the units of interest (e.g., class or grade level), using the mean or median for each assignment, graphing the distribution, and so on. These are quantitative analyses. The school leader and the English department could then inspect these summaries for what they say about student achievement on the assignments they were expected to complete.

But what exactly were they expected to complete? Qualitative analysis is also possible because you have the assignments and rubrics themselves. What topics were students asked to write on? Were the prompts clear? Did the prompts ask students to write about substantive topics or texts, and if so, which ones? Answers to questions like these help interpret students' results in context. For this kind of analysis you could review the assessments themselves, using qualitative methods as well. One qualitative method, coding into categories, also allows you to follow up with simple quantitative analyses like reporting counts or percentages. For example, you might sort the assessments into categories that describe the kinds of writing prompts students were given. You might find that many of the argumentative writing prompts were hypothetical school-based problems (e.g., "Write a letter to your principal arguing for the use of cell phones in school") and there were very few other topics or text-based writing prompts. You might use a simple rating scale to assess the level of rigor of the prompt and might find, for example, that none of the writing prompts called for complex thinking.

You can also use student work samples as data, addressing questions to them about students' strengths and weaknesses, preferred strategies, or really almost anything for which student work could be evidence. In our writing example you might look at several class sets of student argumentative essays to assess the quality of the claims students made or the positions they took. For that you could use a rubric or other quality-level description as the means of analysis. You might look at whether and how well students identified and countered alternative positions to their own, again perhaps using a rubric. Or you could use a more thematic approach, describing students' preferred strategies (e.g., students most often support their arguments with appeals to emotion and personal experience, and when they do use appeals to authority or science, their writing is often more stilted). These kinds of analyses yield more small-grained and more instructionally actionable data and can be a good use of classroom assessment data, either alone or in concert with looking at large-scale data as well.

Any analysis of large-scale or classroom-level data should start with a question—something you want to know that you have reason to believe the data will tell you. In light of your question look at all the relevant information that is available to you. The section below on using information has more detail about how to interpret and use assessment results.

Using Data to Identify and Address Problems

Many authors, evaluators, and researchers have described data-use processes. Some take an action research approach, starting with a question. Others take a data-driven approach, starting with data and generating a question from it. All data-use processes describe some sort of gather-analyze-interpret-use sequence for handling data or, in other words, some version of a basic inquiry process.

In this chapter we will discuss a modified version of Kathryn Boudett et al.'s (2013) Data-Wise Improvement Process, which originated in the Harvard Graduate School of Education and has been used by school leaders around the world. We have modified their process for this chapter for two reasons. One, the first two steps in Boudett and colleagues' Data-Wise process are (1) organizing for collaborative work and (2) building assessment literacy. This whole book is about building assessment literacy, so we have assumed that you will be starting from that point. Two, we have renamed their steps to allow the inquiry process diagram to be more descriptive. Figure 9.2 shows the data-use process as we describe it in this chapter. We do recommend that you consult Boudett and colleagues if you have more detailed questions than are addressed in this chapter.

FIGURE 9.2   A process for using data to identify and address problems

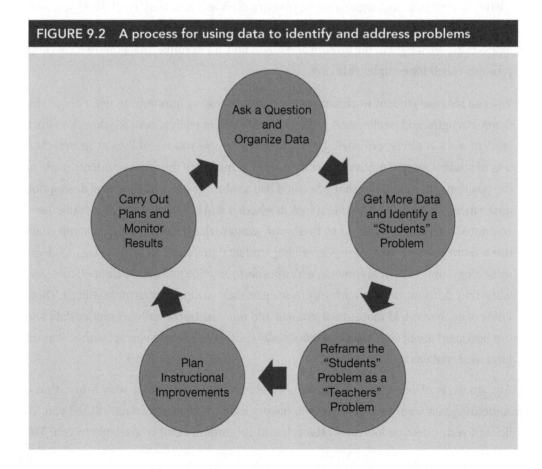

Prerequisites

School leaders should know what student assessment data exist in the assessment system of their building or district, as described in Chapter 1. In addition, school leaders should be organized for collaborative work and organize their school personnel for collaborative work. Using data is best done as a team activity. Finally, team members and other building/district colleagues should continuously work to improve their assessment literacy. Assessment literacy is an important prerequisite for using assessment data to identify and address problems. Once these foundations are in place, you are ready for the inquiry process shown in Figure 9.2: ask a question and organize data, get more data and identify a "students" problem, reframe the "students" problem as a "teachers" problem, plan instructional improvements, and carry out plans and monitor results.

Ask a Question, and Organize Data

Most buildings and districts find themselves drowning in data. The data are often housed in tables in reports, in spreadsheets, and/or in student information systems, organized by variables that may or may not be relevant to the question your team wants to pursue. For example, you may get a spreadsheet of results from the state organized by grade level, year, and school.

The first thing to do is decide what it is you want to find out: create a question that you want to use the data to answer. Next, your team can create a data overview in a form that highlights the answer to the question. The data overview usually takes the form of a visual, perhaps a chart or graph, that focuses viewers on the one question and not all the details in the data spreadsheet, to support a focused discussion.

We'll use a running example here to illustrate the process. The district in our example decided it wanted to know "How are our sixth graders doing in math?" The question arose because several sixth-grade mathematics teachers were wondering why it seemed that a fair number of students were not meeting standards. Teachers in the middle school in our example are organized in grade-level teams and meet regularly, and subject-area teams meet occasionally as well. The question about sixth graders arose in a subject-area meeting. Their first attempt at a data overview looked like Figure 9.3. They created this graph by selecting the overall district percentages at each of four proficiency levels for one grade (sixth) in one year (2019).

This graph clearly focused on the question—sixth-grade math performance—but it didn't provide any more of an answer than the teachers already had intuitively. They decided to add some normative comparison data in the form of the average performance in each category for the state. Their next graph, seen in Figure 9.4, was somewhat more informative.

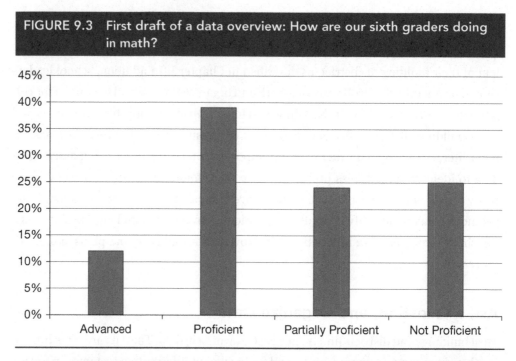

FIGURE 9.3   First draft of a data overview: How are our sixth graders doing in math?

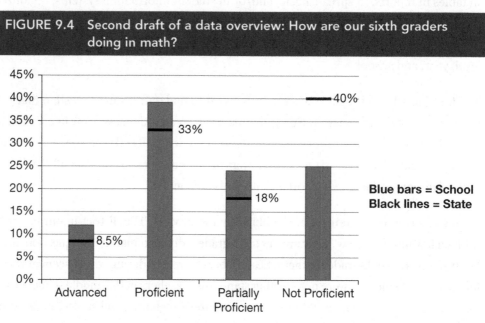

FIGURE 9.4   Second draft of a data overview: How are our sixth graders doing in math?

From Figure 9.4, it's clear that there are several answers to the question "How are our sixth graders doing in math?" Compared with the state proficiency-level averages, this district's students have much fewer Not Proficient students. So one answer to the question might be "Pretty well." But looking at the school data, it still was troubling that there were almost as many Partially Proficient and Not Proficient students as there were Proficient and Advanced students. So another answer might be "Not as well as we'd like." The team tried one more data overview, using four years of data instead of just one, to see if they could get any more insight into their question about sixth-grade math. Figure 9.5 was the result.

FIGURE 9.5   Third draft of a data overview: How are our sixth graders doing in math?

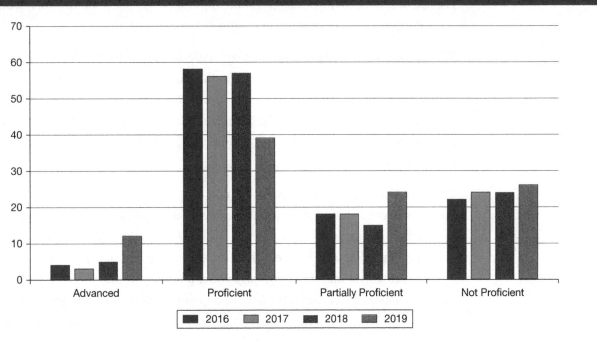

The graph in Figure 9.5 suggests that more students are in the Advanced category in 2019, but fewer are in the Proficient category, and more are in both of the below-Proficient categories. The pattern in 2019 does seem to be a bit of a departure from the pattern in the previous three years, although assessment-literate school leaders know that the changes in percent-in-category may look more dramatic than they actually are (see the section "Distributions" above). Therefore, the team checked the average scale scores for math performance from 2016 through 2019 as well and found that the change in average scale score was actually very small.

Given these deliberations the team decided that the answer to the question "How are our sixth graders doing in math?" was "Not as well as we would like." Of course, this answer raises more questions. In what ways are students not doing as well as we would like? Why? Indeed, it's the why question that the mathematics team really wanted to answer, and none of the data overviews in Figures 9.3 to 9.5 could do that. So the end result of this first step is a refined question: "Why are our sixth graders not doing as well as we would like in math?"

Get More Data, and Identify a "Students" Problem

The problem with "big data," a nickname sometimes given to large-scale test results, is that they only allow you to make broad generalizations. First, the measure itself is broad. In the case of our example the state accountability test measured most of the sixth-grade mathematics standards, many of which were represented by only a few problems each.

Second, the data are highly aggregated, masking any differences by relevant subgroups, classes, or schools. While disaggregation might solve the second problem, it would not solve the first.

This second step in the data-use process is designed to get to instructionally actionable solutions to the refined question created at the end of step 1, in this case why sixth graders are not doing as well as we would like in mathematics. The strategy: get more data of a smaller grain size. They might be data from other external assessments like interims, although as we showed in Chapter 1, interim data might not give you much more insight than you have already from the state test.

More helpful might be data from common assessments and from classroom assessments. Analyze and present these data in ways that might lead to insights about instruction, using the information in the "Classroom Assessment Data" section above. For example, you might check to see whether what was tested matched what was taught, hypothesizing that misalignment might be a potential reason for students not doing as well as desired. This could be done by a qualitative analysis of the content of classroom assignments and assessments, looking to see whether specific learning goals or mathematical practices were reflected in classroom work. Or you might check the rigor of what was taught, hypothesizing lack of rigor as a potential reason, by looking at the cognitive level required by the assessment questions and tasks. This could be done using a simple rubric based on a taxonomy of cognitive levels (e.g., Bloom's) or, perhaps even more useful in this context, a rubric with two or three levels ranging from recall and/or rote application of procedures to extended higher-order thinking. After coding the classroom assignments and assessments with the rubric, you could present the percentage of work in each category that students were asked to do. You may choose to do other analyses, for example, hypothesizing that students aren't doing as well on targets requiring reasoning as on knowledge-level targets. You could then analyze student work, contrasting students' percent correct or quality of performance on recall and rote problems with their percent correct or quality of performance on problems that require extended higher-order thinking.

When your hypotheses, data, and analyses from multiple assessments (and parts of assessments, if you have pulled some assessments apart for analysis) converge on an answer to your question, you have enough information to move to the next step in the process, which is to work toward agreement as a team on a tentative answer to the question. This answer sentence will begin with the subject "Students" and will make it sound like the problem belongs to the students—which isn't entirely true but will help you get to the truth in the next step. Boudett and colleagues (2013) call this a "learner-centered problem" (p. 90). The answer should be a statement about student learning and something that is *within the school's control*. In the case of our example the answer to "Why are our sixth graders not doing as well as we would like in math?" turned out to be "Our students have trouble explaining their mathematical reasoning."

Reframe the "Students" Problem as a "Teachers" Problem

Once you have a problem statement that describes a learning issue for students, flip it around so that the subject of the sentence is "teachers." Because, of course, teaching is the aspect of the learning problem that you have the ability to control and change. Boudett and colleagues (2013) call this a "problem of practice" (p. 110).

You can look at additional data to help you identify a problem of practice, and it doesn't have to be student scores or even necessarily quantitative. In our running example you might look at the kinds of instructional materials and instructional activities, for example, used for sixth graders' mathematics instruction. You might look at lesson plans. Are students asked to explain their mathematical reasoning? Often? Are the standards of sound mathematical reasoning and mathematical communication clear to students? Do they receive feedback aligned to the standards of quality? And so on. The team would brainstorm the links between teaching and learning that are found in the assessments they reviewed, in instructional materials and activities, and so on. For this step most of the sentences should begin with the word "Teachers" or "We," understanding that the problems of practice belong to, and can be improved by, all teachers. This only works, of course, in a school with a culture of inquiry and improvement centered on student learning. Often this brainstorming is done workshop style, using sticky notes or chart paper, and it might result in a chart that looks like Figure 9.6.

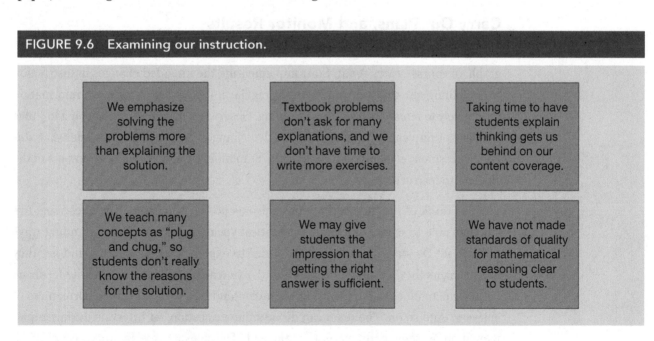

FIGURE 9.6   Examining our instruction.

> We emphasize solving the problems more than explaining the solution.

> Textbook problems don't ask for many explanations, and we don't have time to write more exercises.

> Taking time to have students explain thinking gets us behind on our content coverage.

> We teach many concepts as "plug and chug," so students don't really know the reasons for the solution.

> We may give students the impression that getting the right answer is sufficient.

> We have not made standards of quality for mathematical reasoning clear to students.

The end result of such a brainstorming session should be one or more problems of practice, or "teaching problems." In this case the team might decide that the main instructional issue is that sixth-grade mathematics teachers emphasize solving problems more than explaining the solutions.

Make Instructional Plans

Given the problem you have identified, what are you going to do about it? The sixth-grade mathematics teachers in the school in our example might decide that they are going to work on mathematical reasoning skills and communication about that reasoning by changing instruction in four ways. First, they will include more mathematical vocabulary in their lessons, helping students understand mathematical terms and use them. Second, they will emphasize more conceptual approaches to teaching mathematics, as opposed to rote, algorithmic approaches. Third, they will make the criteria for quality mathematical problem solving *and* quality mathematical explanations clear to students. Fourth, they will make sure that students are exposed regularly to problems that require them to explain their reasoning and that they get feedback on the quality of their explanations.

Finally, decide what you would count as evidence that the plan is working as intended. Don't wait for the state accountability test results next year. What data would you look at as these instructional changes are happening that would let you see how things are going? The team members decide that they need a rubric for mathematical reasoning and mathematical communication, which they can use both in their instructional improvements—using the rubric for teacher feedback and student self-evaluation—and for monitoring whether the instructional changes are leading to improved proficiency.

Carry Out Plans, and Monitor Results

Once you have a plan—with more detail to it than we have put in the previous paragraph, of course—carry it out. Start implementing the intended changes in instruction and anything else that's in your plan. At regular intervals use assessment information formatively to monitor how things are going. Observe the teaching and learning to gauge the level of implementation of the intended changes in instruction. Decide what student assessment evidence you should look at to monitor and evaluate the impact of the changes to instruction.

You can think of the monitoring phase also as posing and answering questions. Are students able to work with the mathematical vocabulary? Are teachers finding ways to teach it? Do students have opportunities to explain their reasoning, and are they improving as they do more and more of it? Are teachers giving high-quality feedback on the explanations and on conceptual understanding as well as on the correctness of answers? And so on. The team can discuss these questions at intervals during implementation. At some point, perhaps at the end of a semester or year, you can circle back to the original questions and see if you have answered them definitively or provisionally, or are still searching. And then, of course, the cycle repeats itself with new data and possibly new questions.

School Leaders' Data-Use Practices

Leithwood and Louis (2012) reported that while almost all reform efforts assume that greater attention to analyzing and using data will result in improved student performance, actual evidence to support this assumption is "thin and mixed" (p. 160). They reviewed studies that showed that data use in districts often suffers because of several obstacles: lack of a shared vision about data use for teaching and learning, lack of the necessary assessment literacy on the part of both leaders and teachers, and lack of collaboration, structures, and a collective will to work on data. However, while current research suggests that data use does not typically have much effect on student learning, it potentially could if these obstacles to its effectiveness were removed. Leithwood and Louis's own research suggested that principal instructional leadership can have an effect on student achievement, but the effect is indirect: principal instructional leadership, including the use of data, affects the teacher professional community in the building, which in turn affects student achievement.

Studies of the use of interim assessments, as reviewed in Chapter 1, have shown very little, if any, effects on student learning. Where data use affects learning the most is in the classroom, when teachers use assessment formatively to focus students on smaller-grained learning goals and immediate next steps (Black & Wiliam, 1998; Brookhart & DePascale, in press). We join Leithwood and Louis (2012), Boudett et al. (2013), and others in suggesting that assessment-literate school leaders know how to use data and do so, with the important insight that "using data" does not only mean using large-scale data but involves problem solving using data at the classroom level as well. In short, assessment-literate school leaders bring a problem-solving orientation and skills in basic data analysis and use to their work, organizing data at all levels of the assessment system to identify and address problems of practice.

Finally, we caution school leaders that analyzing data alone is not a silver bullet, the fix for everything. As the running example showed, skills in curriculum, instructional methods, classroom assessment, and feedback, and disciplinary content knowledge are needed as well. High-quality data analysis, or even a fine diagnosis of a problem, does not help if school personnel lack the means or the time to address the problem.

Success Indicators for Assessment Literacy Goal #9

The school leader

- can create data overviews from school and/or district data reported by the state or from interim assessments and common assessments;

- can offer reasonable interpretations of data displays and reports;

- can lead building/district colleagues in a data-use process that results in improved teaching and learning; and

- does not use assessment results to serve purposes for which the assessment was not designed.

 ## Study Guide Questions

1. As you read the section "Data Analysis Basics," was there anything new for you? Are there any concepts about which you need to find more detailed information?

2. What resources (people, books, computer resources) do you have available in your building/district that you could draw on if you encounter data analysis questions you cannot answer yourself?

3. What data do you currently review in your building/district? How do you do that?

4. How do you use classroom-level data in your building/district?

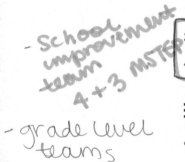

(handwritten margin notes:)
- School improvement team 4 + 3 MSTEP
- grade level teams

 ## Personal Portfolio Entry Suggestions

- An annual school improvement plan that speaks to data use, the professional development provided around it, and the team-based philosophy on which it rests

- Copy of data overviews and reports prepared for collaborative work in your building/district

- Copy of plans resulting from collaborative meetings where data were reviewed, interpreted, and used for suggesting improvements

- Video of yourself explaining and interpreting student assessment results to parents and community members, suitable for posting on the building/district website

---

Activity 9.1
Internet Scavenger Hunt

Learning Target for the Activity

- Explain the basic concepts in quantitative data analysis.

Purpose

The purpose of this activity is to give participants practice with the basic concepts in quantitative data analysis presented in this chapter. The ultimate aim is to increase facility and fluency with the concepts so they become an integral part of school leaders' reasoning about data.

Time

45 minutes

Materials Needed

- Internet access and connected devices (laptops, tablets, or phones) for all participants

Suggested Room Setup

Arrange tables and chairs so they are comfortable for both individual and small-group work.

Directions

Complete each step in the order below:

1. In this activity you will do an internet scavenger hunt, "scavenging" for additional interesting or useful information on these topics: referencing frameworks (norm referencing, criterion referencing, standards referencing), aggregation and disaggregation, unit of analysis, growth measures, and measurement error.

2. First, re-read the section "Data Analysis Basics" in this chapter. Then, as a group decide who will pursue which topic. Every member should have at least one topic to scavenge.

3. Each individual uses an internet browser and search engine to find information about their assigned topic(s). Take about 20 minutes to locate more information on the topic that is understandable to you. Do not worry if some of the information requires advanced statistical knowledge (e.g., you may find some treatments of measurement error that are highly statistical). Focus on scavenging information that is interesting or useful to you and that adds to the understanding of the concept you got from reading this chapter. Make notes (electronically would be easier, because you can copy, paste, and save URLs and other information, but using paper is fine too) to share with the group that tell (a) what you learned about the topic beyond what is in the chapter and (b) why you think that information is interesting, useful, or otherwise worth sharing with the group.

4. Reconvene as a group, and share what you have learned about your topic and why the information is interesting and/or useful to you. Each topic is presented one at a time, by the scavenger who retrieved the information, followed by a brief period for questions and/or discussion.

Closure

Facilitate a discussion based on these questions:

- What did you learn from this activity?

- How will this new knowledge be useful to you as a school leader?

- What new questions do you have?

- How might you find answers to them?

Activity 9.2
Dipping Into Data

Learning Target for the Activity

- Become more conversant with a process for problem solving based on data.

Purpose

The purpose of this activity depends on the will of the group. At a minimum, they will become conversant with the process for problem solving based on the data described in this chapter, so that they can use the process more fluently when the occasion arises in their building/district. However, if the group would like, they can use this activity as an opportunity to begin a "real" application of the process in their work as school leaders.

Time

45 minutes to one hour

Materials Needed

- Student assessment data source—the group may use the data supplied for this exercise, in Figure 9.7, or authentic local data

- Laptop or tablet with spreadsheet capabilities (at least one) and projector

- Chart paper and markers

Suggested Room Setup

Arrange tables and chairs for small-group work. Arrange for projection capability for one of the devices.

Directions

Complete each step in the order below:

1. Re-read the section "Using Data to Identify and Address Problems" in this chapter.

2. In this activity you will do the first step (ask a question, and organize data) of the process, then conduct a brainstorming in anticipation of the second step (get more data, and identify a "students" problem). The group should decide whether they want to do this activity as a practice exercise, using the data provided, or as the beginning of an authentic process for your building/district, using local data.

3. For the first step (ask a question, and organize data) examine the data (either provided here or local to your building/district) in spreadsheet or report form. Create a question you want your data to answer. Write the question on chart paper.

FIGURE 9.7 Sample data: state test results in mathematics from one school

GRADE	PERCENT PROFICIENT 2016	MEAN SCALE SCORE 2016	PERCENT PROFICIENT 2017	MEAN SCALE SCORE 2017	PERCENT PROFICIENT 2018	MEAN SCALE SCORE 2018	PERCENT PROFICIENT 2019	MEAN SCALE SCORE 2019
6	28.8	618.25	33.9	621.15	35.7	623.46	42.7	626.11
7	23.2	716.27	25.8	719.66	26.9	718.14	47.3	728.40
8	16.6	811.35	16.4	810.76	21.5	814.71	23.1	812.19

(Continued)

(Continued)

4. Summarize the data in a form that focuses on that question, using some sort of visual display or data overview (e.g., a line or bar graph, or a chart). Use a spreadsheet to do this, and project the results for the group to see.

5. Discuss the data overview. What, if anything, can you conclude? Can you refine your question or ask a further question? Can you float some hypotheses about the answers to your questions that you could investigate? Typically, these further questions and hypotheses would be about the reasons underlying what you see in the "big data" and would require additional classroom-level data to answer. Record the results of your deliberation on the chart paper.

6. The second step in the data-use process is to get more data and identify a "students" problem. At this point, since you will not have additional data at the ready, the activity continues as a thought experiment. This is the case whether you are using the furnished data or your own local data.

   • What additional data would be required to answer the new question? Include classroom-level data sources.

   • How would you identify, locate, and get the additional data?

   • How would you analyze the additional data? What would you be looking for?

Closure

Facilitate a discussion based on these questions:

• What did you learn from trying out the beginning of the data-use process?

• How will this new knowledge be useful to you as a school leader?

• For those using their own local data for this activity: make plans to continue the data-use process through the rest of the steps to action.

• For those using the data provided as an exercise: make plans, as appropriate, to use this process in your building/district.

Activity 9.3
Scenario Discussions

Learning Target for the Activity

• Lead and support teachers in understanding and problem solving with data.

Purpose

The purpose of this activity is to give participants practice in applying the data analysis skills learned in this chapter to scenarios that may arise in schools or districts. That is, participants will practice leading and supporting others in understanding and problem solving with data.

Time

45 minutes

Materials Needed

- Copies (paper or electronic) of the handout "Responding to Scenarios About Data" (Figure 9.8)

FIGURE 9.8   Responding to scenarios about data

Scenario 1

You are the superintendent of a school district that has just received large-scale test results. An associate superintendent approaches you and points out that a third of the students in the district are below the 40th percentile in reading and is concerned that parents or school board members may be upset. The associate superintendent proposes that the district hire an additional reading specialist and initiate a program for students who are reading below the 40th percentile on this test.

a. What data analysis issues are raised in this scenario?

b. How would you respond (and/or what would you do)?

Scenario 2

You are a building principal in a middle school. A mathematics teacher approaches you with last year's state test results for the students in their classes and is very concerned that the scores are lower than they would like. The teacher asks for your help in analyzing the data and figuring out how the students might receive better test scores next year.

a. What data analysis issues are raised in this scenario?

b. How would you respond (and/or what would you do)?

Scenario 3

You are a district administrator in a well-resourced suburban school district. The school board regularly receives pressure from parents and community members to make sure the district shows up well and is considered the best in the area. This year's state accountability assessment results have just come out, and they are disappointing. The superintendent hires a local university expert to write a memo explaining that test scores are just estimates, that decisions should not be made on the basis of one test score, and so on.

a. What data analysis issues are raised in this scenario?

b. How would you respond (and/or what would you do)?

(Continued)

(Continued)

Suggested Room Setup

Arrange tables and chairs so they are comfortable for pairs and small-group work.

Directions

Complete each step in the order below:

1. Participants review the contents of this chapter, which they have read prior to this activity. The group should entertain any questions people have about the meaning or content of the chapter text.

2. In pairs, consider each of the scenarios in the handout "Responding to Scenarios About Data" (Figure 9.8).

3. For each scenario, the group reconvenes after individuals (or pairs) have considered the scenarios. A volunteer facilitator calls on each individual (or pair) in turn to facilitate a discussion on one of the scenarios. Participants should choose a scenario that is difficult for them, raises an issue they think is especially important to discuss, and/or resonates with something in their own experience as school leaders. They should identify the scenario they would like to discuss, explain why, and ask any specific questions they have about it.

Closure

Participants should refer back to the learning target for this activity and also to the chapter learning goals. Each one should perform a self-evaluation: am I closer to this learning goal now than before the activity? Participants should share out briefly what they have learned that has brought them closer to their assessment literacy goal of facility with problem solving that involves data.

Some facilitators may find it useful to have a fact sheet, so we offer one here (see Figure 9.9). It should not be used to grade or score participants but only to assist in discussions where needed. It is not necessary to use this fact sheet in the activity at all, especially if discussions are lively and on point. Notice that the fact sheet identifies issues of data analysis and interpretation and makes some suggestions but does not definitively state what to do, which would vary by local context.

FIGURE 9.9   Data analysis issues in the scenario questions

Scenario 1

- Find out what the composition of the norm group was: how many students were in it, how they were sampled, and what population they were intended to represent.

- If the school was representative of the norm group, one would expect 40% of students to score below the 40th percentile. Therefore, if only 33% did, the district is doing somewhat better than the norm.

- Never make a major decision on the basis of one assessment. Look for additional evidence. For example, the assistant superintendent says nothing about the efficacy of the current reading program, the text adoption series, the supplemental materials, the reading instruction philosophy (and practice) in schools, whether this has happened previously (and for how many years), and so on. What additional data would be helpful?

Scenario 2

- Data analysis should be a team effort, so help the teacher identify suitable colleagues with whom to investigate the assessment results.

- Identify what types of test scores are in the class report (scale scores, proficiency levels, etc.) and whether there is any report of potential error (e.g., confidence bands around the scale scores).

- Find out whether this year's data are an anomaly or are similar to previous years' data.

- Find out whether this mathematics class's data are similar to other mathematics class data in the school/district.

- Identify an addressable problem, for example, whether the learning goals were clear (and taught), whether the classroom curriculum matched what's on the state test, and so on.

- Help the team identify additional data, including classroom-level data, to more precisely specify the problem and suggest solutions.

Scenario 3

- The professor's points are correct. However, construing the problem as a public relations problem may not satisfy parents and local community members. Based on the data-use process in this chapter, what else could be done? For example, the district could assume ownership of the problem, proactively creating an improvement plan for the next year. Examples of student work could showcase what students know and can do.

Definitions

Aggregation: Combining several data points to make one statistic for reporting.

Criterion referencing: Interpreting students' performance by comparing it with a defined standard.

Disaggregation: Separating summary data into component parts, typically separating test results for all students tested into results by subgroup.

Distribution: A description of a set of scores over the range of performance.

Error (in measurement): Variation in assessment results due to chance or other factors.

Growth measure: A measure of change in performance over time.

Norm referencing: Interpreting students' performance by comparing it with the performance of other students.

Reliability: The degree to which scores are consistent across various factors influencing measurement (e.g., time, occasions, scorers, forms).

Standards referencing: Interpreting students' performance by comparing it to clearly defined levels of proficiency that are set by using a combination of criterion-referencing and norm-referencing techniques.

Unit of analysis: The entity being measured or studied (e.g., individual students, classes, schools).

 This chapter's online resources are available for download from **resources.corwin.com/10GoalsLeaders**

School and District Assessment Policies

10

Assessment Literacy Goal #10: *The leader develops and implements sound assessment and assessment-related policies.*

In earlier chapters we have referred to systems, using descriptive terms like *congruent*, *comprehensive*, and *coherent*, and other terms sometimes associated with systems, like *compliance* and *regulation*. School and district policies are often seen as serving the regulatory and compliance requirements of the organization. But policies can also help advance the academic mission and promote the written learning goals of the system. District and school policy can act as a comprehensive and coherent network, helping to set and communicate standards, expectations, and procedures that are most relevant to increasing student achievement and, for our purposes, improving student assessment. Thus, how school leaders approach policy development is central to their ability to use it as a school improvement tool. The integration of school district processes such as goal setting, strategic planning, and policy development is fundamental to helping build a standards-based, comprehensive and balanced assessment system (Chappuis, 2007).

Chapter Learning Goals

1. Know how to review a school or district policy for alignment with sound assessment practice.

2. Understand how the school or district policy manual can act as a system of policies that support sound assessment practice.

3. Describe how and where assessment fits into numerous policies related to student learning and well-being.

The Long Policy Reach of Student Assessment

As school leaders know, policy drives practice, or at the very least, it can. If we want quality assessment practices in every classroom, then district and school policies must support the implementation and continued use of such practices. Quality assessment works to secure student well-being, and well-written policies that have an assessment connection can do the same. Sound and unsound assessment practices both matter because, as we have already noted, assessment done poorly harms students. Many policies at both the school and the district level have the potential to support the effective and appropriate use of sound assessment, but they might also unwittingly support practices that are not in the best interest of students. Below are a few examples:

- Consider an attendance policy that permits seat time to be factored into student grades based on the assumption that students can't learn unless they are in school, an assumption being tested daily across the country during the 2020 pandemic crisis. The policy is punitive in nature as it allows a behavioral variable to distort and therefore misrepresent student achievement (O'Connor, 2007). As a solution, schools and individual teachers have created guidelines and rubrics for behavioral variables so they can be reported separately from the academic subject, preventing those variables, such as attendance, from "hiding" in the report card grade. Rubrics can be used for conduct, class participation, effort, perseverance, and attitude, among other things. Figure 10.1 is one example of a rubric that can be used to report on effort, another behavioral variable often factored into grades.

 *what we talked about last wk*

- Consider a policy on homework that ignores the purposes of homework and allows (or, in some policies we've seen, requires) teachers to grade homework that is meant for practice and include those scores in the gradebook. Furthermore, if a homework policy allows individual teachers to determine their own systems of rewards (e.g., extra points) and punishments (e.g., zeroes) for the completion of homework, some students are set up for failure regardless of their mastery of the content.

- What if the lesson plan policy had no requirement for including how students would be assessed on what is to be taught? Or what if a policy makes no mention of the established learning goals of the subject area and grade level as the foundation for all lesson plans? Either or both omissions create mysteries for students (and perhaps for the teacher) in what they are to learn and how they will be assessed. If the learning goals are fuzzy for students or not well communicated, you can expect assessments to be problematic for them as well.

- A policy on promotion and retention that states a student will not be promoted unless a certain score or rating is achieved on the state accountability assessment ignores the practice of using multiple measures when making a decision of this magnitude. Promotion and retention decisions could consider multiple factors such as the following:

  o Achievement of the learning goals as demonstrated through classroom assessments, common assessments, standardized tests, portfolios, performances, exhibitions, projects, and other modes of school or classroom assessment

  o The student's overall academic achievement record

  o The social and emotional maturity of the student

- ○ What benefits might be accomplished by retention

- ○ Participation and success in remedial programs, tutoring, summer school, and/or other opportunities for success

- The school or district assessment policy is the principal driver in a large group of policies relating to student assessment. Ideally, it reflects the notions of "systems" of assessment, balance, and quality, and aligns with the comprehensive assessment plan described in Chapter 1. If so, it might open with a statement like this:

> "The board believes quality assessment is the core of teaching and learning. The assessment system of _____ School District is designed to communicate to students, educators, parents and other stakeholders regarding areas of student strength, individual student and group growth, and areas in need of support and improvement."

Contrast that with the following:

> "The district assessment program should provide information necessary to allow district staff to evaluate the effectiveness of curriculum and instructional programs and strategies."

The first statement contains a broad, more inclusive view of assessment with both success and improvement in mind. The second statement is largely focused on using assessment for program evaluation. Those two mindsets are likely to continue throughout the remainder of the policy language and are also likely to influence language in other policies that relate to student assessment. We'll return to the importance of the student assessment policy itself later in this chapter.

FIGURE 10.1   Sample rubric for effort

LEVEL 4: ACCOMPLISHED	LEVEL 3: PROGRESSING	LEVEL 2: BEGINNING	LEVEL 1: NOT YET
The student *consistently*	The student *frequently*	The student *sometimes*	The student *does not yet*
Completes work on time	Completes work on time	Completes work on time	Complete work on time
Shows attention to neatness in work	Shows attention to neatness in work	Shows attention to neatness in work	Show attention to neatness in work
Uses class time effectively—stays on task	Uses class time effectively—stays on task	Uses class time effectively—stays on task	Use class time effectively—stay on task
Engages productively in group activities	Engages productively in group activities	Engages productively in group activities	Engage productively in group activities
Persists in the face of difficulty	Persists in the face of difficulty	Persists in the face of difficulty	Persist in the face of difficulty
Seeks out resources when needed	Seeks out resources when needed	Seeks out resources when needed	Seek out resources when needed
Acts on feedback provided	Acts on feedback provided	Acts on feedback provided	Act on feedback provided
Strives to make work better	Strives to make work better	Strives to make work better	Strive to make work better

Directions: Highlight the phrases that best describe the student's level of effort for each category.

In each of the examples in Figure 10.1 decisions are made about students that affect them every bit as much as the quality of instruction they receive every day. Earlier in the book we described how poor data can lead to poor decisions about students. It is the same with policies that relate to student assessment. Policies like those above can either support quality assessment, acting in concert to describe a system of beliefs and practices, or act in opposition to each other, creating inconsistency and conflict.

As a reminder, just as any assessment can be audited for quality, the same is true for any rubric you encounter or may develop on your own. Next in this chapter (and in Activity 10.1) you'll have opportunities to review policies with a critical eye, using the lens of quality assessment. It's also a good practice to engage in a similar review of rubrics that are used to both evaluate and communicate a behavior or disposition. For further reference on using a "rubric for rubrics" you can consult Chappuis and Stiggins (2020, chap. 7).

Reviewing Policies With Student Assessment in Mind

It is one of the school leader's assessment responsibilities to regularly review and revise policies as needed so they provide a framework for sound assessment practice. Part of that responsibility extends to a regular review with staff of the policies at the district and building levels that are most germane to daily school operation and classroom instruction. As we have seen, assessment is at the core of many school and district policies. A list of policies that have a strong connection with student assessment include those in Figure 10.2.

FIGURE 10.2

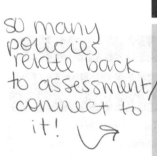
so many policies relate back to assessment/ connect to it!

Assessment	Teacher evaluation
Curriculum	Program evaluation
Instruction	Strategic planning
Grouping for instruction	Individualized Education Plan
Lesson planning	Student placement
Grading	Pupil records
Homework	Attendance
Instructional materials	Gifted/talented
Communicating student progress	Promotion and retention
Remediation and intervention	Accountability
Professional development	Graduation requirements
Teacher selection and hiring	

Each of the policies in Figure 10.2 could be written or revised so that they are in concert with the assessment vision, beliefs, and practices of the organization. To achieve the horizontal, policy-to-policy congruence in the policy manual that can help unify a system of assessments, it is helpful to identify those policies that require alignment of assessment theory or practice, and review or revise small groups of those policies at the same time. For example, in the scenarios used earlier in this chapter it's not difficult to see the need for consistency between a homework policy and a grading policy. Or think of a lesson plan policy: would we expect to see reference to how the lesson will be assessed, how the assessment is scored, and what the learning goals are? If so, there's a connection to both the grading policy and the assessment policy as well as the curriculum policy.

Another example: assume a high school or district is rewriting an attendance policy. The grading policy must be in alignment, the homework policy needs consideration, and there may need to be a connection with the graduation requirements policy and the promotion/retention policy.

trickling effect

When reviewing policies, it can be helpful to establish in advance a set of criteria. For this purpose we have chosen to generate policy review criteria in the form of questions such as "What do we want to achieve in assessment through school or district policies?" and "What would constitute a strong policy?" Other questions might include those below:

Does this policy

- support the vision of assessment in the school or district as defined in the comprehensive assessment plan?

- reflect the assessment balance called for in the plan?

- support the use of high-quality assessment tools and procedures?

- have a direct impact on student learning?

- have a connection to other policies that need to be considered?

- encourage the use of multiple measures of student learning, leading to judgments about student achievement based on combinations of data sources?

- require clear, meaningful, and frequent communication about learning?

- link standards, instruction, and assessment?

- require any specialized professional development for implementation success?

Another tool that can be used to conduct a policy review is a rubric, or a set of them. For example, the rubric below on a 5-point scale is a part of Nebraska's school effectiveness assessment. This rubric assesses to what extent standards-driven grading policies are shared with students and parents. Activity 10.1 provides an opportunity to practice a policy review using policies selected for that task. You may want to consider completing that activity before turning your attention to your own policies.

FIGURE 10.3   School rubric for evidence-based analysis: ASSESS-4

0	Grading policies are not driven by standards. Grading policies are not disseminated to students and parents in writing.
1	Grading policies reflect a consideration of standards. Grading policies are disseminated to students and parents only on request.
2	Grading policies reflect a consideration of mastery of standards. Grading policies, standards, and student progress are disseminated to students and parents periodically and also on request.
3	Grading policies promote standards-driven mastery of content. Grading policies, standards, and student progress are disseminated to students and parents regularly, on request, and via multiple media outlets. Student progress is continually accessible by students and parents.
4	Grading policies prioritize standards-driven mastery of content. Standards are written with student-friendly language to promote student and parent understanding of expectations. Grading policies, standards, and student progress are disseminated to students and parents systemically and regularly, on request, and via multiple media outlets. Student progress toward mastery of standards is continually communicated to and accessible by students and parents.

Source: Office of Data, Research and Evaluation, Nebraska Department of Education (2020, p. 35). Used with permission.

Developing an Assessment Policy to Help Guide Other Policies

Essential for quality assessment practices at all levels is a document that states assessment beliefs and provides guiding principles and policies for both large-scale testing and classroom practice based on that set of beliefs. As noted in Chapter 1, a written comprehensive assessment plan

- confirms that the learning goals of the district should be the basis for the majority of assessments;
- clarifies the purposes of assessment, how assessment both measures and supports effective teaching and learning and continuous improvement;
- emphasizes the value of multiple measures, and thereby sources of information, with which to make decisions about students and educational programs; and
- describes the benefits of a balanced system, including summative and formative assessment, and the student's role in classroom assessment.

The comprehensive assessment plan should form the foundation for the assessment policy itself and also inform all assessment-related policies.

Your comprehensive plan may call for assessment practice to stay current with research in the field. But unlike the formative assessment and leadership research we have reviewed, research that reports a causal relationship between actual assessment policy and student academic performance is minimal. One higher education study reports not finding any academic performance differences between two groups of students in courses with different assessment policies, although it did find differences in student motivation and self-regulatory factors (Kickert et al., 2019). Related to motivation, students in one group expected higher grades for themselves and had higher enjoyment of the tasks and learning. They also displayed higher "time and study environment management," referring to student capacity to plan study activities and manage time. The course assessment policy differences were these: this group had additional opportunities to retake assessments (see Chapter 5), the course had higher stakes in terms of acting as a gateway to other courses, and it required higher academic performance in terms of grades to be considered successful. The conclusion of the authors is that student motivation and self-regulation are sensitive to the details of assessment policy. They also recommend that educators keep this influence in mind as they develop standards, expectations, and policies.

The assessment policy content should be overarching, reflecting the "big-picture" vision of a balanced assessment system as expressed in a comprehensive plan. School board policy at the district level is intended to be brief and concise; with limited space it cannot contain the detail a written plan or report to the board might. School-level policies generally have more leeway when it comes to length, often incorporating procedures into the policy itself, unlike board policy, where procedures are usually separate. You can evaluate your own assessment policy at either school or district level against some or all of the criteria below, posed as questions:

- Does your current assessment policy provide a definition of assessment? Does it extend the definition to further describe what the characteristics are of effective assessment? Does it speak to the assessment literacy requirement for quality assessment?

- Does it speak to the purpose(s) of assessment? If it speaks to the purposes of assessment, does it also speak to the different types of assessment, including formative?

- Is there a "philosophy" of assessment or a set of beliefs about assessment in or referenced in the policy? What are the "big ideas" around assessment that are present? For example, is the policy weighted toward assessment's role in measurement, or is it a balanced view that considers assessment's role in promoting learning in the classroom, where the vast majority of assessments take place?

- Does the policy speak to the relationship assessment has with curriculum and instruction, with an explicit link to the learning goals of the district?

- Does it list or speak to other policies with a connection to student assessment?

- Does it contain an explicit understanding of the professional development necessary to support the assessment literacy needs of all staff?

Other subsections of a district assessment policy might contain the following:

- List of assessment information stakeholders

- Parent and student rights related to assessment

- Assessment selection

- Opt-out and exemption procedures

- Assessment calendar

- Communication of assessment results

- Confidentiality protections or assurances of safeguarding

- Accommodations

Summary

The school board policy manual is a framework through which the school district is led and governed. The board establishes rules and procedures for each policy, which provide the structure and day-to-day guidance necessary to operate a complex system. A school or district policy manual is the perfect place to apply a systems-thinking approach to leadership. And at both levels there is a need for assessment-literate thinking given the many policies that directly rely on quality student assessments to achieve their purpose.

Most of the assessment literacy goals presented in this book have a connection to one or more school or district policies and, through that, a connection to sound or unsound assessment practice. Chapter 1 begins the book with a goal of developing a comprehensive and balanced assessment system that also encompasses the subsequent goals. Chapter 10 ends the book in the same manner: student assessment is improved when assessment literacy is in place and when student assessment is planned and organized with the coordination of school and district policy.

 Success Indicators for Assessment Literacy Goal #10

The school leader

- can lead a policy review process;

- knows the key features of an assessment policy;

- can identify sound and unsound assessment practices that may be present in school or district policy;

- can develop or revise policies using quality assessment as a guide; and

- can implement new or revised policies via staff communication and discussion and with appropriate professional development.

Study Guide Questions

1. Assessment reform initiatives can be assisted by policy support. What examples can you think of in your experience that did or did not have policy support? What happened, and what were the results?

2. Often schools revise policy only in response to a crisis or legislative enactment. Both situations are valid. Make a list of other circumstances that might prompt an assessment policy review.

3. In the absence of a comprehensive assessment plan in your district, how might you go about revising assessment-related policies?

4. Does policy really drive practice? Think of examples where it did or did not. What happened, and what were the results?

 ## Personal Portfolio Entry Suggestions

- Policy review memos or sessions with staff

- Examples of policies recently reviewed for sound assessment practice

- Summary of professional development provided for staff related to new or revised policies

- Faculty handbook references to assessment, with their adherence to principles of assessment literacy highlighted

Activity 10.1
Using School/District Policies to Support Quality Assessment

Learning Target for the Activity

- Understand how assessment literacy can serve as a guide in the development or revision of school or district policy.

Purpose

This activity extends the policy review process introduced in Chapter 10. In the examples that follow some context is missing without the implementation procedures that usually accompany board policies, but the main concepts and priorities are still apparent. The intention of the activity is not to entirely perfect each policy but rather to practice reviewing policies with quality assessment as the filter.

Time

60 minutes

(Continued)

(Continued)

Materials Needed

- Optional: policies from your school or district

Suggested Room Setup

Tables and chairs

Directions

Read each of the four policies in this activity, taking one at a time to process. After reading each, pause and consider the following three questions with your team. Do this with the remainder of the sample policies in this activity. If desired, you can add other criteria you may have developed for policy review or those that have been offered in Chapter 10 for a deeper review. For each policy scenario there are multiple points of discussion (and possible disagreement), which is in part the purpose of the activity. Still, there are some elements in each policy that are contrary to quality assessment. Our purpose here is not to create a comprehensive list of all the possible points of discussion in terms of pros, cons, and possible policy amendments but to alert the reader to the main pitfalls of each policy from an assessment literacy perspective.

1. From an assessment literacy perspective, what are the strong points of the policy the way it is currently written? How does it support quality assessment?

2. What are the weak areas of the policy relative to student assessment? For instance, does the policy contain any assessment practices deemed to be unsound?

3. What language could be omitted and what language might be added to make it more supportive of sound assessment?

Policy #1: Lesson Plans

To ensure proper planning and continuity of instruction, the board requires that each teacher prepare lesson plans for daily instruction. To facilitate more effective instruction, lesson plans must be prepared in advance of the actual class presentation. The format for the lesson plan will be specified by the building principal and shall be reviewed on a regular basis. The plan book must be readily available when a substitute teacher is needed.

Policy #2: Homework

The board believes that homework is a constructive tool in the teaching/learning process when geared to the age, health, abilities, and needs of students. Purposeful assignments not only enhance student achievement but also develop self-discipline and associated good working habits. Because homework is viewed as an extension of the classroom, students are expected to complete all assigned work. Homework must be planned and organized, must be viewed as purposeful to the students, and must be returned to the student in a timely manner with appropriate feedback.

Make-up work, due to illness, is not to be considered as homework, as is work begun in the classroom that carries over beyond the school day. Students shall be given the opportunity to make up assignments missed during excused absences.

Policy #3: Communication About Student Achievement

_____ School District is a standards-driven district with the goal of communicating effectively about student achievement. It is the intent of the district to provide timely, understandable, and meaningful information about student progress toward clearly articulated achievement standards to students, parents, and education professionals. Grades and report cards represent only one of a number of ways to communicate student progress toward standards. All communications home from schools or the district about student achievement should, when appropriate, strive to

- communicate to parents/guardians in ways that describe student progress toward district standards and provide an accurate description of learning;

- provide information students can use for self-evaluation and improvement;

- provide data for the selection, identification, or grouping of students for certain educational paths or programs; and

- provide information for evaluation of the effectiveness of instructional programs.

Policy #4: Classroom Formative Assessment

In each class students will complete a daily formative assessment to demonstrate their learning for that day. Teachers are to make sure that the formative assessments

- assess the learning target;

- are valid and appropriate demonstrations of what students should know and be able to do;

- provide data to drive future instruction;

- provide meaningful feedback to students, including opportunities to reflect, self-evaluate, set goals, and strengthen their performance; and

- are a part of the regular learning process, with separate activities used only when embedded ones are not feasible.

Teachers will make adjustments in instruction to meet student learning needs as a result of daily formative assessments.

Closure

Below are just a few of the points of conversation that might arise during this activity, as well as a few of the pitfalls to be aware of in each policy review.

Policy #1: Lesson Plans

- The board's aim for "continuity of instruction" isn't just ensured by daily lesson plans. Longer-term planning is needed for students not to see one class period after another unconnected to a bigger picture. Daily learning targets are part of a larger system of learning goals.

- The fact that the building principal specifies the format of the lesson plan is problematic on multiple levels, one being that commonly accepted elements of

(Continued)

(Continued)

effective lesson planning (clear and appropriate learning goals, monitoring of student progress and understanding, aligned assessment strategies, etc.) may be omitted.

- The policy makes no mention of state standards or district learning goals as the primary source of instructional planning and assessment.

Policy #2: Homework

- Properly structured, homework can also be a part of the classroom assessment process, including formative assessment, in which case the homework would not be graded if it is still part of an ongoing learning process.

- There is less correlation between amount of homework and student achievement in elementary grade levels than in the upper grade levels. Purposes of homework, therefore, should differ depending on grade level.

Policy #3: Communication About Student Achievement

- Although the policy acknowledges that there are other communication methods beyond grades and report cards, it fails to help promote different communication strategies that could include student portfolios, the use of rubrics, parent engagement, progress reports, student-led conferences, and so on.

- No mention is made in the policy of the difference between summative and formative information, the various purposes of assessment, or the use of results.

Policy #4: Classroom Formative Assessment

- The first paragraph twice suggests that formative assessment is a tool, administered like a test.

- The purposes of formative assessment are at odds with the requirement that the teacher conduct a formative assessment at the end of the day to see what students know and can do.

- The policy in effect mandates that teachers will use formative assessment, ensuring that it is done through a daily requirement. Is that the best way? Are there other ways to ensure this requirement is met?

- The goals or the desired characteristics of formative assessment in the bulleted list are far more complex and comprehensive than can be achieved in a daily assessment. There is only partial understanding that formative assessment is less an event than a process.

Source: Adapted from Chappuis et al. (2017).

Appendix

A Guide to Learning With the Book

We have written this book with the needs of school leaders in mind, whether you are reading it independently or working through the chapters in collaboration with others. We do recommend that, if possible, you study the text as an Assessment Leadership Learning Team. The learning team approach to developing assessment expertise we advocate is based on best practice as reflected in professional development literature and research: educators learn best when the experience is collaborative and provides active contextualized opportunities for application of the ideas studied.

The Assessment Leadership Learning Team Process

In the learning team approach participants engage in a combination of independent study and ongoing small-group collaboration, with a commitment to helping all group members gain expertise. Team members read a portion of the text individually and then meet to share thoughts, questions, potential actions, and reflections. In addition, teams discuss the chapter study guide questions and carry out selected chapter activities.

Time Frame

Using the text as the basis for learning team study requires a long-term commitment of time. Developing assessment literacy is not an initiative; it is an essential and powerful component of the work we do as educators. We recommend that you plan a reading and meeting schedule that spans a year or more. We suggest that teams meet every two to three weeks, with assigned reading to be done between meetings.

Leading an Assessment Leadership Learning Team

Effective learning teams don't all look alike, but they do have several things in common, one of which is a designated facilitator. Another is careful prior planning, either by the facilitator or by a small group of people who may rotate facilitatorship responsibilities. Any school leader can facilitate a learning team. For example, if you are a district or area superintendent, an assistant superintendent, or a director, you may wish to study the book with principals and assistant principals. If you are a building administrator, you may wish to form a group with other building administrators or a group of those in leadership positions within your building. If you are in charge of instructional coaches, you may wish to form groups with them.

The Facilitator's Role

As a learning team facilitator, you are acting for the good of the team to manage and organize the process. The text, materials, activities, and participants' expertise all come together to create the learning experience, without requiring instruction from a leader. So facilitators are not the team's content experts but rather "guides on the side." Tasks that successful facilitators typically undertake (or ensure are done) when the teams are in place include the following:

1. Posting a schedule of team meetings

2. Bringing materials needed for the meeting

3. Monitoring meeting time so all members have opportunity to participate

4. Reviewing the next assignment at the end of each meeting

5. Completing and posting a meeting summary, noting actions the participants committed to, after each meeting

The facilitator may set the meeting agenda and determine the reading to be completed before the next meeting, or the team may do that collaboratively. *In all cases it is recommended that the facilitator do the work along with the team.*

Planning to Lead a Team

We recommend that facilitators take the following planning steps:

1. Review the book *Ten Assessment Literacy Goals for School Leaders* in advance.

2. Identify participants.

3. Plan a reading and meeting schedule.

4. Create meeting agendas.

5. Determine how team members will track, reflect on, and share their learning.

1. Reviewing the Text

Prior to meeting with a learning team, as the team's facilitator it is a good idea to familiarize yourself with the content the team will be studying and the resources available. Read through the text, noting the learning goals and success indicators for each chapter and reviewing the end-of-chapter study questions and activities, considering which will be of greatest importance to your group.

2. Identifying Participants

Assessment Leadership Learning Teams can be made up of individuals in leadership roles, including administrators, counselors, learning specialists, instructional coaches, and professional development specialists.

The size of the team is a function of how much time you schedule for each meeting. The team should be large enough to offer a variety of ideas, viewpoints, and expertise but small enough to allow each member to participate meaningfully during the meeting. If your meeting time falls within the range of 45 minutes to an hour and a half, keep the team size between three and six members to maximize participation opportunities. If that is not practical, give members time to discuss and work in smaller groups.

When inviting participants, be clear about the learning team process. Make sure potential team members understand the commitments involved:

- Working between meetings, with each member completing an agreed-on assignment

- Meeting regularly—every two to three weeks

- Engaging in partner or whole-group activities during meetings to further their learning, to conduct needs assessments, and to create resources for use in improving assessment practices

During the first team meeting, it is a good idea to agree to group operating principles such as the following:

- To make team time a priority and to honor the meeting time commitment

- To do the agreed reading between meetings, for personal benefit as well as for the benefit of the other team members

- To come prepared to contribute during meetings

3. Planning the Reading and Meeting Schedule

We recommend that you read the book chapter by chapter, in the order it is written. Members of your team may have previously mastered some of the learning goals addressed, or portions of them. If so, you could give those sections less time. We don't recommend skipping sections, but rather participants should review the topics they are familiar with in those sections, noting and discussing new ideas or useful tips.

The question "How should I pace the study of the text?" comes up frequently. Don't rush through the text or march to the pace of a predetermined schedule if it means sacrificing learning and implementation. Plan for *learning* as opposed to *coverage*. The point is not to finish the book but rather to master the learning goals and apply the content successfully.

To select the readings and activities, after reviewing a chapter, determine how many pages of the chapter team members will read for the next meeting and which activity they will complete during the meeting. Select activities by considering the learning goals and success indicators, and then decide which activities are best suited to the needs of your team. Study questions can be used as part of a reading assignment or as discussion prompts during the meeting, or both. Refer to Table A.1 for information on how the activities and study guide questions relate to the chapter learning goals and success indicators. You may wish to use these chapter charts to guide your planning.

If possible, schedule meetings two to three weeks apart to give people enough time to read and reflect, without having so much time elapse between meetings that members lose track of the thread of their learning.

4. Creating Meeting Agendas

When each meeting follows a reading assignment, you can set up a three-part agenda:

1. Discuss responses to the reading. You may want to use one or more study questions to focus the discussion.

2. Share thoughts about desired actions to take based on the chapter content.

3. Complete one of the chapter activities.

It may be that your team will read a chapter and then take several meetings to complete one or more chapter activities. Again, select activities to meet the learning and implementation needs of team members. Note that some activities are designed for the school leader to conduct with teachers. It can be helpful to practice those during the leadership learning team meeting before conducting them with staff.

5. Tracking, Reflecting on, and Sharing Learning

We have shared personal portfolio entry suggestions at the end of each chapter. We recommend that each team member establish a portfolio and decide which entries to include to reflect their accomplishment of each chapter's assessment literacy goal. Each portfolio artifact should be accompanied by a short explanation of which chapter learning goal it relates to and perhaps a reflection on how creating the artifact contributed to their learning. As explained in Chapter 4, engaging in these processes deepens commitment to the learning, increases the learning, and offers intrinsic reward along the way by developing a sense of accomplishment.

At the end of the learning team experience, we encourage participants to review their portfolios and plan for a way to share the highlights. Two options are to share with other learning teams or with colleagues who are not part of this experience.

TABLE A.1	Alignment of chapter learning goals, success indicators, activities, and study guide questions		
CHAPTER LEARNING GOAL	**ALIGNED SUCCESS INDICATORS**	**SUPPORTIVE CHAPTER ACTIVITIES**	**RELEVANT STUDY GUIDE QUESTIONS**
Chapter 1			
1. Understand the five levels of a comprehensive and balanced assessment system and what each level contributes to the system.	Can describe a model for a comprehensive local assessment system and can speak to components of the system such as assessment balance, coherence of learning goals, accurate assessment, and student involvement. Can explain the differences and similarities among the five levels of assessment.	Activity 1.1: An Abbreviated Assessment Audit Model	#1 #4
2. Recognize that learning goals form the backbone of a comprehensive and balanced assessment system.	Can describe a model for a comprehensive local assessment system and can speak to components of the system such as assessment balance, coherence of learning goals, accurate assessment, and student involvement.	Activity 1.1: An Abbreviated Assessment Audit Model	#4
3. Understand the function of assessment audits and how they are necessary to a comprehensive and balanced assessment system.	Can describe a model for a comprehensive local assessment system and can speak to components of the system such as assessment balance, coherence of learning goals, accurate assessment, and student involvement.	Activity 1.1: An Abbreviated Assessment Audit Model	#1
4. Recognize how classroom formative assessment acts as the foundation for a comprehensive and balanced assessment system.	Can explain why classroom formative assessment acts as the foundation of the system. Can explain the differences and similarities among the five levels of assessment.	Activity 1.1: An Abbreviated Assessment Audit Model	#2 #3 #4
Chapter 2			
1. Understand how state standards are deconstructed into smaller-grain-size learning goals in the curriculum in use in your building/district.	Ensures that school curriculum documents are aligned with state standards.	Activity 2.1: Exploring the Relationship Between Learning Goals and Assessment	#1 #2

(Continued)

TABLE A.1 (Continued)

CHAPTER LEARNING GOAL	ALIGNED SUCCESS INDICATORS	SUPPORTIVE CHAPTER ACTIVITIES	RELEVANT STUDY GUIDE QUESTIONS
2. Describe how state standards and the learning goals in your district's curriculum are assessed in your building/district.	Ensures that school curriculum documents are easily accessible to staff. Secures staff training in the use of classroom materials relative to state standards. Differentiates for staff teaching the written curriculum from teaching a textbook.	Activity 2.1: Exploring the Relationship Between Learning Goals and Assessment	#1 #3
3. Understand the role of student-friendly learning targets and success criteria in connecting classroom-level instruction and learning with broader learning goals.	Monitors lesson plans and classroom instruction for clear communication of learning targets. Publishes learning goals/targets for parents in student-friendly language.	Activity 2.2: Learning Targets and Success Criteria Activity 2.3: Recognizing the Formative Learning Cycle in Action	#1 #4
4. Understand how clear academic learning goals form the basis for developing sound assessments.	Provides staff training in selecting or creating assessments that are matched to the learning goals.	Activity 2.1: Exploring the Relationship Between Learning Goals and Assessment	#1 #2
Chapter 3			
1. Describe the five keys to quality assessment, understand how they relate to one another, and know why they should underpin assessments at all levels.	Can describe the five keys to classroom assessment quality. Can explain how each of the keys contributes to assessment accuracy and effective use. Can offer a compelling rationale for the importance of following the guidelines within each key.	Activity 3.1: Connecting Your Own Experiences to the Keys to Quality	#2
2. Conduct an audit with teachers to identify the strengths and weaknesses of an assessment according to quality indicators.	Understands the conditions necessary for effective formative use of the assessment process and its results. Knows how to audit an assessment for the match to what was taught. Can determine the appropriate assessment method(s) to use based on the types of learning goals taught. Knows how to audit an assessment for standards of quality. Identifies sources of bias that can distort assessment results.	Activity 3.2: Auditing an Assessment for a Clear Purpose Activity 3.3: Auditing an Assessment for Clear Learning Goals and Appropriate Sample Size Activity 3.4: Practicing With Target-Method Match Activity 3.5: Auditing an Assessment for Quality Activity 3.6: Auditing an Assessment for Bias and Distortion	#3

CHAPTER LEARNING GOAL	ALIGNED SUCCESS INDICATORS	SUPPORTIVE CHAPTER ACTIVITIES	RELEVANT STUDY GUIDE QUESTIONS
Chapter 4			
1. Understand formative assessment practices and their role in increasing student achievement.	Can describe the six critical components of formative assessment. Can offer a compelling rationale for the importance of the student as informed decision maker.	Activity 4.1: Identifying Talking Points for Critical Components of Formative Assessment	#2
2. Identify effective uses of formative assessment within the context of instruction.	Knows what to look for in the classroom for each of the six critical components.	Activity 4.2: Looking for Evidence of Effective Formative Assessment Practices in the Classroom	#3
3. Engage in discussions with teachers to enhance and expand their use of formative assessment.	Has a repertoire of questions to ask of teachers and students to deepen their understanding of the application of formative assessment practices.	Activity 4.1: Identifying Talking Points for Critical Components of Formative Assessment Activity 4.2: Looking for Evidence of Effective Formative Assessment Practices in the Classroom Activity 4.3: Discussing Formative Assessment Practices With Students	#3
4. Analyze the current formative assessment practices in a school and plan for ways to build formative assessment capacity.	Establishes a baseline for formative assessment practices in the school from which to build formative assessment capacity.	Activity 4.4: Establishing a School Baseline	#3
Chapter 5			
1. Understand the principles of sound grading practices.	Can articulate my district's official grading policies and explain why they are sound and can work with colleagues to improve them as needed.	Activity 5.1: Grading Stories	#1 #2
2. Lead teachers and others in implementing sound grading practices.	Can recognize the sound and unsound grading practices in use in my building/district and can work with colleagues to improve them as needed.	Activity 5.2: Grading Policies and Practices in My District Activity 5.3: Grading in Classrooms and Courses	#1 #3 #4 #5
3. Communicate grading policies and practices to students, parents, and community members.	Can explain to students, parents, and other educators the purpose and meaning of grades in my building/district.	Activity 5.1: Grading Stories Activity 5.2: Grading Policies and Practices in My District	#1 #4 #5

(Continued)

TABLE A.1 (Continued)

CHAPTER LEARNING GOAL	ALIGNED SUCCESS INDICATORS	SUPPORTIVE CHAPTER ACTIVITIES	RELEVANT STUDY GUIDE QUESTIONS
Chapter 6			
1. Understand the differences between parent involvement and family/parent engagement.	Understands the value of a school culture that honors and encourages parent engagement, with consistent communication to families. Is aware of the difficulties and barriers that exist that can impede a shift from parent involvement to parent engagement.	Activity 6.1: Beyond the Report Card	#1
2. Become familiar with teacher-to-home communications that can promote family engagement.	Can share agendas, memos, professional development descriptions, or other documentations that reflect the effort by the school leader to help teachers understand the benefits to student learning of school-to-home communications and/or show opportunities provided for teachers to learn and practice strategies that support that effort. Is aware of the difficulties and barriers that exist that can impede a shift from parent involvement to parent engagement.	Activity 6.1: Beyond the Report Card	#2 #3
3. Understand which assessment topics may be of most interest to parents at both the building and the classroom level and consider communication strategies for potential use.	Understands the value of a school culture that honors and encourages parent engagement, with consistent communication to families. Can point to multiple sources of evidence of student learning beyond the traditional report card.	Activity 6.1: Beyond the Report Card	#3
Chapter 7			
1. Understand the rationale for ethical and appropriate use of student assessment.	Can explain how ethical and appropriate use of student assessment supports students and their learning.	Activity 7.1: Recognizing the Ethical and Appropriate Use of Student Assessment	#1
2. Be familiar with professional standards for the use of both large-scale and classroom assessment.	Can reference relevant professional standards in assessment when dealing with assessment issues in school leadership.	Activity 7.2: *The Classroom Assessment Standards*	#1 #2

CHAPTER LEARNING GOAL	ALIGNED SUCCESS INDICATORS	SUPPORTIVE CHAPTER ACTIVITIES	RELEVANT STUDY GUIDE QUESTIONS
3. Understand the following concepts in assessment use and be able to lead others in their ethical and appropriate use: fairness, opportunity to learn, accommodations and modifications, confidentiality, test preparation.	Can create a school climate in which fairness and opportunity to learn are the hallmarks of student assessment. Can ensure that students in their school receive assessment accommodations as needed. Can lead teachers and others to provide ethical and appropriate test preparation.	Activity 7.1: Recognizing the Ethical and Appropriate Use of Student Assessment Activity 7.3: Assessment Accommodations Activity 7.4: Ethical and Unethical Test Preparation	#3 #4 #5
Chapter 8			
1. Understand the implications of recent teacher evaluation reforms for the evaluation of classroom assessment knowledge and skill and how that may affect professional development in assessment literacy.	Can explain the standards of sound classroom assessment practice (Chapters 2–5) on which evaluations of teacher performance can/should be based. Creates ways to observe, analyze, evaluate, and provide feedback on classroom assessment processes and instruments. Facilitates the conditions for effective adult learning in schools and secures professional development characterized by a long-term *process* that teaches new ideas and strategies through interaction with appropriate materials, hands-on practice, coaching, and collaboration.	Activity 8.1: Practicing With Teacher and Principal Evaluative Criteria in Assessment Activity 8.2: Personal Reflection on Classroom Assessment, Teacher Evaluation, and Professional Development Activity 8.4: Verifying Teachers' Content Knowledge and Assessment Competence	#2 #3 #4 #5
2. Become familiar with various measures used for teacher evaluation and their connection to assessment literacy.	Can explain the standards of sound classroom assessment practice (Chapters 2–5) on which evaluations of teacher performance can/should be based. Considers interview questions that relate to the classroom assessment literacy of candidates for teaching positions.	Activity 8.3: Practicing Linking Evaluation Results to Professional Development Recommendations Activity 8.4: Verifying Teachers' Content Knowledge and Assessment Competence	#3
3. Understand how the evaluation process can connect to and drive the district staff development program, and why.	Facilitates the conditions for effective adult learning in schools and secure professional development characterized by a long-term *process* that teaches new ideas and strategies through interaction with appropriate materials, hands-on practice, coaching, and collaboration.	Activity 8.1: Practicing With Teacher and Principal Evaluative Criteria in Assessment Activity 8.2: Personal Reflection on Classroom Assessment, Teacher Evaluation, and Professional Development Activity 8.3: Practicing Linking Evaluation Results to Professional Development Recommendations Activity 8.4: Verifying Teachers' Content Knowledge and Assessment Competence	#1 #2 #4 #5

(Continued)

TABLE A.1   (Continued)

CHAPTER LEARNING GOAL	ALIGNED SUCCESS INDICATORS	SUPPORTIVE CHAPTER ACTIVITIES	RELEVANT STUDY GUIDE QUESTIONS
4. Know how to unpack teacher evaluative criteria.	Can explain the standards of sound classroom assessment practice (Chapters 2–5) on which evaluations of teacher performance can/should be based. Considers interview questions that relate to the classroom assessment literacy of candidates for teaching positions (see Activity 8.3).	Activity 8.1: Practicing With Teacher and Principal Evaluative Criteria in Assessment Activity 8.2: Personal Reflection on Classroom Assessment, Teacher Evaluation, and Professional Development Activity 8.3: Practicing Linking Evaluation Results to Professional Development Recommendations	#1 #2
Chapter 9			
1. Understand basic concepts in quantitative data analysis.	Can offer reasonable interpretations of data displays and reports	Activity 9.1: Internet Scavenger Hunt	#1 #2
2. Understand a process for problem solving based on data.	Can create data overviews from school and/or district data reported by the state or from interim assessments and common assessments. Can offer reasonable interpretations of data displays and reports. Can lead building/district colleagues in a data-use process that results in improved teaching and learning. Does not use assessment results to serve purposes for which the assessment was not designed.	Activity 9.2: Dipping Into Data	#3 #4
3. Lead and support teachers in understanding and problem solving with data.	Can create data overviews from school and/or district data reported by the state or from interim assessments and common assessments. Can offer reasonable interpretations of data displays and reports. Can lead building/district colleagues in a data-use process that results in improved teaching and learning. Does not use assessment results to serve purposes for which the assessment was not designed.	Activity 9.2: Dipping Into Data Activity 9.3: Scenario Discussions	#3 #4

CHAPTER LEARNING GOAL	ALIGNED SUCCESS INDICATORS	SUPPORTIVE CHAPTER ACTIVITIES	RELEVANT STUDY GUIDE QUESTIONS
Chapter 10			
1. Know how to review a school or district policy for alignment with sound assessment practice.	Can lead a policy review process. Knows the key features of an assessment policy. Can identify sound and unsound assessment practices that may be present in school or district policy. Can develop or revise policies using quality assessment as a guide.	Activity 10.1: Using School/District Policies to Support Quality Assessment	#2 #3
2. Understand how the school or district policy manual can act as a system of policies that support sound assessment practice.	Can identify sound and unsound assessment practices that may be present in school or district policy. Can develop or revise policies using quality assessment as a guide. Can implement new or revised policies via staff communication and discussion and with appropriate professional development.	Activity 10.1: Using School/District Policies to Support Quality Assessment	#1
3. Describe how and where assessment fits into numerous policies related to student learning and well-being.	Knows the key features of an assessment policy. Can identify sound and unsound assessment practices that may be present in school or district policy.	Activity 10.1: Using School/District Policies to Support Quality Assessment	#1 #3 #4

References

Overview

Au, W. (2007). High-stakes testing and curricular control: A qualitative metasynthesis. *Educational Researcher, 36*(5), 258–267. https://doi.org/10.3102/0013189X07306523

Chappuis, J., & Stiggins, R. (2020). *Classroom assessment for student learning: Doing it right, using it well* (3rd ed.). Pearson.

Educational Testing Service. (2018). *Understanding balanced assessment systems.* https://www.ets.org/s/k12/pdf/ets-k-12-understanding-measurement-white-paper.pdf

Leithwood, K., & Louis, K. S. (2012). *Linking leadership to student learning.* Jossey-Bass.

No Child Left Behind Act. (2001). Pub. L. No. 107–110, 115 Stat. 1425 (2002).

Chapter 1

Brookhart, S., McTighe, J., Stiggins, R., & Wiliam, D. (2019). *The future of assessment practices: Comprehensive and balanced assessment systems.* Learning Sciences International.

Carlson, D., Borman, G. D., & Robinson, M. (2011). A multistate district-level cluster randomized trial of the impact of data-driven reform on reading and mathematics achievement. *Educational Evaluation and Policy Analysis, 33*(3), 378–398. https://doi.org/10.3102/0162373711412765

Chappuis, J., & Stiggins, R. (2020). *Classroom assessment for student learning: Doing it right, using it well* (3rd ed.). Pearson.

Chappuis, S., Commodore, C., & Stiggins, R. (2017). *Balanced assessment systems: Leadership, quality, and the role of classroom assessment.* Corwin. https://doi.org/10.4135/9781071800508

Dadey, N., & Diggs, C. R. (2019). *A rapid review of interim assessment use.* National Center for the Improvement of Educational Assessment.

Educational Testing Service. (2018). *Understanding balanced assessment systems.* https://www.ets.org/s/k12/pdf/ets-k-12-understanding-measurement-white-paper.pdf

Erkens, C. (2016). *Collaborative common assessments: Teamwork, instruction, results.* Solution Tree.

Herman, J., Osmundson, E., & Dietel. R. (2010). *Benchmark assessment for improved student learning* (AACC Report). University of California. https://doi.org/10.1037/e685212011-001

Jones, K. D. (2013). *The myth of benchmark testing: Isomorphic practices in Texas public school districts' use of benchmark testing* [Doctoral dissertation, Texas State University]. Digital Collections Repository. https://digital.library.txstate.edu/handle/10877/4856

Konstantopoulos, S., Li, W., Miller, S. R., & van der Ploeg, A. (2016). Effects of interim assessments across the achievement distribution: Evidence from an experiment. *Educational and Psychological Measurement, 76*(4), 587–608. https://doi.org/10.1177/0013164415606498

Konstantopoulos, S., Miller, S. R., & van der Ploeg, A. (2013). The impact of Indiana's system of diagnostic assessments on mathematics achievement. *Educational Evaluation and Policy Analysis, 35*(4), 481–499. https://doi.org/10.3102/0162373713498930

Konstantopoulos, S., Miller, S. R., van der Ploeg, A., & Li, W. (2016). Effects from interim assessments on student achievement: Evidence from a large-scale experiment. *Journal of Research on Educational Effectiveness, 9*(Supp. 1), 188–208. https://doi.org/10.1080/19345747.2015.1116031

Leithwood, K., & Louis, K. S. (2012). *Linking leadership to student learning.* Jossey-Bass.

Perie, M., Marion, S., Gong, B., & Wurtzel, J. (2007). *The role of interim assessments in a comprehensive assessment system.* Aspen Institute.

SCHILLS. (n.d.). *Ensuring rigor in local assessment systems: A self-evaluation protocol.* https://www.oercommons.org/authoring/57127-ensuring-rigor-in-local-assessment-systems-a-self-/view

Chapter 2

Anderson, L. W., & Krathwohl, D. R. (Eds.). (2001). *A taxonomy for learning, teaching, and assessing: A revision of Bloom's Taxonomy of Educational Objectives.* Longman.

Bloom, B. S., Englehart, M. D., Furst, E. J., Hill, W. H., & Krathwohl, D. R. (1956). *Taxonomy of educational objectives: The classification of educational goals. Handbook 1: Cognitive domain.* Longman.

Bloom, B. S., Hastings, J. T., & Madaus, G. F. (1971). *Handbook on formative and summative evaluation of student learning.* McGraw-Hill.

Common Core State Standards Initiative. (2020). *Common core state standards initiative: Preparing America's students for college and career.* http://www.corestandards.org/

Chappuis, J., & Stiggins, R. (2020). *Classroom assessment for student learning: Doing it right, using it well* (3rd ed.). Pearson.

Moss, C. M., & Brookhart, S. M. (2012). *Learning targets: Helping students aim for understanding in today's lesson.* ASCD.

Moss, C. M., & Brookhart, S. M. (2015). *Formative classroom walkthroughs: How principals and teachers collaborate to raise student achievement.* ASCD.

Moss, C. M., Brookhart, S. M., & Long, B. A. (2011). Knowing your learning target. *Educational Leadership, 68*(6), 66–69. http://www.ascd.org/publications/educational-leadership/mar11/vol68/num06/Knowing-Your-Learning-Target.aspx

No Child Left Behind Act. (2001). Pub. L. No. 107–110, 115 Stat. 1425 (2002).

Porter, A. C. (1993). School delivery standards. *Educational Researcher, 22*(5), 24–30. https://doi.org/10.2307/1176948

U.S. National Commission on Excellence in Education. (1983). *A nation at risk: The imperative for educational reform.* https://www2.ed.gov/pubs/NatAtRisk/risk.html

Chapter 3

Chappuis, J., & Stiggins, R. J. (2020). *Classroom assessment for student learning: Doing it right, using it well* (3rd ed.). Pearson.

Chappuis, J., & Stiggins, R. J. (2021). *An introduction to student-involved assessment for learning* (7th ed.). Pearson.

Stiggins, R. J., Arter, J. A., Chappuis, J., & Chappuis, S. (2004). *Classroom assessment for student learning: Doing it right—Using it well.* Assessment Training Institute.

Chapter 4

Akron Global Polymer Academy. (2011). *Best teaching practices: Wait time.* https://uakron.edu/polymer/agpa-k12outreach/best-teaching-practices/wait-time

Andrade, H. (2013). Classroom assessment in the context of learning theory and research. In J. H. McMillan (Ed.), *The SAGE handbook of research on classroom assessment* (pp. 17–34). Sage. https://doi.org/10.4135/9781452218649.n2

Andrade, H. L., Bennett, R. L., & Cizek, G. J. (Eds.). (2019). *Handbook of formative assessment in the disciplines.* Routledge.

Black, P., & Wiliam, D. (1998). Assessment and classroom learning. *Assessment in Education, 5*(1), 7–74. https://doi.org/10.1080/0969595980050102

Blackwell, L., Trzesniewski, K., & Dweck, C. (2007). Implicit theories of intelligence predict achievement across an adolescent transition: A longitudinal study and an intervention. *Child Development, 78*(1), 246–263. https://doi.org/10.1111/j.1467-8624.2007.00995.x

Brown, G., & Harris, L. (2013). Student self-assessment. In J. McMillan (Ed.), *The SAGE handbook of research on classroom assessment* (pp. 367–393). Sage. https://doi.org/10.4135/9781452218649.n21

Burkhardt, H., & Schoenfeld, A. H. (2019). Formative assessment in mathematics. In H. L. Andrade, R. L. Bennett, & G. J. Cizek (Eds.), *Handbook of formative assessment in the disciplines* (pp. 35–67). Routledge. https://doi.org/10.4324/9781315166933-3

Butler, R. (1988). Enhancing and undermining intrinsic motivation: The effects of task-involving and ego-involving evaluation on interest and performance. *British Journal of Educational Psychology, 58*(1), 1–14. https://doi.org/10.1111/j.2044-8279.1988.tb00874.x

Chappuis, J. (2015). *Seven strategies of assessment for learning* (2nd ed.). Pearson.

Chappuis, J. (Forthcoming). Student involvement in assessment. In S. Brookhart (Ed.), Assessment section; D. Fisher (Ed.), *Routledge Encyclopedia of Education* (online). Taylor & Francis.

Chappuis, J., & Stiggins, R. J. (2020). *Classroom assessment for student learning: Doing it right, using it well* (3rd ed.). Pearson.

Cizek, G. J., Andrade, H. L., & Bennett, R. L. (2019). Formative assessment: History, definition, and progress. In H. L. Andrade, R. L. Bennett, & G. J. Cizek (Eds.), *Handbook of formative assessment in the disciplines* (pp. 3–19). Routledge. https://doi.org/10.4324/9781315166933-1

Deane, P., & Sparks, J. R. (2019). Scenario-based formative assessment of key practices in the English language arts. In H. L. Andrade, R. L. Bennett, & G. J. Cizek (Eds.), *Handbook of formative assessment in the disciplines* (pp. 68–96). Routledge. https://doi.org/10.4324/9781315166933-4

Dewey, J. (1933). *How we think* (Rev. ed.). Heath.

Halvorson, H. G. (2012). *Succeed: How we can reach our goals.* Penguin.

Harlen, W., & James, M. (1997). Assessment and learning: Differences and relationships between formative and summative assessment. *Assessment in Education: Principles, Policy, & Practice, 4*(3), 365–379. https://doi.org/10.1080/0969594970040304

Hattie, J. (2009). *Visible learning: A synthesis of over 800 meta-analyses relating to achievement.* Routledge.

Hattie, J. (2012). *Visible learning for teachers: Maximizing impact on learning.* Routledge. https://doi.org/10.4324/9780203181522

Hattie, J., & Timperley, H. (2007). The power of feedback. *Review of Educational Research, 77*(1), 81–112. https://doi.org/10.3102/003465430298487

Heritage, M., Kim, J., Vendlinksi, T., & Herman, J. (2009). From evidence to action: A seamless process in formative assessment? *Education Measurement: Issues and Practices, 28*(3), 24–31. https://doi.org/10.1111/j.1745-3992.2009.00151.x

Heritage, M., & Wylie, C. (2019). Teacher preparation in mathematics. In H. L. Andrade, R. L. Bennett, & G. J. Cizek (Eds.), *Handbook of formative assessment in the disciplines* (pp. 207–242). Routledge.

Keeley, P., Sneider, C., & Ravel, M. (2020). *Uncovering student ideas about engineering and technology.* NSTA Press.

Kluger, A. N., & DeNisi, A. (1996). The effects of feedback interventions on performance: A historical review, a meta-analysis, and a preliminary feedback intervention theory. *Psychological Bulletin, 119*(2), 254–284. https://doi.org/10.1037/0033-2909.119.2.254

Locke, E. A., & Latham, G. P. (2002). Building a practically useful theory of goal setting and task motivation. *American Psychologist, 55*(9), 705–717. https://doi.org/10.1037/0003-066X.57.9.705

Moss, C. M., & Brookhart, S. M. (2019). *Advancing formative assessment in every classroom: A guide for instructional leaders.* ASCD.

Moss, C. M., Brookhart, S. M., & Long, B. A. (2013). Administrators' roles in helping teachers use formative assessment information. *Applied Measurement in Education, 26*, 205–218. https://doi.org/10.1080/08957347.2013.793186

Rowe, M. B. (1986). Wait time: Slowing down may be a way of speeding up. *American Educator, 37*(1), 43–50. https://doi.org/10.1177/002248718603700110

Sadler, D. R. (1989). Formative assessment and the design of instructional systems. *Instructional Science, 18*, 119–144. https://doi.org/10.1007/BF00117714

Sadler, D. R. (1998). Formative assessment: Revisiting the territory. *Assessment in Education, 5*(1), 77–84. https://doi.org/10.1080/0969595980050104

Shepard, L. A. (2001). The role of classroom assessment in teaching and learning. In V. Richardson (Ed.), *Handbook of research on teaching* (4th ed., pp. 1066–1101). American Educational Research Association.

Shepard, L. A. (2008). Formative assessment: Caveat emptor. In C. Dwyer (Ed.), *The future of assessment: Shaping teaching and learning* (pp. 279–303). Lawrence Erlbaum. https://doi.org/10.4324/9781315086545-12

Shepard, L. A., Penuel, W. R., & Davidson, K. L. (2017). Design principles for new systems of assessment. *Phi Delta Kappan, 98*(6), 47–52. https://doi.org/10.1177/0031721717696478

Stiggins, R. J. (2008). *An introduction to student-involved assessment for learning* (5th ed.). Pearson.

Walsh, J. A., & Sattes, B. D. (2005). *Quality questioning: Research-based practice to engage every learner.* Corwin.

White, B. Y., & Frederiksen, J. R. (1998). Inquiry, modeling, and metacognition: Making science accessible to all students. *Cognition and Instruction, 16*(1), 3–118. https://doi.org/10.1207/s1532690xci1601_2

Wiliam, D. (2013). Feedback and instructional correctives. In J. H. McMillan (Ed.), *The SAGE handbook of research on classroom assessment* (pp. 197–214). Sage.

Wiliam, D. (2018). *Embedded formative assessment* (2nd ed.). Solution Tree Press.

Wiliam, D. (2019). Conclusion: Why formative assessment is always both domain-general and domain-specific and what matters is the balance between the two. In H. L. Andrade, R. L. Bennett, & G. J. Cizek (Eds.), *Handbook of formative assessment in the disciplines* (pp. 243–264). Routledge. https://doi.org/10.4324/9781315166933-10

Wylie, C., & Lyon, C. (2016, February). *Using the formative assessment rubrics, reflection and observation tools to support professional reflection on practice (revised).* Formative Assessment for Students and Teachers (FAST) State Collaborative on Assessment and Student Standards (SCASS) of the Council of Chief State School Officers (CCSSO). https://center.ncsu.edu/ncfalcon/pluginfile.php/2/course/section/57/FAROP_Revised_2016.pdf

Chapter 5

Bowers, A. J. (2011). What's in a grade? The multidimensional nature of what teacher-assigned grades assess in high school. *Educational Research and Evaluation, 17*(3), 141–159. https://doi.org/10.1080/13803611.2011.597112

Brookhart, S. M. (1993). Teachers' grading practices: Meaning and values. *Journal of Educational Measurement, 30*(2), 123–142. https://doi.org/10.1111/j.1745-3984.1993.tb01070.x

Brookhart, S. M. (2009). *Grading* (2nd ed.). Merrill.

Brookhart, S. M. (2013). *Grading and group work.* ASCD.

Brookhart, S. M. (2015) Graded achievement, tested achievement, and validity. *Educational Assessment, 20*(4), 268–296. https://doi.org/10.1080/10627197.2015.1093928

Brookhart, S. M. (2017). *How to use grading to improve learning.* ASCD.

Brookhart, S. M., Guskey, T. R., Bowers, A. J., McMillan, J. H., Smith, J. K., Smith, L. F., Stevens, M. T., & Welsh, M. E. (2016). A century of grading research: Meaning and value in the most common educational measure. *Review of Educational Research, 86*(4), 803–848. https://doi.org/10.3102/0034654316672069

Chappuis, J., & Stiggins, R. (2020). *Classroom assessment for student learning: Doing it right, using it well.* Pearson.

Crooks, A. D. (1933). Marks and marking systems: A digest. *Journal of Educational Research, 27*(4), 259–272. https://doi.org/10.1080/00220671.1933.10880402

Donohoe, K., & Zigmond, N. (1990). Academic grades of ninth-grade urban learning disabled students and low-achieving peers. *Exceptionality, 1*(1), 17–27. https://doi.org/10.1080/09362839009524739

Forsell, J., Frykedal, K. F., & Chiriac, E. H. (2020). Group work assessment: Assessing social skills at group level. *Small Group Research, 51*(1), 87–124. https://doi.org/10.1177/1046496419878269

Galla, B. M., Shulman, E. P., Plummer, B. D., Gardner, M., Hutt, S. J., Goyer, J. P., D'Mello, S. K., Finn, A. S., & Duckworth, A. L. (2019). Why high school grades are better predictors of on-time college graduation than are admissions test scores: The roles of self-regulation and cognitive ability. *American Educational Research Journal, 56*(6), 2077–2115. https://doi.org/10.3102/0002831219843292

Glaser, R. (1963). Instructional technology and the measurement of learning outcomes: Some questions. *American Psychologist, 18*(8), 519–521. https://doi.org/10.1037/h0049294

Guskey, T. R. (2015). *On your mark: Challenging the conventions of grading and reporting.* Solution Tree.

Guskey, T. R., & Brookhart, S. M. (Eds.). (2019). *What we know about grading: What works, what doesn't, and what's next.* ASCD.

Jung, C. (2017). *Differentiated Assessment and Grading Model (DiAGraM).* Lead Inclusion. https://www.leadinclusion.org/single-post/2017/05/17/Differentiated-Assessment-and-Grading-Model-DiAGraM

Strijbos, J.-W. (2016). Assessment of collaborative learning. In G. T. L. Brown & L. R. Harris (Eds.), *Handbook of human and social conditions in assessment* (pp. 302–318). Routledge.

Chapter 6

Association of Washington School Principals (2020). *The ASWP leadership framework: To support principal development.* https://www.awsp.org/docs/default-source/member-support-documents/Leadership-Framework/awsp_framework_version_2-0.pdf

Bergman, P. (2021). Parent-child information frictions and human capital: Evidence from a field experiment. *Journal of Political Economy, 129*(1). The University of Chicago.

Bergman, P., & Chan, E. W. (2019). Leveraging parents through low-cost technology: The impact of high-frequency information on student achievement. *Journal of Human Resources.* https://doi.org/10.3368/jhr.56.1.1118-9837R1

Brenner, M., & Quirk, A. (2020). *One size does not fit all: Analyzing different approaches to family-school communication.* Center for American Progress.

Chappuis, J. (2015). *Seven strategies of assessment for learning.* Pearson.

Graham-Clay, S. (2005). Communicating with parents: Strategies for teachers. *School Community Journal, 15*(1), 117–129.

Hattie, J. (2009). *Visible learning: A synthesis of over 800 meta-analyses relating to achievement.* Routledge.

Kraft, M. A., & Bolves, A. (2019). *Can technology transform teacher-parent communication? Evidence from a randomized field trial.* Brown University.

Kraft, M. A., & Dougherty, S. M. (2013). The effect of teacher-family communication on student engagement: Evidence from a randomized field experiment. *Journal of Research on Educational Effectiveness, 6*(3), 199–222. https://doi.org/10.1080/19345747.2012.743636

Kraft, M. A., & Rogers, T. (2014). *The underutilized potential of teacher-to-parent communication: Evidence from a field experiment.* Harvard Kennedy School. https://doi.org/10.2139/ssrn.2528688

Learning Heroes. (2018, December). *Parents 2018: Going beyond good grades.* https://r50gh2ss1ic2mww8s3uvjvq1-wpengine.netdna-ssl.com/wp-content/uploads/2018/12/2018_Research_Report-final_WEB.pdf

Leithwood, K., & Louis, K. S. (2012). *Linking leadership to student learning.* Jossey-Bass.

MetLife (2012). *The Metlife survey of American teachers: Teachers, parents and the economy.* https://files.eric.ed.gov/fulltext/ED530021.pdf

Sirvani, H. (2007). The effect of teacher communication with parents on students' mathematics achievement. *American Secondary Education, 36*(1), 31–46.

Wardlow, L. (2013). *The positive results of parent communication: Teaching in a digital age.* Pearson.

York, B. N., & Loeb, S. (2014). *One step at a time: The effects of an early literacy text messaging program for parents of preschoolers* (CEPA working paper). Stanford University. https://doi.org/10.3386/w20659

Chapter 7

American Counseling Association. (2014). *2014 ACA code of ethics.* https://www.counseling.org/Resources/aca-code-of-ethics.pdf

American Educational Research Association, American Psychological Association, & National Council on Measurement in Education. (2014). *Standards for educational and psychological testing.* American Educational Research Association.

Carroll, J. B. (1963). A model of school learning. *Teachers College Record, 64*(8), 723–733.

Elliott, S. N., & Bartlett, B. J. (2018). Opportunity to learn. *Oxford Handbooks Online, May.* https://doi.org/10.1093/oxfordhb/9780199935291.013.70

Klinger, D., McDivitt, P., Howard, B., Munoz, M., Rogers, T., & Wylie, C. (2015). *The classroom assessment standards for PreK–12 teachers.* Joint Committee on Standards for Educational Evaluation; Kindle Direct Press.

McLaughlin, M. W., & Marsh, D. D. (1978). Staff development and school change. *Teachers College Record, 80*(1), 69–94.

National Association of School Psychologists. (2020). *The professional standards of the National Association of School Psychologists.* file:///C:/Users/SHAMIL~1/AppData/Local/Temp/2020_Professional_Standards_Web.pdf

Rasooli, A., Zandi, H., & DeLuca, C. (2018). Re-conceptualizing classroom assessment fairness: A systematic meta-ethnography of assessment literature and beyond. *Studies in Educational Evaluation, 56,* 164–181. https://doi.org/10.1016/j.stueduc.2017.12.008

Thompson, S. J., Morse, A. B., Sharpe, M., & Hall, S. (2005). *Accommodations manual.* Washington, DC: Council of Chief State School Officers. https://nceo.umn.edu/docs/OnlinePubs/AccommodationsManual.pdf

Thurlow, M. L., Lazarus, S. S., Christensen, L. L., & Shyyan, V. (2016, January). *Principles and characteristics of inclusive assessment systems in a changing assessment landscape* (NCEO Report 400). National Center on Educational Outcomes. https://nceo.umn.edu/docs/OnlinePubs/Report400/NCEOReport400.pdf

Wang, S., Rubie-Davies, C. M., & Meissel, K. (2018). A systematic review of the teacher expectation literature over the past 30 years. *Educational Research and Evaluation, 24*(3–5), 124–179. https://doi.org/10.1080/13803611.2018.1548798

Chapter 8

Bolton, D. (1973). *Selection and evaluation of teachers.* McCutcheon.

Cantrell, S., & Kane, T. J. (2013). *Ensuring fair and reliable measures of effective teaching: Culminating findings from the MET project's three-year study.* Bill and Melinda Gates Foundation.

Castellano, K., & Ho, A. (2013, February). *A practitioner's guide to growth models.* Council of Chief State School Officers.

Center for Educational Leadership. (2016). *5D+™ rubric for instructional growth and teacher evaluation.* University of Washington.

Center on Great Teachers and Leaders, American Institutes for Research. (2019, February 16). *Improving instruction for all students through educator evaluation as meaningful support.* https://files.eric.ed.gov/fulltext/ED597296.pdf

Curtis, R. (2012). *Building it together: The design and implementation of Hillsborough County Public Schools' teacher evaluation system.* Aspen Institute.

Darling-Hammond, L., Hyler, M., & Gardner, M. (2017). *Effective teacher professional development.* Learning Policy Institute.

Donaldson, M. L., Cobb, C. D., LaChasseur, K., Gabriel, R., Gonzales, R., Woulfin, S., & Makuch, A. (2014). *An evaluation of the pilot implementation of Connecticut's system for educator evaluation and development.* University of Connecticut Center for Educational Policy Analysis.

Garet, M. S., Wayne, A. J., Brown, S., Rickles, J., Song, M., & Manzeske, D. (2017). *The impact of providing performance feedback to teachers and principals.* U.S. Department of Education, National Center for Education Evaluation and Regional Assistance.

Goe, L., Biggers, K., & Croft, A. (2012). *Linking teacher evaluation to professional development: Focusing on improving teaching and learning.* Educational Testing Service.

Goe, L., Wylie, E. C., Bosso, D., & Olson, D. (2017). *State of the states' teacher evaluation and support systems: A perspective from exemplary teachers*. Educational Testing Service. https://doi.org/10.1002/ets2.12156

Honig, M., Copland, M., & Rainey, L. (2010). *Central office transformation for district-wide teaching and learning improvement*. University of Washington.

Hull, J. (2013). *Trends in teacher evaluation: How states are measuring teacher performance*. Center for Public Education.

Interstate Teacher Assessment and Support Consortium. (2021, January 15). *InTASC model core teaching standards and learning progression for teachers 1.0*. https://ccsso.org/resource-library/intasc-model-core-teaching-standards-and-learning-progressions-teachers-10

Jackson, C., & Cowan, J. (2018). *Assessing the evidence on teacher evaluation reforms* (CALDER Policy Brief No. 13-1218-1). CALDER Policymakers Council; American Institutes for Research. http://caldercouncil.org/assessing-the-evidence-on-teacher-evaluation-reforms/#.YAH2lBZS_IU

Kachur, D., Stout, J., & Edwards, C. (2013). *Engaging teachers in classroom walkthroughs*. ASCD.

Kraft, M. A. (2018). *What have we learned from the Gates-funded teacher evaluation reforms?* Education Next. https://www.educationnext.org/learned-gates-funded-teacher-evaluation-reforms/

Kraft, M. & Gilmour, A. (2016). Can principals promote teacher development as evaluators? A case study of principals' views and experiences. *Educational Administration Quarterly, 52*(5), 711–753. https://doi.org/10.1177/0013161X16653445

Leithwood, K., & Louis, K. S. (2012). *Linking leadership to student learning*. Jossey-Bass.

Marsh, J. A., Bush-Mecenas, S., Strunk, K. O., Lincove, J. A., & Huguet, A. (2017). Evaluating teachers in the big easy: How organizational context shapes policy responses in New Orleans. *Educational Analysis and Policy Development, 39*(4), 539–570. https://doi.org/10.3102/0162373717698221

Minnici, A. (2018). Toward teacher evaluation that promotes professional learning and growth. *The Source*. Cognia.org

No Child Left Behind Act. (2001). Pub. L. No. 107–110, 115 Stat. 1425 (2002).

Ross, E., & Walsh, K. (2019). *State of the states 2019: Teacher and principal evaluation policy*. National Council on Teacher Quality.

Rowan, B., & Raudenbush, S. W. (2016). Teacher evaluation in American schools. In D. H. Gitomer & C. A. Bell, *Handbook of research on teaching* (5th ed., chap. 19). AERA. https://doi.org/10.3102/978-0-935302-48-6_19

Stecher, B. M., Garet, M. S., Hamilton, L. S., Steiner, E. D., Robyn, A., Poirier, J., Holtzman, D., Fulbeck, E. S., Chambers, J., & Brodziak de los Reyes, I. (2016). *Improving teacher effectiveness: Implementation—the intensive partnerships for effective teaching through 2013–2014*. RAND Corporation. https://doi.org/10.7249/RB9908-1

Steinberg, M. P., & Sartain, L. (2015). Does better observation make better teachers? *Education Next, 15*(1), 70–76.

Tuma, A. P., Hamilton, L. S., & Tsai, T. (2018). *A nationwide look at teacher perceptions of feedback and evaluation systems* (Research report). RAND Corporation.

Will, M. (2016, December 30). Assessing quality of teaching staff still complex despite ESSA's leeway. *Education Week*. https://www.edweek.org/policy-politics/assessing-quality-of-teaching-staff-still-complex-despite-essas-leeway/2016/12

Chapter 9

Black, P., & Wiliam, D. (1998). Assessment and classroom learning. *Assessment in Education: Principles, Policy and Practice, 5*(1), 7–74. https://doi.org/10.1080/0969595980050102

Boudett, K. P., City, E. A., & Murnane, R. J. (2013). *Data wise: A step-by-step guide to using assessment results to improve teaching and learning*. Harvard Education Press.

Brookhart, S. M., & DePascale, C. A. (in press). Assessment to inform teaching and learning. In L. Cook & M. J. Pitoniak (Eds.), *Educational measurement* (5th ed.). Oxford University Press.

Castellano, K. E., & Ho, A. D. (2013, February). *A practitioner's guide to growth models*. Council of Chief State School Officers.

Ho, A. D. (2008). The problem with "Proficiency": Limitations of statistics and policy under No Child Left Behind. *Educational Researcher, 37*(6), 351–360. https://doi.org/10.3102/0013189X08323842

Leithwood, K., & Louis, K. S. (2012). *Linking leadership to student learning*. Jossey-Bass.

National Forum on Education Statistics. (2016). *Forum guide to collecting and using disaggregated data on racial/ethnic subgroups* (NFES 2017-017). U.S. Department of Education, National Center for Education Statistics.

No Child Left Behind Act. (2001). Pub. L. No. 107 -110, 115 Stat. 1425 (2002).

Chapter 10

Chappuis, J., & Stiggins, R. (2020). *Classroom assessment for student learning: Doing it right, using it well* (3rd ed.). Pearson.

Chappuis, S. (2007). Sound assessment through proper policy. *The School Administrator, 64*(1), 24–26.

Chappuis, S., Commodore, C., & Stiggins, R. (2017). *Balanced assessment systems: Leadership, quality, and the role of classroom assessment*. Corwin. https://doi.org/10.4135/9781071800508

Kickert, R., Meeuwisse, M., Stegers-Jager, K., Koppenol-Gonzalez, G., Arends, L., & Prinzie, P. (2019). Assessment policies and academic performance within a single course: The role of motivation and self-regulation. *Assessment and Evaluation in Higher Education, 44*(8), 1177–1190. https://doi.org/10.1080/02602938.2019.1580674

O'Connor, K. (2007). *A repair kit for grading: Fifteen fixes for broken grades*. Pearson.

Office of Data, Research and Evaluation, Nebraska Department of Education. (2020, January 6). *School rubric for the 2019–2020 evidence-based analysis (EBA)*. AQuESTT for Nebraska. https://aquestt.com/wp-content/uploads/2020/01/2019-2020-School-EBA-Rubric-FINAL-v0.01.pdf

Index

ABCDF scale, 127
Academic achievement targets, 4, 5 (table), 29–50.
    See also Learning goals
Accommodations, 130, 163–164, 173–175 (activity)
Accountability assessment, 12–13
Accuracy, 54–66
    bias and distortion, 56, 63–64, 64 (figure)
    learning goals, 56
    purpose, 54, 56
    sampling and, 63
    sound assessment design, 56–64
Aggregation, 208–211
    distribution, 210
    measures of central tendency, 208–209
Alignment, 10, 17
American Counseling Association, 158
American Educational Research Association (AERA), 158
American Psychological Association (APA), 158
Assessment, 1, 53
    audit. *See* Audit, assessment
    blueprint, 70, 71 (figure)
    classroom. *See* Classroom assessment
    information, 3, 157–158
    instruction and, 3
    inventory, 18
    learning goals and, 38–40, 41–44 (activity)
    principals' assessment methods, 38, 57
    tools/instruments, 38
Assessment Leadership Learning Team, 245–248
    facilitator's role, 246
    group operating principles, 247
    meeting agendas, 248
    meeting schedule, 245, 247–248
    participants, identifying, 247
    planning reading, 247–248
    planning steps, 246–248
    process, 245
    size of, 247
    text, reviewing, 246–247
    tracking, self-reflection and sharing learning, 248
Assessment literacy, 185, 217
    definition, 2
    overview, 2–4
    school-to-parent communication and, 144–145
Assessment literacy goals
    academic achievement targets, 29–50
    comprehensive and balanced assessment system, 9–26

effective communication, 141–155
ethical and appropriate assessment, 157–177
formative assessment, 81–116
overview, 4–6, 5 (table)
policies, assessment, 233–244
quality standards, assessment, 53–78
sound grading, 117–138
student assessment information, 205–231
teacher evaluation and professional development, 179–203
Assessment methods, 38, 63
    constructed-response, 38, 58–59, 59 (figure)
    performance assessment, 34, 37–38, 60–61
    personal communication, 38, 62
    quality and, 57–62
    selected-response, 38, 57, 57–58 (figure)
Assessment system, 9
    effectiveness of, 10
    overview, 9–10
    prerequisites, 10–11
    See also Comprehensive and balanced assessment system
Attendance policy, 234
Audit, assessment, 18–19, 21–26 (activity), 69–73, 75–78
    bias and distortion, 77–78 (activity)
    learning goals and sample size, 70–73 (activity)
    purpose, 69–70 (activity)
    quality, 75–76 (activity)
AWSP Leadership Framework, 149 (figure)

Balanced assessment system. *See* Comprehensive and balanced assessment system
Benchmark assessment, 13–14, 158
Bias and distortion, 56, 63–64, 64 (figure), 161, 213
    audit, assessment, 77–78 (activity)
Bloom's taxonomy, 35
Boudett, K., 216, 220–221, 223
Bowers, A., 120
Brainstorming, 221
Brookhart, S., 119
Butler, R., 96

Carroll, J., 162
"Carroll's model" of instruction, 162
Castellano, K., 212
Central tendency, measures of, 208–209
Class discussions, 62

Classroom
    dialogue, 88
    formative assessment, 17, 159, 165
    instruction, learning goals and, 34
    observations, 180, 182, 187
    quality, assessment. *See* Quality standards,
        assessment
    questioning, 88–91, 91–92 (figure)
    summative assessment, 16–17, 126, 159, 164
    walk-throughs, 191
Classroom assessment, 16
    communication about, 146–147
    competencies. *See* Teacher evaluation and professional
        development
    fairness in, 161–162
Classroom Assessment Standards, The, 159–160 (figure), 159–161,
    172–173 (activity)
Cognitive Process dimension, learning goals, 35
Collaborative Inquiry Guide for Learning Targets and Success
    Criteria, 41, 48–49
Collaborative learning, 124
Common assessments, 15–16, 159, 164
Communication. *See* Effective communication
Competency testing, 31
Compounding error, 213–214
Comprehensive and balanced assessment system,
    3–4, 5 (table), 9–26, 141
    audit, 18–19, 21–26 (activity)
    common assessments, 15–16
    communication and, 141
    designing, 18–19
    effectiveness of, 10
    formative classroom assessment, 17
    interim/benchmark assessments, 13–14
    learning goals and, 17
    levels of, 10–17, 12 (figure)
    overview, 9–10
    personal portfolio on, 21
    prerequisites, 10–11
    state accountability/district standardized assessments,
        12–13
    success indicators, 20
    summative classroom assessment, 16–17
Comprehensive assessment plan, 18, 238
Confidentiality, 164
Constructed-response assessment, 38
    quality guidelines, 58–59, 59 (figure)
Construct-irrelevant variance, 161
Corrective feedback, 99
Council of Chief State School Officers, 158
Craft knowledge, 95
Criteria, 59
Criterion referencing, 118–119, 124, 206–207, 207 (figure)
Curriculum
    evaluation, 31
    instruction and, 3, 13–14
    learning goals for, 36–37
    theory, 30
Curriculum-based assessment, 31
Cut scores, 210

Data analysis, 206–216
    aggregation and disaggregation, 208–210
    classroom assessment data, 214–216
    growth models, 212–213
    measurement error, 213–214
    qualitative, 215
    quantitative, 214–215, 224–225 (activity)
    referencing framework, 206–208
    unit of analysis, 210–211
Data-based decision-making, 205
Data-use process for problem solving, 216–223, 216 (figure),
    226–231 (activity)
    identifying problem, 219–220
    implementation, plan, 222
    instructional plans, 222
    prerequisites, 217
    question creation and data organization, 217–219
    reframing as teachers problem, 221
    school leaders' data-use practices, 223
Data-Wise Improvement Process, 216
Decision making, 205
Deeper thinking, 88
DeNisi, A., 97
Diagnosing learning needs, 92–95
Differentiated Assessment and Grading Model (DiAGraM),
    131, 132 (figure)
Disaggregation, 208–210
Distortion, bias and. *See* Bias and distortion
Distribution, 207 (figure), 210
District administrator, 7, 211
District assessment policy. *See* Policies, assessment
District standardized assessment, 12–13
Domain of learning, 30
Donohoe, K., 130

Effective communication, 4, 5 (table), 141–155
    barriers, 149–150
    classroom assessment, about, 146–147
    family engagement, 141, 143–144, 147–148
    information sources for reporting student learning to parents,
        154–155 (activity)
    large-scale assessment, about, 145–148
    mode of, 144, 147–149
    parent engagement and student learning, 142–149
    personal portfolio on, 153
    quality and, 65–66
    school-to-parent communication, 144–145
    scoreboard mode of display, 142–143
    student-led conferences, 151–152, 151–152 (figure)
    students as communicators, 151–152
    success indicators, 152–153
    teacher-to-parent communication, 144, 147–148
    texting, 144, 148
    using technology for, 143–144, 148–150
Effective feedback, 96–99, 99 (figure)
    characteristics, 96 (figure)
    definition, 96
    grading, 97
    intended learning and, 97–98
    intervention feedback, 98

next-step feedback, 98–99, 98 (figure)
strength feedback, 98, 98 (figure)
timing of, 96–97
Ensuring Rigor in Local Assessment Systems, 19
Equity, 3, 56, 162
Error, measurement, 213–214
Ethical and appropriate assessment, 4, 5 (table), 157–177
    accommodations and modifications, 163–164, 173–175 (activity)
    Classroom Assessment Standards, The, 159–160 (figure),
        159–161, 172–173 (activity)
    confidentiality, 164
    fairness, 161–162
    OTL, 162–163
    personal portfolio on, 167
    professional standards, 158
    recognizing, 167–172 (activity)
    standardized testing, preparation for, 164–166
    success indicators, 166
    test preparation, ethical and unethical, 175–177 (activity)
Every Student Succeeds Act, 1, 205, 208
Extended-response questions, 58

Fairness, 161–162
Family Educational Rights and Privacy Act, 164
Family engagement, 141, 143
    principal evaluation criteria, in, 149
    teacher-to-parent communication and, 144, 147–148
    using technology for communication and, 148–149
Feedback, 85, 148
    corrective, 99
    effective, 96–99, 99 (figure)
    learning-oriented, 98
    loop, 92
    mindfulness, 96
    next-step, 98–99, 98 (figure)
    peer, 102–103, 104–105 (figure)
    point of intervention, 98
    self-focused, 98
    strength, 98, 98 (figure)
Fill-in questions, 58 (figure)
Formative assessment, 2, 4, 5 (table), 10, 35, 81–117, 126, 146
    classroom, 17, 159, 165
    classroom questioning, 88–91, 91–92 (figure)
    communication and, 65
    critical components of, 82, 109–111 (activity)
    definition, 81
    effective feedback, 96–99, 99 (figure)
    faulty, 3
    goal setting, 103–104, 104–105 (figure)
    implementation of, 106–107
    leader support for, 106–107
    learning goals and success criteria, 84–87, 87 (figure)
    learning needs, diagnosing, 92–95, 96 (figure)
    learning target for, 85
    overview, 81–83
    peer feedback, 102–103
    personal portfolio on, 108
    practices in classroom, 111–112 (activity)
    practices in school, 114–116 (activity)
    practices with students, 113–114 (activity)

prerequisites for effectiveness of, 83–106
    self-assessment, 100–101, 101–102 (figure),
        104–105 (figure)
    student as decision maker, 82–83
    student tracking and self-reflection, 105–106, 106 (figure)
    success indicators, 108
    teacher evaluation, 181, 185
Formative feedback, 126–127
Formative learning cycle, 47–50 (activity), 83, 125
Framework for Teaching from the Danielson Group, 183

"Garbage in, garbage out" syndrome, 20, 124
General rubric, 59
Glaser, R., 119
Goal setting, 85, 103–104, 104–105 (figure)
Grades, 117
    accuracy of, 127–130
    formative feedback relationship and, 126–127
    group, 124
Grading, 97
    absolute standards, on, 119
    communication *vs.* motivational aspect, 118
    criterion referencing, 118–119, 124
    definition, 117
    DiAGraM model, 131, 132 (figure)
    grades to ability relationship, 119–120
    group grades, 124
    growth, 123
    historical perspective, 117–121
    issues, 117–121
    norm referencing, 118–119, 130
    policies, 131, 133
    purpose, 118
    referencing scheme, 118–119
    reliability, 120–121
    retaking/revision and, test, 126
    scale, 127
    self-referencing, 118–119
    sound, 4, 5 (table), 117–138
    standards-based, 124–125, 127, 130
    students' involvement in, 125–126
    unsound, 3
Group grades, 124
Growth measures, student, 181
Growth models, 180–181, 212–213
Guskey, T. R., 119, 121, 123, 129

Halvorson, H. G., 104
Handbook of Formative Assessment in the Disciplines, 89
Hattie, J., 92, 151
Ho, A., 212
Homework policy, 234
Honig, M., 191
Hybrid referencing, 207

Individualized Education Program, 163
Instruction
    assessment and, 3
    "Carroll's model" of, 162
    curriculum and, 3, 13–14

learning goals and classroom, 34
    learning goals for, 36–37
Instructional adjustment, 92
Instructional content, 163
Instructional leadership, 2
Instructional objectives, 32 (figure), 33–34
Instructional quality, 163
Instructional questions, 62
Instructional time, 1, 163
Instructional traction, 93
Instruments, assessment, 38
InTASC Model Core Teaching Standards, 183, 189
Intended learning, 15, 40, 56, 62, 85, 87
    effective feedback and, 97–98
    goal, 60–61, 121–122
Interim assessment, 13–14, 19, 54, 158, 165, 223
Interpretive questions, 58
Interrater reliability, 213
Interstate Teacher Assessment and Support Consortium
        (InTASC), 183
Inventory, assessment, 18
Item bank, 14–15

Joint Committee on Standards for Educational
        Evaluation, 159
Jung, L. A., 131

Kluger, A., 97
Knowledge dimension, learning goals, 35
Knowledge learning goals, 36, 85

Large-scale assessment, 65, 214
    communication about, 145–148
    fairness in, 161
Latham, G., 103
Learner-centered problem, 220
Learning
    collaborative, 124
    cycle, formative, 47–50 (activity), 83, 125
    domain of, 30
    progressions, 84
Learning goals, 10, 29–30, 63
    assessment and, 38–40, 41–44 (activity)
    assessment system and, 17
    audit for, assessment, 70–73 (activity)
    classification, 35–36
    classroom instruction and, 34
    Cognitive Process dimension, 35
    constructed-response assessment, 38
    curriculum/instruction/assessment, for, 36–37
    formative assessment, 84–87
    formative learning cycle, 47–50 (activity)
    grain size, 32 (figure)
    historical perspective, 30–31
    intended, 60–61
    knowledge, 36, 85
    Knowledge dimension, 35
    learning targets, 29, 32 (figure), 33–35,
        45–46 (activity)
    overview, 31–32

performance assessment, 37–38, 60
performance skill, 36, 86
personal communication, 38
personal portfolio on, 41
product, 36, 86
quality assessment and, 56, 66
questions/tasks categories, 38
reasoning, 36, 86
sample size and, 70–73 (activity)
selected-response assessment, 38
sharing, 85, 87
sound grading and, 122
state standards, 32
success criteria and, 84–87, 127, 185
success indicators, 40
target-method match, 39, 39 (figure), 73–75 (activity)
teacher instructional objectives, 32 (figure), 33
two levels of, 33 (figure)
unit learning goals, 32–33
Learning needs, 92–95, 96 (figure)
    information source for identifying, 92–95
    time for addressing, 95
Learning-oriented feedback, 98
Learning targets, 29, 32 (figure), 33–34
    formative assessment, for, 85
    lesson, 35
    success criteria, and, 34–35, 45–46 (activity), 85
Leithwood, K., 205, 223
Lesson learning targets, 35
Lesson plan policy, 234
Lesson plan review, 185
Locke, E., 103
Logic rule, 129 (figure)
Louis, K. S., 205, 223

Marsh, J., 182
Matching questions, 57, 57 (figure)
Mean, 129 (figure), 208–209
Measures of central tendency, 208–209
Median, 129 (figure), 208–209
Model of School Learning, A (Carroll), 162
Modifications, 130, 163–164
Multiple-choice questions, 57, 57 (figure)
Multiple measures, 121, 128

National Association of State Directors of Special
        Education, 158
National Board for Professional Teaching Standards, 183
National Center on Educational Outcomes, 158
National Council on Measurement in Education (NCME), 158
Nation at Risk, A, 31
Next-step feedback, 98–99, 98 (figure)
No Child Left Behind (NCLB) Act, 1, 31, 180, 184–185, 208
Norm-referenced assessment, 13, 146
Norm referencing, 118–119, 130, 206, 207 (figure), 225

Observation rubrics, 180, 187–188
Opportunity to learn (OTL), 161–163
Oral presentation rubric, 61
Ordinal measures, 209

Parent engagement, 142–149. *See also* Family engagement
Parent involvement, 143, 147
Pattern of learning, 129 (figure)
Peer feedback, 102–103, 104–105 (figure)
Percentile ranks, 206
Performance assessment, 34, 37–38
   rubric quality guidelines, 61, 61–62 (figure)
   task quality guidelines, 60–61, 60 (figure)
Performance skill learning goals, 36, 86
Personal communication, 38
   quality, 62
Policies, assessment, 4, 5 (table), 233–244
   academic performance and, 238–239
   attendance, 234
   comprehensive assessment plan and, 238
   development, 238–240
   evaluation criteria, 239
   homework policy, 234
   lesson plan, 234
   manual, 240
   personal portfolio on, 241
   promotion and retention, 234–235
   quality assessment and, 235–236,
      241–244 (activity)
   reviewing, 236–237
   rubric, 237, 238 (figure)
   student assessment, 233–236
   subsections of district, 240
   success indicators, 240
Portfolio, 187
Practitioner's Guide to Growth Models, A
      (Castellano & Ho), 212
Praising, 98
Principals
   assessment-literate, 2–4
   assessment methods. *See* Assessment methods
   instructional leadership, 223
   responsibility for assessment leadership, 15–16
Principles and Characteristics of Inclusive Assessment Systems in a
      Changing Assessment Landscape, 158
Problem of practice, 221
Process criteria, 123
Product criteria, 123
Product learning goals, 36, 86
Professional development, 15, 17, 145, 150
   teacher evaluation and, 4, 5 (table), 179–203
Professional standards, 158
Professional Standards of the National Association of School
      Psychologists, The, 158
Progress criteria, 123
Progress reports, 123
Promotion and retention policy, 234–235
Psychological safety, 100
Purpose, assessment, 11, 63
   audit for, assessment, 69–70 (activity)
   grading, 118
   interim/benchmark, 13
   quality, 54, 56, 66, 69–70 (activity)
   summative classroom, 16

Qualitative data analysis, 215
Quality standards, assessment, 4, 5 (table), 53–78, 238
   accuracy, 54–66
   audit, assessment, 75–76 (activity)
   bias and distortion, 56, 63–64, 64 (figure), 77–78 (activity)
   constructed-response assessment, 58–59, 59 (figure)
   effective communication, 65
   effective use of information, 64–66
   formative assessment, 64–65
   keys of, 54–66, 55 (figure), 67–68 (activity)
   learning goals, 56, 70–73 (activity)
   performance assessment, 60–61, 60 (figure), 61–62 (figure)
   personal communication, 62
   personal portfolio on, 67
   policy and, 235–236, 241–244 (activity)
   purpose, 54, 56, 66, 69–70 (activity)
   sampling, 62–63
   selected-response assessment, 57, 57–58 (figure)
   sound assessment design, 56–64
   success indicators, 66
   target-method match, practicing with, 73–75 (activity)
Quantitative data analysis, 214–215, 224–225 (activity)
Questioning, 88–91, 91–92 (figure)
   deeper thinking, 88
   learning, for, 90–91
   misconceptions and, 88–89
   student-to-student discussion, 89–90
   student understanding and, 88–89
Questions
   constructed-response, 38, 58–59, 59 (figure)
   extended-response, 58
   fill-in, 58 (figure)
   instructional, 62
   interpretive, 58
   matching, 57, 57 (figure)
   multiple-choice, 57, 57 (figure)
   performance assessment, 34, 37–38, 60–61
   personal communication, 38, 62
   posing, 90–91
   selected-response, 38, 57, 57–58 (figure)
   short-answer, 58
   true/false, 57, 57 (figure)

Race to the Top, 180
Randomizing respondents, 91
Rasooli, A., 162
Raudenbush, S., 181
Reasoning learning goals, 36–37
   student-friendly language, into, 86
Reflective thinking, 105 (figure)
Reliability, 213
Report cards, 123, 142, 146
Retaking, test, 126
Rowan, B., 181
Rubrics, 54, 65, 146, 235 (figure)
   constructed-response assessment, 59
   instructional traction, as, 93–95
   observation, 180, 187–188
   oral presentation, 61

performance assessment, 61, 61–62 (figure)
policy review, 237, 238 (figure)
student-friendly language, into, 86
success criteria, 86
task-specific, 59

Sadler, D. R., 85, 98
Sadler, R., 83
Sample, 62–63
    audit for, assessment, 70–73 (activity)
Sampling, 62–63
School assessment policy. *See* Policies, assessment
School-to-home communications, 141
School-to-parent communication, 144–145
SCILLSS (Strengthening Claims-Based Interpretations and Uses of
    Local and Large-Scale Science Assessment Scores), 19
Score pollution, 161
Scoring guides, 56, 95
Selected-response assessment, 38
    quality guidelines, 57, 57–58 (figure)
Self-assessment, 3, 17, 35, 85, 100–101, 101–102 (figure),
    104–105 (figure)
    student, 188 (figure)
    teacher, 186
Self-efficacy, 100
Self-focused feedback, 98
Self-referencing, 118–119
Shepard, L., 97
Short-answer questions, 58
6+1 Trait Writing Rubric, 65
Sound assessments, 11, 29, 56–64, 66
    assessment methods and quality, 57–62
    bias and distortion, 63–64, 64 (figure)
    sampling, 62–63
Sound grading, 4, 5 (table), 117–138
    accuracy of grades, 127–130
    achievement, reporting, 121–122
    classrooms and courses, in, 137–138 (activity)
    combinatory method, 127–130, 129 (figure)
    current status, reporting, 122–126
    DiAGraM model, 131, 132 (figure)
    formative feedback and grades relationship, 126–127
    grading stories, 134–135 (activity)
    learning goals, clear, 122
    personal portfolio on, 134
    policies, 131, 133
    policies and practices in district, 136 (activity)
    students' involvement in, 125–126
    students with special needs, 130–131
    success indicators, 133
Standardized achievement tests, 119–120
Standardized assessment, 12–13, 161
Standardized testing, 164–166
    teacher evaluation, in, 186
Standards, 29–50
    movement, 31
    professional standards, 158
    quality, assessment, 4, 5 (table), 53–78, 238
    referencing, 206–207, 207 (figure)
    state standards, 32, 32 (figure), 37
    See also Learning goals

Standards-based assessment, 142–143
Standards-based grading, 124–125, 127, 130
Standards for Educational and Psychological Testing, 158, 161
State accountability assessment, 12–13, 34, 158, 165, 234
State standards, 32, 32 (figure), 37
Stecher, B., 182
Stiggins, R., 83
Student artifacts, 186
Student assessment information, 3–4, 5 (table), 205–231
    data analysis, 206–216
    data-use process for problem solving, 216–223, 216 (figure),
        226–231 (activity)
    internet scavenger hunt, 224–225 (activity)
    personal portfolio on, 224
    success indicators, 223–224
Student current status, reporting, 122–126
    assessment evidence for, using, 124
    base grades, 124
    standards-based records, 124–125
    students' involvement in, 125–126
Student growth measures, 181
Student-involved parent conference, 151
Student learning, 3, 6, 14, 53, 182, 223
    formative assessment and, 17
    grading practices, 121 (figure)
    parent engagement and, 142–144
Student-led conferences, 151–152, 151–152 (figure)
Student-to home communication, 151–152
Success criteria, 29, 84
    formative assessment, 84–87
    learning goals and, 84–87, 127, 185
    learning targets and, 34–35, 45–46 (activity)
    rubrics, 86
Summative assessment, 12, 35, 87, 117, 146
    checking up, 126
    classroom, 16–17, 126, 159, 164
    communication and, 65
    summing up, 126
    teacher evaluation, 181
System, 9

Target-method match, 39, 39 (figure), 73–75 (activity)
Task-specific rubric, 59
Taxonomy, 31
Teacher evaluation and professional development,
    4, 5 (table), 179–203
    administrator and observer training, 191–194
    assessment literacy problem in, 193, 200–201 (activity)
    classroom observations, 180, 182, 187
    classroom walk-throughs, 191
    continued professional growth, 183–184, 190–191
    criterion-based measures, 181–182
    feedback and, 187
    formative purpose, 181, 185, 192
    4-point rubric, 188 (figure)
    implications, 185–194
    lesson plan review, 185
    observation rubrics, 180, 187–188
    personal portfolio on, 195
    personal reflection on, 198–199 (activity)
    portfolios, teacher, 187

postobservation conference and, 187, 191
principal criteria and, 190
procedures/factors for teacher effectiveness, 180–182, 185–188
purposes of, 181
reforms of, 180, 185 (figure)
standardized testing in, 186
student artifacts, 186
student growth measures, 181
student/parent surveys, 186
student self-assessment, 188 (figure)
success indicators, 194–195
summative purpose, 181, 192
teacher and principal evaluative criteria in assessment, 196–198 (activity)
teachers' content knowledge and assessment competence, 201–203 (activity)
teacher self-assessment, 186
teaching standards and evaluation criteria, 182–183, 188–190
Teacher instructional objectives, 32 (figure), 33
Teacher-to-parent communication, 144, 147–148
using technology for, 148–149

Technology, communication, 143–144, 148–150
Text Types and Purposes, 37
Think time, 90
Tools, assessment, 38
True/false questions, 57, 57 (figure)
2014 ACA Code of Ethics, 158
Tyler, R., 30

Unit learning goals, 32–33, 32 (figure)
Unit of analysis, 210–211
Unit test, 34, 38
Unsound assessment, 20
U.S. National Commission on Excellence in Education, 31

Validity, 70
Value added growth models, 212

Wait time, 90
What We Know About Grading (Guskey & Brookhart), 119
Wiliam, D., 82, 90

Zigmond, N., 130

A SAGE Publishing Company

Helping educators make the greatest impact

CORWIN HAS ONE MISSION: to enhance education through intentional professional learning.

We build long-term relationships with our authors, educators, clients, and associations who partner with us to develop and continuously improve the best evidence-based practices that establish and support lifelong learning.

Solutions YOU WANT | Experts YOU TRUST | Results YOU NEED

EVENTS

>>> **INSTITUTES**

Corwin Institutes provide large regional events where educators collaborate with peers and learn from industry experts. Prepare to be recharged and motivated!

corwin.com/institutes

ON-SITE PD

>>> **ON-SITE PROFESSIONAL LEARNING**

Corwin on-site PD is delivered through high-energy keynotes, practical workshops, and custom coaching services designed to support knowledge development and implementation.

corwin.com/pd

>>> **PROFESSIONAL DEVELOPMENT RESOURCE CENTER**

The PD Resource Center provides school and district PD facilitators with the tools and resources needed to deliver effective PD.

corwin.com/pdrc

ONLINE

>>> **ADVANCE**

Designed for K–12 teachers, Advance offers a range of online learning options that can qualify for graduate-level credit and apply toward license renewal.

corwin.com/advance

Contact a PD Advisor at (800) 831-6640 or visit www.corwin.com for more information